D1087786

EXISTENTIAL EPISTEMOLOGY

EXISTENTIAL EPISTEMOLOGY

A HEIDEGGERIAN CRITIQUE OF THE CARTESIAN PROJECT

JOHN RICHARDSON

CLARENDON PRESS · OXFORD
1986

Oxford University Press, Walton Street, Oxford OX2 6DP

Oxford New York Toronto
Delhi Bombay Calcutta Madras Karachi
Petaling Jaya Singapore Hong Kong Tokyo
Nairobi Dar es Salaam Cape Town
Melbourne Auckland

and associated companies in
Beirut Berlin Ibadan Nicosia

Oxford is a trade mark of Oxford University Press

Published in the United States
by Oxford University Press, New York

© John Richardson 1986

All rights reserved. No part of this publication may be reproduced,
stored in a retrieval system, or transmitted, in any form or by any means,
electronic, mechanical, photocopying, recording, or otherwise, without
the prior permission of Oxford University Press

British Library Cataloguing in Publication Data

Richardson, John
Existential epistemology: a Heideggerian critique of the Cartesian project.
1. Heidegger, Martin
I. Title
193   B3279.H49
ISBN 0-19-824906-3

Set by Thomson Litho Ltd, East Kilbride, Scotland
Printed in Great Britain
at the University Printing House, Oxford
by David Stanford
Printer to the University

SKIDMORE COLLEGE LIBRARY

TO PAMELA

ACKNOWLEDGEMENTS

BECAUSE this book began as part of my thesis at Berkeley, my original and greatest debts in it are to my principal advisers there, Hubert Dreyfus and Thompson Clarke. These debts are quite different in type, but I feel them about equal in scope.

To the former I owe my first introduction to *Being and Time*, and guidance in my next early workings through that text—these surely have shaped my understanding of Heidegger, in ways I can scarcely step back to see. Later, at several stages in the growth of this book, he has helped with detailed suggestions (though I have not always been able to satisfy his doubts). And I am also more generally grateful for the overflowing energy and enthusiasm he so successfully shares with his students.

To the latter I owe a certain basic conception of the nature and limits of epistemology, which has shaped the overall structure of this book, and guided some of its concrete arguments (though I am afraid the extension to this other philosophical mode might make these contacts unnoticeable or unappealing to him). He has also offered a model of a type of seriousness in philosophy—of a persistence, independence, and abiding concern for its problems—which has seemed worth pursuing, and so has helped to sustain me in the field.

More recently and concretely, I have been helped by the criticisms of several readers of drafts of this book. I would particularly like to acknowledge those of Thomas Nagel and Michael Graves, and by two anonymous reviewers (though once again, I have not always managed to right the wrongs they have noted).

CONTENTS

REFERENCES

FOR reasons I shall mention in the Introduction, I have confined my references to the following English translations of works by Heidegger. Citations will be given in parentheses in the text, using an abbreviated title, and page numbers.

All quotations are from *Being and Time* (translated by John Macquarrie and Edward Robinson; Harper & Row; New York, 1962), abbreviated as *BT*.

Additional supporting references are to:

The Basic Problems of Phenomenology (translated by Albert Hofstadter; Indiana University Press; Bloomington, 1982), abbreviated as *BPP*.

The Essence of Reasons (translated by Terrence Malick; North western University Press; Evanston, 1969), abbreviated as *ER*.

The Metaphysical Foundations of Logic (translated by Michael Heim; Indiana University Press; Bloomington, 1984), abbreviated as *MFL*.

'What is Metaphysics?' (translated by David Krell in: *Martin Heidegger: Basic Writings*, edited by Krell; Harper & Row; New York, 1977), abbreviated as *WIM*.

INTRODUCTION

MY aim is to develop a Heideggerian response to the central problem in epistemology.

What do I mean by this problem, and by such a response?

The problem is the familar one, which may be stated so: can we know the existence of physical objects? But it is either capable of a variety of formulations, or belongs to a cluster of closely related problems: can we know any objective empirical facts? can we prove the existence of a world external to our minds? can we arrive at the way things are in themselves? Without confronting the question how such problems are to be individuated, I shall use such expressions as "the central problem in epistemology" to distinguish *any* of these issues from such 'secondary' epistemological puzzles as those concerning other minds and induction. I hope to discuss these central issues at a level of generality that makes them in effect interchangeable, and that abstracts still more clearly from such subsidiary versions as those stated in terms of sense-data or ideas. Eventually I shall be offering an account of the basic character or aim of epistemological inquiry, and only then will it be appropriate to consider which of these formulations might have priority.

My 'Heideggerian response' to this central problem will be developed from out of *Being and Time* in particular, with lesser use of the more minor works of that 'early' period (1927–30). This project will be made more manageable by completely suppressing all questions as to Heidegger's evolution in his later writings; we thereby avoid an additional dimension of intricacy that would complicate the discussion exponentially. The importance of *Being and Time*, both in its own right and for an understanding of those later writings, gives a more positive justification for this focus. Because Heidegger's system in this early period is crucially 'existential'—in a sense that needs to be explained—so too will be my handling of epistemology. Thus this book's title implies not an epistemology for existentialism (as an analysis how we might know that movement's claims to be true), but rather a critique of epistemology from an existential stance.

Now, this response I develop will be 'Heideggerian', and not 'Heidegger's', in that I shall not be simply recounting his own explicit remarks on epistemology in those early writings. Rather, I shall attempt to construct as strong a position as I can, extrapolating beyond these explicit discussions. This procedure is required for several reasons. In the first place, Heidegger's direct comments on that traditional problem are brief and dismissive. They need considerable elaboration if they are to present a full response, and supplementation if they are to present a response sufficiently sympathetic to that problem to interest those who have been captivated by it. Moreover, even where *Being and Time* develops and supports its positions more fully than here, it is with a style of argument that may seem not argument at all, but oracular assertion. This style must be recast, the sequence of presentation rearranged, if these positions are to be seriously entertained by some audiences; I must avoid if I can the more aggravated form of this style so common among Heideggerians, of breaking off argument too soon, by supposing it clinched with the lemma "Heidegger says so". And finally, Heidegger's explicit comments on epistemology bring in too little of the wide-ranging system elaborated in his writings themselves. But fortunately, by working to correct this last inadequacy I can hope to deal with the others as well.

Our task will be to work our way into the system of *Being and Time*, and to see what its response to that traditional problem must be. By taking account of implications for this problem that points all through the deep structure of this system can be seen to bear, and by arranging these implications into argument more familiar in form, I shall attempt to present both a far fuller reply to the problem than Heidegger himself expresses, and one that does more justice to the very strong attraction this problem has exercised. (We shall eventually see, indeed, that Heidegger's general view on the appropriate response to traditional philosophical problems requires just such a more sympathetic handling of this problem as well). I shall try to show that this system can be adapted to argue epistemological issues in a way that can be grasped and evaluated in its own right, without reliance on the historical pedigree of its parts—on the fact that such-and-such eminent associates of Heidegger have shared in such views. Such emphasis on historical supports, along with the notion that Heidegger's views are justified just as Heidegger's, is one of the features of much writing in the field, that inclines analytic philosophers to suppose this genre to be quite removed from their own, in its standards for argument and defence. This book's procedure will still be rather distinct, but to emphasize that its argument is at least intended to be self-sufficient in this way, I have dispensed with secondary references.

My argument involves, then, a considerable amount of extrapolation beyond the views Heidegger directly expresses; this amount increases from each chapter to the next. There is obviously room for disagreement as to whether this projection has been faithfully drawn. I shall quote Heidegger's words where my development lies close to the texts, and then hope that extensions will appear as organically continuous with his remarks. But while confident in an overall faithfulness, my main aim is to develop as strong and coherent a response to the problem as I can offer. In this way, I hope not merely to present Heidegger's system, but to use it constructively: to show how this network of exotic concepts can be developed and put to work. This project will look suspicious to those who suppose one must either be an expositor faithfully presenting a philosopher's system, or original by diverging critically from it, and who therefore would rule illegitimate any effort at constructive exposition. Against this doubt, this book will have to be justified mainly by itself, if at all. But I may add that this is also (notoriously) Heidegger's own way with the philosophers he presents—so that such a critic might at least enjoy the irony in seeing Heidegger himself subjected to the 'illegitimate' handling he imposes on others.

Why do I single out this problem, and why am I interested in Heidegger's response?

The fact that Heidegger's treatment of this problem is so sketchy may make it seem an inappropriate or even self-defeating choice. Why not focus on some other problem that he handles at greater length—for example the question of what human beings essentially are, which is the central topic of (the published part of) *Being and Time* itself? First, the very fact that this problem is peripheral in Heidegger's discussion presents a peculiar advantage. Were I handling a question so much in the foreground in Heidegger's own presentation, my treatment would more extensively mirror or parallel his, and would lose an independence that can help to illuminate. By bringing his system to bear on an issue it is not already presented with respect to, we approach that system in a fresh way, along an unfamiliar dimension, and so, we may hope, can see it and judge it for a moment more clearly.

But of course there are many philosophical problems that Heidegger treats only briefly; this freshness could be had by attending to any of these. Moreover, with respect to certain broader substantive interests, it may not matter which such traditional issue we orient Heidegger's system towards. One general aim of this book will be to uncover the difference between the traditional and phenomenological methods as such, and this aim even requires that parts of the argument be applicable to uses of the former method in other fields as well. Thus I shall claim that what might be called the central problem in traditional ethics—whether we can know that some particular action is right—is susceptible to a treatment that closely parallels the one I shall give to the problem in epistemology; at convenient points in the following I shall quickly sketch the corresponding stage in that parallel story.

However, there are also reasons favouring the choice of epistemology for focused discussion. It is often said that epistemology is the central and guiding discipline in the modern philosophical tradition beginning with Descartes. The enterprise or undertaking at the core of this discipline, and the parameters most commonly adopted in working it through, are thus of an especially broad significance and interest. If parallel treatments of such other fields as ethics are possible, we may plausibly expect the reason to lie in the influence of epistemology on these other disciplines, or at least in the influence of an orientation that manifests itself first and most prominently in epistemology. And we shall see that despite Heidegger's relative inattention to this field, we can develop out of his early system a treatment of it that recognizes and accounts for this pre-eminence within the modern tradition.

I have a range of ambitions in developing such a Heideggerian treatment. An acquaintance with *Being and Time* cannot plausibly be supposed, and so the discussion, particularly in its first chapter, will attempt to serve as an introduction to the terms and claims of that work. Although I omit some important topics, and treat others much more briefly than they deserve, the core of Heidegger's early system will be presented in the course of this book. I hope to make this system more accessible to an analytic audience, by adopting (so far as I am able, and so far as the material permits) the latter's own standards for care and clarity and concreteness of exposition. And I hope also to convey, on occasion, an intuitive force or vividness which these points must possess if they are to be grasped in the manner we shall see the phenomenological method to demand.

Nevertheless, this aim of introducing to Heidegger's vocabulary and viewpoint is secondary to my interest in several more substantive points. Of course, I hope that this Heideggerian response to epistemology will be plausible in its own right, and will contribute to debate in the field by approaching its problems from an unaccustomed direction. If it were not both presumptuous and unrealistic, I might even hope for the more radical effect we shall see phenomenology's treatment of the field to intend. These aims are obvious, and need no elaboration, but I also have some more general and methodological interests which require a fuller account. And in introducing these, I shall be giving a first look at the overall structure to this Heideggerian response.

In *Being and Time* we find, almost inextricably intertwined, the twin orientations of phenomenology and existentialism. Each of these historical movements attempts in its own way an attack on traditional philosophical problems and approaches; each attempts to turn philosophy in new directions, to substitute new problems and goals for those of the philosophical tradition. But of course these problems are not totally new. We rather find, in most cases, a transformation of the traditional problems into descendent ones, which are divergent and continuous with their predecessors to different degrees, along different dimensions. Now, for recurring reasons of simplicity I shall ignore the historical context these two movements provide for *Being and Time*; I lay aside Heidegger's relationship to other existentialists and other phenomenologists: the complex similarities and differences, the lines of influence and reaction. But by developing Heidegger's response to the traditional problem in epistemology, we put ourselves in a position to examine the concrete forms these two radical methods take, in the most important work by the most important of existential phenomenologists. If I am able to structure his response in a clear and plausible way, I shall have organized the problems and positions so as to allow an easy extension to other figures as well; whether such an extension is worth pursuing will depend on the worth of this organization, to which it therefore seems best to give our first attention.

Now one basic feature of Heidegger's method will be that he attempts to *undermine* our representative traditional problem; he argues that the problem itself is an illegitimate one, and that the proper response is not straightforwardly to answer it, but to diagnose our tendency to raise this problem at all. And in this respect the radical or anti-traditional character of Heidegger's approach is shared in by certain commonsensical or ordinary language philosophy writing in the analytic mode. Moreover, this continuity goes further: Heidegger too will view the traditional philosopher's problems and claims as illegitimate divergences from a basic pre-philosophical or everyday position or condition. The epistemologist is attempting to escape this condition, to overcome a felt inadequacy in it, in a way not allowed us; the new philosophy's proper role is (in part) to show us that this route must not be attempted. Similarly, the scheme of at least some ordinary language philosophers is to argue that the traditional epistemological difficulties only arise when our everyday linguistic procedures are illegitimately stretched or abandoned. But while these latter philosophers would probably most typically see philosophy's new and proper role as purely critical, as aiming solely to return us to those everyday uses from the tradition's abuses, Heidegger assigns to the new philosophy a more positive and constructive task as well. The existential phenomenologist does not merely seek to return us to our everyday position from those traditional puzzles and proposals; he recognizes the unsatisfactory character of that position, which the tradition has responded to, and seeks a more adequate response. There is, according to Heidegger, also a legitimate route out of our everyday condition, one that answers to the most basic dissatisfactions that have given rise to the traditional projects. And the search for this other route will then constitute the 'descendent' problem spoken of above. These very general similarities and differences between Heidegger's strategy and those of ordinary language philosophers provide a more particular motive for interest in the radical approach of existential phenomenology. Although once again it seems best to avoid the added dimension of complexity that would be required to discuss these relationships explicitly, we may hope that a clear sketch of Heidegger's methodology, distinguishing it from various neighbouring routes, will at least provide a framework of alternatives with respect to which those commonsensical and ordinary language approaches can be fruitfully treated.

What is the general plan of my discussion, and what are its
subsidiary themes?

This overall outline of Heidegger's strategy explains the sequence
of my own discussion. The three chapters will deal respectively
with *everydayness*, as our basic, pre-philosophical position, with
epistemology, as a traditional philosophical project trying to improve upon this position by overcoming an unsatisfactoriness
rooted deeply within it, and with *phenomenology*, as a more
favoured response to this dissatisfaction, and the only appropriate
exit from everydayness. But since an adequate grasp of any of these
three requires that it be contrasted with both of the others, my
treatment cannot afford to deal with them in quite so simple and
isolating a sequence. Even everydayness cannot serve us as an
absolute starting-point, to be firmly laid in place with a description that will act as foundation for the others; we most profitably
progress towards a full view of everydayness by glancing ahead at
its borders with epistemology and phenomenology. Similarly, that
epistemological project is best approached by looking first at the
way everydayness quite naturally leads into it, and later at its
contrast with phenomenology's quite different removal from everydayness. Then the final advance on phenomenology should
progress through sketches of that defect in everydayness which
it responds to, and of the inadequate response attempted in
epistemology. Thus within each of the chapters themselves I shall
be dealing with each of these three broad stances, though with an
emphasis on and orientation towards some one among them. This, I
hope, will lift us through progressively higher perspectives upon all
three, in their complex relationships with one another.

The structure of my discussion will therefore be somewhat involved, with cycles set into the overall advance. It is of course
important to keep this full structure in view. For although—as I
mentioned—I shall try to give arguments that can be judged for
themselves, it remains true that *Being and Time* presents a system
of the old sort, some of whose power to persuade lies in the unity
and breadth of its vision, and in its surprising ability to explain at
once a great diversity of phenomena. Both in that work and here,
this system is unfolded layer by layer—its accounts are deepened in
stages, by being restated in increasingly basic terms. This unor-
thodox sequence is intended to allow the most basic account, which

is also the most novel and radical, to be led to by steps that allow one to keep an intuitive grasp. But it also makes the system especially difficult to hold in overall view. I shall try to keep clear the context of individual points, in particular by recalling an earlier appearance of a topic, and by anticipating its later development. This will, though, produce a quantity of back and forth references that may irritate some. It is tempting to try to defend this advice in some terms from the discussion itself: such reviews and previews can help us to reach out explicitly in time, in the way (we shall see) Heideggerian 'authenticity' demands—but this defence could too plausibly be thought to reduce that ideal to absurdity. It is in fact just my own inability to hold otherwise together in mind the various strands and stages of the overall system, that has pressed me into this practice.

Working across the grain of this overall sequence will be several secondary concerns. As mentioned, I hope this discussion may also serve as an introduction to Heidegger's early system. Conveniently, the bulk of exposition of his concepts and claims can come in the opening chapter, since its topic—everydayness— is also the initial subject in *Being and Time*, and the one with reference to which most of the book's terms are introduced. There will therefore be far more straightforward exposition in this first chapter than in the following two; indeed, a reader confident in his grasp of that Heideggerian system might prefer to skim through or skip over this account, to the considerably denser discussions that follow. But there are also some important Heideggerian notions that are presented only later in *Being and Time* (often in its second Division), and that will only be needed at later points in my own discussion as well; prominent among these are anxiety, authenticity, and temporality. It seems best to delay presenting these terms until the relevant points in my argument, even though this divides the straightforward exposition of his system, and makes the first chapter still less complete as such. In fact, this could not be genuinely avoided, for even those terms that are introduced early in the discussion, will usually be given new aspects as we proceed. Thus exposition of *Being and Time* will recur as a theme throughout the treatment of substantive topics.

This secondary aim of introducing Heidegger's system poses problems of a different sort as well: we must make some decisions about translation. To facilitate access to the English edition of

Being and Time, I shall follow the Macquarrie and Robinson translation throughout, noting dissatisfactions with their choices as we meet them. I shall also retain much of this (translated) Heideggerian terminology in my handling of the issues themselves—it might have been possible to switch to a less ponderous and idiosyncratic vocabulary in extracting my position from the texts, but such a switch would introduce new questions of equivalence between terms, and of faithfulness to the Heideggerian perspective. Generally, Heidegger adopts his odd vocabulary for good reason: he is suggesting a perspective that divides things differently than we are accustomed to do. Interpreting his points back into the terms of our customary perspective will often strip them of their force and point.

Now I mentioned that Heidegger's relationship to other existentialists and other phenomenologists will not be addressed, and that I shall also forgo any explicit comparisons with ordinary language philosophers; either project would be made unwieldy in our present context, by the necessity of adding an exposition of those other figures as well. But comparison with other philosophical stances will still be useful in presenting my Heideggerian response, and is made feasible by confining discussion to certain very major figures whose general views may be noted without exposition. Thus I shall characterize Heidegger's stance by occasionally contrasting it with those of Kant, Descartes, and Aristotle. These are appropriate choices because it was Heidegger's own intent to treat just them in the projected Part Two of *Being and Time*. But more importantly, they are also respectively relevant to the topics of my three chapters. And so I shall present Heidegger's description of our everyday understanding with occasional comparisons to Kant's account of our grasp of the synthetic a priori; I shall develop the Heideggerian critique of epistemology with reference to Descartes' version of that enterprise; and I shall give a sense of Heidegger's positive conception of phenomenology by contrasting it with the philosophical understanding at which Aristotle aims.

I

EVERYDAYNESS

EVERYDAYNESS is an appropriate starting-point for my discussion for at least three reasons. First and most important, it is presented by Heidegger as a sort of base condition, in which human beings initially find themselves, and in which they mainly remain. My other chief topics will be epistemology and phenomenology, and we shall see that these contrasting philosophical projects arise secondarily out of everydayness, and in response to deficiencies intrinsic to it. Although this priority of everydayness is not such as to permit a really full account of it in isolation from those two alternatives, it still makes this condition our best beginning. Second, Heidegger's interest in everydayness is the source of certain methodological interests that will implicitly guide the course of this discussion. It is Heidegger's attention to our everyday condition, and the priority he conspicuously gives it over the traditional philosopher's stance (though the exact character of this priority is, as we shall see, less immediately clear), that serve as a first clue there may be interesting relationships between his views and those of analytic philosophers writing in the commonsensical and ordinary language modes. For it is characteristic of the latter to take our everyday beliefs or ways of speaking as a standard against which the traditional philosopher's conclusions or uses of words are to be judged (and, deviating from which, to be rejected). Does Heidegger's description of everydayness resemble those given by these analytic philosophers? Does he single out the same aspects of everydayness as his standard? And what justification does he give for holding philosophy to such a standard? These and many further questions are prompted by notice of this first superficial parallel, and although I shall not explicitly pursue such relationships, I shall orient this presentation of Heidegger towards them in such a way as to interest, perhaps, an analytic audience. And last and most concrete, everydayness is a suitable starting-point because it is Heidegger's own in *Being and Time*, and indeed the focus for most of the book's first Division. Its choice therefore offers the opportunity to lay out at my beginning the central core of that Division's terminology and system, which we shall need in the discussions to follow. As a result, this first chapter will be far more thorough in summary and explication than those that follow, and will make a much heavier use of quotation from Heidegger's works, in justifying its presentation of them.

Let us begin, then, with a summary of Heidegger's description of everydayness, one that doubles as an introduction to his system of concepts and claims; these, though often seeming quite removed from my topics, will eventually be brought to bear upon them. Now in part, this description portrays our everyday relationship to the entities around us—our everyday way of encountering them. But more importantly, it concerns a background understanding that is a 'condition of the possibility' for all this everyday experience. Heidegger is obviously indebted here to a parallel account in Kant, though he tries to improve upon this historical precedent, by applying its insight at a deeper level. In presenting his description of this everyday understanding, it will therefore be helpful and appropriate to compare it with this Kantian analogue. Very roughly, we shall see that Heidegger differs in attributing to our everyday experience a 'pragmatic' character; this radically alters the account of the understanding that makes such experience possible. Because we are much more accustomed to view our everyday relationships as basically 'theoretical' (as Kant also has viewed them), Heidegger's summary of everydayness will challenge our ability to adopt a quite different perspective and vocabulary—a 'pragmatic' conception that indeed will guide all the rest of this book. This summary of everydayness constitutes the first and by far the largest part in this chapter. In the second and third parts we shall glance ahead to the topics of the following chapters—epistemology and phenomenology—and shall take our first bearing towards these by noticing certain broad relations in which they stand to our everyday condition. That is, we shall notice (in the second part) the general way in which everydayness is used by Heidegger as a standard for the epistemologist's reasoning, and we shall see (in the third) how the choice of everydayness as starting-point is grounded in the general character of Heidegger's phenomenological method. This series of topics—everydayness, epistemology, phenomenology—has a logic that was sketched in the introduction, and will emerge more fully as we proceed; this sequence corresponds not only to the three chapters, but to the divisions within each of them. By focusing upon each topic in turn, but also discussing the others in their relationship to it, we progressively deepen our understanding of all three.

1. Everydayness: an account of our basic condition, and introduction to Heidegger's terms

a. How the task of describing everydayness arises. Heidegger says that the aim of his book is 'to work out the question of the meaning of *Being* and to do so concretely' (*BT* 19). But this project was not completed, either in *Being and Time* itself or in the other works of this 'early period'. I am thus at an immediate disadvantage in explaining his use of this crucial term "**Being**" [Sein]—a term that analytic readers will find especially aggravating, and that therefore stands in particular need of clarification. Heidegger will use it in conjunction with the (in German) etymologically-related word "**entity**" [Seiendes], which he will apply to anything that is, in any way or sense whatsoever. And the 'Being' of an entity will then be, roughly, that most general way in which this entity is, in which it is most basically like or distinct from others. We shall soon see that Heidegger distinguishes three such possibilities of Being, so that there will be three most basic types to which entities can belong. The structure of each of these alternatives, and how just these three come to be, will be central topics in this first chapter; the use of "Being" should become more concrete as we proceed to these instances of it. We shall also see as we go that there are strong continuities between this basic level of the Being of entities, and the a priori or transcendental level in Kant. Heidegger will claim that these types of Being are laid out by us, and not originally extracted from entities themselves; as in Kant, this provision indeed makes possible all discovery or experiencing of entities. And these continuities will also be helpful in clarifying this Heideggerian use of "Being".

As he examines this guiding question of the meaning of Being, Heidegger soon introduces another crucial term—"**Dasein**"—as referring to the entity that enters upon this inquiry: 'This entity which each of us is himself and which includes inquiring as one of the possibilities of its Being, we shall denote by the term "*Dasein*".' (*BT* 27). It refers, that is, to what we would commonly call "human beings", but one of Heidegger's motives in substituting his own term is that he views that and other familiar expressions for this entity as corrupted by their association with a misinterpretation of the Being of this entity (cf. for example *BT* 72). As we shall see later in this part, Heidegger's own term is chosen for its appropriateness to the basic structure he will soon be attributing to us. Now while an account of the meaning of Being is the ultimate aim of *Being and Time*, Heidegger adopts as his intermediate task a working-out of the Being of Dasein, and it is towards this that all the published part of the book's plan—two of three Divisions, within the first of two Parts—is directed.

In order not to prejudice his treatment of this entity by describing some *special* condition it may be in, he determines to look first at Dasein's 'averageness', or '**everydayness**' [Alltäglichkeit]:

> At the outset of our analysis it is particularly important that Dasein should not be Interpreted with the differentiated character of some definite way of existing, but that it should be uncovered in the undifferentiated character which it has proximally and for the most part.... Out of this kind of Being—and back into it again—is all existing, such as it is. We call this everyday undifferentiated character of Dasein "*averageness*". (*BT* 69).

Heidegger supposes, that is, that there are several key conditions—or 'modes'—that are possible for us. Later, when he gives his account of our essential structure, he will try to explain each of these modes as a different basic 'modification' of this structure. But now, as he works towards that account of our Being, he provisionally assumes that this Being will be most visible or accessible in that ordinary and undeveloped condition in which we initially and most often find ourselves. He thus focuses first on this way we live most of our lives, on the way we are 'proximally and for the most part'; this is our 'average everydayness'. And he leaves aside, for the moment, certain more developed or 'special' conditions or modes we occasionally pass into; for my purposes, the most important of these will be the 'theoretical attitude', and 'authenticity'.

Thus Heidegger's account of our everydayness, provided in his book's first Division, is at the same time a preliminary description of the Being that belongs to Dasein as such: 'In this everydayness there are certain structures which we shall exhibit—not just any accidental structures, but essential ones which, in every kind of Being that factical Dasein may possess, persist as determinative for the character of its Being' (*BT* 38). By examining this everyday condition, he lays out structures that are essential, and will be retained when the scope of his account is later widened to include those developed alternatives to everydayness. But he also describes these structures with an eye to the particular 'modifications' they take in the condition of everydayness, so that parts of this description will need to be subtly revised when he later attempts to accommodate those alternatives within these structures. This gives to his discussion a (mostly unacknowledged) complexity, which poses an early challenge to my own undertaking: in reviewing the structures presented in Division I, I must try to distinguish the extent to which they characterize Dasein quite generally, and the extent to which their presentation is oriented towards everydayness. But the distinction is a difficult one to confront here at our beginning, for a fully adequate grasp of what is peculiarly everyday itself depends upon clarification of the contrast between that condition and the special alternatives to it—alternatives not to be introduced until later. For this reason the bulk of this part will follow Heidegger's own procedure of outlining Dasein's essential structures by reference to their everyday modifications, but without explicitly distinguishing the essential from the everyday. Treatment of this distinction, in the preparatory and somewhat obscure form that alone is possible for us as yet, will be confined to two brief passages, at the end of each of the main sections of my primary exposition.

Now Heidegger believes that this problem of characterizing our everyday condition has been neglected by the philosophical tradition: 'This task [of an analysis of Dasein] includes a *desideratum* which philosophy has long found disturbing but has continually refused to achieve: *to work out the idea of a 'natural conception of the world'.' (BT 76)*. As we shall see, Heidegger holds that traditional philosophy has neglected everydayness precisely by focusing its attention on one of those special conditions possible for us, the condition into which the philosophizing philosopher has placed himself. Roughly, the tradition has treated our relation to entities as basically 'theoretical', rather than 'pragmatic'. And when it *has* undertaken an account of everydayness, or of our Being in general, its own insertion within this special theoretical attitude has inevitably led it to further distortions of a quite particular sort. These missteps, moreover, are not peculiar to philosophers, but are motivated from deep within our essential structure itself. Heidegger's effort to resist these compelling distortions is responsible for his demand that we learn unfamiliar terms, and grasp familiar ones in radically new ways. I shall return later, and repeatedly, to his account of the common character of these misinterpretations, and to his explanation for the way they thrust themselves upon the philosophical tradition, and upon us. Indeed, one of my central concerns will be to trace back to its roots this prominent anti-traditional strain in Heidegger, which we shall shortly begin to see manifesting itself. For as will be quickly obvious, much of Heidegger's own description of everydayness consists precisely in rulings-out of insistent and pervasive traditional interpretations of ourselves.

b. Everydayness as Being-in-the-world: the world. Most generally, Heidegger's account of everydayness is an elaborate description of the way we are essentially '**Being-in-the-world**' [In-der-Welt-sein], a central concept in *Being and Time* which will figure prominently in its treatment of epistemology, and which therefore must be developed in some detail. First, by way of general orientation, this expression does not say that we 'are in' anything by being spatially contained in it, and does not mean by "world" the earth or our physical environment. Heidegger himself, and very typically, begins his development of this term with just these denials (cf. *BT* 79 ff.)—ruling out the most obvious and natural interpretation of these words, because he wishes to reject the most familiar and accepted interpretations of ourselves. Now, as we follow him by considering in sequence these two elements of the expression, "world" and "Being-in", we must even resist the temptation to take them as naming distinct entities. As we shall see, they penetrate one another so thoroughly that the world will turn out to belong to our own structure.

The notion of world is best arrived at by beginning with a description of our everyday relationship to entities within-the-world. (It will help, though, to bear in mind from the beginning that the world is not simply made up of these entities, and that these entities are 'within' the world in a quite different sense than Dasein is 'in' it.) We here enter on what I shall loosely call Heidegger's "pragmatism", for he claims that this basic everyday relationship lies in our employment of tools, or '**equipment**' [Zeug]. But he uses these terms to encompass much more than we ordinarily associate with them, so that they cover for example not merely hammers and chisels, but also chairs, clothes, books, pavements, timber, and even the sun—i.e. all those entities of which we make use in order to realize our purposes (cf. e.g. *BT* 100). In more overtly technical jargon, Heidegger also refers to these entities as "the **ready-to-hand**" [das Zuhandene]. What determines an entity as such ready-to-hand equipment, then, is that we have adopted a certain attitude or relationship to it. And Heidegger will try to convince us that this attitude is both more pervasive and more basic than we might ordinarily suppose. He will encourage us to attend to the intricate details of our everyday lives, and to notice the wealth of equipmental dealings we more usually overlook. Although it will be convenient to focus on equipment of the type that a craftsman handles, we should therefore bear in mind that the class is in fact far broader. Similarly, the purposes for which these entities are used will extend well beyond those productions of further equipment (as in the carpenter's construction of a house) of which we perhaps first think.

Our relationship to such equipment, as we are occupied in our dealings with it, is called by Heidegger "**concern**" [Besorgen], a term whose sense will emerge as we proceed, but that should initially suggest the way these equipmental dealings, and their results, *matter* to us. We employ equipment for a diverse range of purposes towards which we aim, and the importance of which gives significance as well to the means of achieving them. This concernful relation to the ready-to-hand has two characteristic features that will be of particular importance to us later on. First, in these manipulations of the ready-to-hand our attention is typically directed ahead to those purposes, so that the tools themselves are 'inconspicuous', and are in fact more effectively employed the less we explicitly reflect upon them (cf. *BT* 99, 106; *BPP* 309). We notice the weight to a hammer most when we find difficulty in driving nails; we notice the look or sound of words most when we are failing to follow their sense. It is this typical inconspicuousness, indeed, that partly explains our failure to notice the pervasiveness of our relations to the ready-to-hand. We are constantly employing a great range of equipment in the course of our activities—intellectual activities as well—but out attention normally passes *through* these entities so that our encounter with them remains merely implicit. A second key feature of our relationship to equipment is that we encounter any particular tool within a broader context of equipment that is employed all together in pursuit of our ends. Our attention is spread out across a ready-to-hand system, and not focused in upon any particular tool within it. We use the hammer along with the nails, the wood, the workbench, the light; we encounter it primarily in its role within this network, as part of a background from which it again stands out only if something goes wrong. Thus it is always a totality of equipment with which we are familiar first: 'What we encounter as closest to us (though not as something taken as a theme) is the room . . . as equipment for residing. Out of this the 'arrangement' emerges, and it is in this that any 'individual' item of equipment shows itself. *Before* it does so, a totality of equipment has already been discovered.' (*BT* 98; cf. also *BPP* 163). This context-embeddedness of ready-to-hand entities also contributes to our tendency to overlook our relationship to them; it means that our attention is typically diffused.

Now in claiming that our everyday and basic relation to entities lies in such concernful dealings, Heidegger is not simply marking off our actions as opposed to our perceptions and thoughts; there is a kind of seeing, for example, that is proper to such concern, and that Heidegger calls "**circumspection**" [Umsicht]: the craftsman *'looks about'* to be sure that his tools are in order, or to select the one best suited to his task (cf. *BT* 98; *BPP* 163). Such seeing is characterized by the same features as our actual use of equipment, and is not a detached scrutiny of these entities for and by themselves. Circumspection discovers a knife as appropriate for a particular job of cutting; it does not dwell on this entity as it is in its own right, but passes through or beyond it to the business at hand. And when we look to the traffic signal before crossing a road we discover this tool only as part of an intricate network of equipment which has sense or significance for us as a whole: kerb, crossing, turning traffic, and other pedestrians are all present together for our circumspective sight.

All such concernful doing and seeing displays still another feature that will play a prominent role for us later on. When the craftsman thus sees that his tools are in place, or arranges them about him to be most readily accessible, he operates upon them in a crucial general way that Heidegger (in awkward translation) calls "**desevering**" [Entfernen]. This term refers to an essential tendency in us to *'bring close'* the entities with which we are concerned. But we must understand this bringing close not as a diminishing of the measurable distance at which these entities lie from us, but as a process of making these entities maximally available to our manipulations of them. 'Proximally and for the most part, de-severing is a circumspective bringing-close—bringing something close by, in the sense of procuring it, putting it in readiness, having it to hand. . . . *In Dasein there lies an essential tendency towards closeness.*' (*BT* 139–40). Such closeness can be achieved either by physically operating upon equipment, or by discovering it and its uses through circumspective sight. When we wash, dry, and stack dishes we are desevering this equipment, by readying it for a later use; when we learn the plan and transportation systems of a city we desever its parts by making them more accessible to us. In all such ways, we put ourselves in a better position to realize our ends, by 'bringing close' the equipment we shall need as means; indeed, desevering is a preparatory stage in our pursuit of those ends.

With this special sense of "bringing close" we also touch the edges of the peculiar spatiality belonging to the ready-to-hand, according to which the *distance* of an entity from us consists not in some objectively measurable interval, but in its accessibility or availability to us, while the *direction* in which it lies is determined not by the reading on any compass or co-ordinate system, but by reference to the locations of whole contexts of equipment. An office is in a certain building in the centre of the town; it is located as belonging within some larger unit of equipment we know our way towards (cf. *BT* 140). And this unit is near or distant according to the ease with which we may reach it; it is further in heavy traffic than in light (cf. *BT* 136–7; *BPP* 310). It is in such space that we principally act and reckon, and not in that of the geometer or physicist. I shall return to this spatiality of the ready-to-hand and to Dasein's desevering in the next chapter; now we must proceed to see how the concept of world is developed on the basis of this account of equipment.

Heidegger expresses the principle underlying this classification of entities in this way: 'Equipment is essentially 'something in-order-to . . .'.' (*BT* 97). That is, an entity is determined as equipment by virtue of our adopting an attitude that assigns it a certain use or function. We understand this entity primarily in terms of a certain purpose that may be realized with it. By virtue of this understanding, equipment thus has an '**assignment**' [Verweisung] to what it is for, or as Heidegger also puts it, there is always an '**involvement**'

SKIDMORE COLLEGE LIBRARY

[Bewandtnis] with the equipment in its 'towards-which' [Wozu]. When we see some hammer *as* a hammer, it is because we are already familiar with the function that hammers are for, and because we can thus view this entity in terms of that use. But this assignment to a towards-which, although definitive, is only one among a great number of assignments in terms of which we grasp the ready-to-hand. We always understand any tool by reference to several other relationships it enters into. Thus there is an assignment also to the 'totality' of equipment with which (as we have seen) a ready-to-hand entity always belongs—that is, to the other equipment with which it is typically encountered, and often, only in conjunction with which it is able to function properly. 'Equipment—in accordance with its equipmentality—always is *in terms of* its belonging to other equipment: ink-stand, pen, ink, paper, blotting pad, table, lamp, furniture, windows, doors, room.' (*BT* 97). Further, a ready-to-hand entity has an assignment to the other Dasein that has produced it, to the materials it has been produced out of, to the nature these materials have been extracted from, and so on (cf. *BT* 100). And most importantly, the assignment to what the equipment is for can be traced onward, in Aristotelian fashion, through the 'purposes' mentioned above:

> ... *with* this thing, for instance, which is ready-to-hand, and which we accordingly call a "hammer", there is an involvement in hammering; with hammering, there is an involvement in making something fast; with making something fast, there is an involvement in protection against bad weather; and this protection 'is' for the sake of providing shelter for Dasein—that is to say, for the sake of a possibility of Dasein's Being. (*BT* 116).

This last assignment, in the teleological chain stretching beyond a tool's towards-which, is some possible way for Dasein itself to be. This **'possibility'** [Möglichkeit] is called by Heidegger "the **for-the-sake-of-which**" [das Worum-willen], and as we shall see it plays a very special role in his account. We must from the beginning keep in mind an important point about it: this end need not be some definite state that Dasein intends to realize at some future date; it may rather, for example, be a role Dasein plays in the very process of carrying out its equipmental dealings. That carpenter may hammer not only for-the-sake-of completing the house and receiving his wages, but also because he takes pride in, or views himself in terms of, his skilful use of the tools of his trade. This point leads on to another: Dasein need not explicitly recognize, or be able to articulate, this for-the-sake-of-which; thus "purpose" has been only a first, potentially misleading approximation. The carpenter may never be able to announce to himself that he works for so subtle an end, but may still 'understand' his tools as assigned to this end, in the technical sense I shall soon introduce for "understanding".

Any ready-to-hand entity thus possesses a great range of assignments beyond itself; these assignments will intersect with those belonging to other equipment in a most complex pattern. We recognize and employ all the countless tools through which we live, by virtue of a prior familiarity with the assignments these types of equipment possess. This familiarity is at work in the most casual, rapid, and implicit of our equipmental dealings; tying our shoes, we 'know' what these laces are for, and this assignment relates this equipment to the shoes, and through them to the pavement and other surfaces our day will lead us across. Heidegger refers to the intricate system of all these assignments belonging to the sum of our equipment as "the **referential totality**" [die Verweisungsganzheit] (I shall also use the expressions "involvement structure" and "system of assignments"). We may view this system, or any portion of it, as oriented towards some for-the-sake-of-which, which is that way for Dasein to be, the 'realization' of which is the final end of some particular network of equipment.

But while this for-the-sake-of-which lies at the 'end' of one or more chains of assignments, it also occupies a certain prior or privileged position within the entire involvement structure. For Dasein always 'begins' by assigning *itself* to such a for-the-sake-of-which (i.e. by taking up some end), and from that to the rest of the involvement structure (as, roughly, the means for achieving that end) (cf. *BT* 119). In assigning itself to an end in this way, Dasein understands itself in terms of this end, and then in turn understands equipment by reference to the contribution it makes to this end. It is at this point that we ourselves are drawn into the involvement structure, in a way that will have important consequences for Heidegger's account; here, it is what allows the concept of world to at last be arrived at. For this is only grasped when we recognize that the involvement structure does not stand independently over and against us as something we may have a detached acquaintance with, but that our familiarity with it is precisely a familiarity with our own ends and with the means for achieving them. The assignments which make up this structure are not properties or relations that we discover in ready-to-hand entities, as may have at first appeared; they are rather constituted by our directedness towards certain ends and by our capacity for realizing them. A hammer's assignment to its towards-which, for example, is not anything we originally discover in some particular hammer, by observing its structure, or what we and other Dasein do with it; it is rather already contained in our prior directedness towards the ends that may be achieved with hammers (in conjunction with other equipment), and in our prior ability or preparedness to employ hammers in achieving those ends. Indeed, Heidegger claims that it is only on the basis of this 'a priori' familiarity with the assignments belonging to hammers, that it is possible for us to see or use some particular hammer as a hammer. This familiarity, that is, plays an analogous role to that Kant assigns to our grasp of the concepts of the understanding. But Heidegger's account both of this founding transcendental understanding and of the founded empirical experience diverges drastically from this Kantian precedent; Heidegger intends it to do better justice to the way we live through the bulk of our lives. We discover some entity as a tool not because we have mastered any concepts, but because we are already pursuing some set of ends, and have a generalized competence over the system of equipment needed to achieve them. This pursuit and this competence have as their object the whole system of assignments belonging to this and other equipment. And it is precisely this system of assignments, understood as embodied within this competent directedness, that Heidegger refers to as "**world**" [Welt]. We can now see clearly, then, that this term does not refer to the sum of entities (for which Heidegger often will use the word in scare quotes, however; cf. *BT* 93); it is instead what we must have an a priori understanding of, before such entities can be encountered. As Heidegger also puts it, this understanding '**frees**' [freigibt] these entities, entities that we can then go on to encounter '**within-the-world**' [innerweltlich].

Now Heidegger claims further that the Being or essence of equipment is provided by this system of assignments (cf. *BT* 116), so that our understanding of the world is an understanding of the Being of entities within-the-world. This puts us in a position to grasp his sharp distinction between '**disclosedness**' [Erschlossenheit], as the a priori familiarity we have with our world, and '**discovering**'

[Entdecken], as the encountering of entities within-the-world which is possible only on the basis of disclosedness (cf. *BT* 105, 118, 263). This distinction runs parallel to another, between the terms "**ontological**" [ontologisch] and "**ontical**" [ontisch]: the latter applies to any relation to entities within-the-world, while the former applies to any relation to the Being of those entities. So we can ontically discover some particular hammer only because the Being of hammers, i.e. the place of their various involvements within the structure of the world in general, is already ontologically disclosed to us.

But moreover, because these involvements are all oriented towards some for-the-sake-of-which, as a way for us to be, to which we assign ourselves, and in terms of which we understand ourselves, this understanding of the world equally involves an understanding of ourselves, and of our own Being. That carpenter's understanding of the involvements belonging to his equipment is at the same time an understanding of himself, in terms of that for-the-sake-of-which towards which these involvements point: he may identify himself, for example, as the proficient manipulator of his equipment, or by reference to that standard of living his work permits him to enjoy. It is his competent directedness towards certain ends that specifies both who he is, and what the ready-to-hand entities about him are; the Being of the former is delineated in his striving towards ends, the Being of the latter in his mastery of the means to those ends. This reciprocity between the Being of Dasein and the Being of entities within-the-world, which arises from the way in which an understanding of one always involves an understanding of the other, will be an important theme in the discussions to follow, and should grow progressively clearer as we proceed. Heidegger summarizes this, and several other of the above points, in this typically cryptic way:

Dasein always assigns itself *from* a 'for-the-sake-of-which' *to* the 'with-which' of an involvement; that is to say, to the extent that it *is*, it always lets entities be encountered as ready-to-hand. *That wherein* Dasein understands itself beforehand in the mode of assigning itself is *that for which* it has let entities be encountered beforehand. *The 'wherein' of an act of understanding which assigns or refers itself, is that for which one lets entities be encountered in the kind of Being that belongs to involvements; and this 'wherein' is the phenomenon of the world.* (*BT* 119).

The preceding should allow us to make some sense of these seemingly impenetrable lines.

Before leaving this notion of world we must consider, however, how much of the above account describes a structure essential to Dasein as such, and how much instead an everyday 'filling' to this structure. For while everydayness is the mode in which we mainly live our lives, and while our essential structure may therefore be expected to be most accessible in it, there still are other modes of existence possible for us, to which parts of this description may turn out not to apply. Our perspective is still too narrow to allow or justify treating this question in detail here, but I shall briefly note a pair of points that will be of particular importance later on.

First, we shall see as soon as the next part that ready-to-hand equipment is not the only type of entity that we can discover within-the-world, and correspondingly that an understanding of the involvement structure is not the only way in which the Being of entities can be disclosed. Roughly speaking, there are 'theoretical' analogues to both of these, so that entities may be differently discovered, and their Being differently disclosed, in a special attitude distinct from everydayness. It is this attitude in which the scientist discovers his objects, and whose grounding disclosure was described by Kant. However, as we shall also eventually see, this does not mean that in this 'theoretical' stance we dispense with our understanding of the involvement structure altogether; this is retained, and that special disclosure of the Being of entities is possible only on the basis of it. Indeed, this dependence of the theoretical discovery of entities on our concernful understanding of the world will be a key claim in the next chapter's response to epistemology. So a familiarity with the involvement structure described above is essential to us, but this familiarity only exhausts our understanding when we are in the condition of everydayness.

Second, we shall see in the third chapter that there is a quite different way in which we may step out of everydayness, and one with quite different implications for our relationship to the involvement structure; this way will be called "authenticity". Here it is not that we base upon our understanding of our world a secondary way of disclosing the Being of entities, but rather, as I shall provisionally put it, that we recognize a certain contingency or lack of secure grounding as belonging to this world. More specifically, in this second special state we do not narrowly identify ourselves with the

for-the-sake-of-which lying at the apex of the involvement structure, but recognize that this could as easily be any other end, and is
by no means established as what we ourselves most basically are.
And reciprocally, we do not take the Being of entities within-the-
world to be conclusively settled by their assignment towards any
particular such end. Thus this second alternative to everydayness
also serves to confirm that an understanding of the system of
assignments is essential to us, but it suggests that a particular
attachment to or immersion in this understanding is distinctive of
everydayness. We cannot hope for full clarity on these points until
this discussion has achieved a much broader perspective, however.

c. Everydayness as Being-in-the-world: Being-in. Such then is
Heidegger's account of the world which, as he claims, we are
essentially Being-in. We may now turn to his development of this
latter notion—that is to his explanation of the manner in which we
are *in* this world. We are after, in other words, the nature of our
familiarity with our world, or the structure of the disclosedness of
that world—a structure running along a different dimension than
the internal structure of the world, so far discussed. And Heidegger
offers still another formulation for this topic: it is the question, in
what way Dasein is its '**there**' [Da]. For he explains: 'In the expression "there" we have in view this essential disclosedness.' (*BT* 171).
It is because the world is 'there' or disclosed to Dasein alone among
entities, and because this disclosure is necessary for there to be any
entities at all, that Heidegger has adopted this term "Dasein". This
'there' that we essentially are, is also characterized as the '**clearing**'
[Lichtung] within which it first becomes possible for entities to be
discovered. Our familiarity with the system of assignments creates a
'space' or locale within which both equipment and we ourselves can
then appear. In the absence of such familiarity we could not see or
use chairs as chairs; this type of entity would simply not occur. And
similarly, it is only our familiarity with the ends such equipment is to
be used for, and with the standard manner of its use, that provides
us with the types within which we can encounter or identify ourselves and one another; only so can there be carpenters, or even
'persons' at all.

So far we have been looking at the overall lay-out of this clearing
or 'there'—at its internal structure as a system of assignments. Now
we must see just how it is laid out for us, or how we are in it. I have

already remarked that world and Being-in are not fully separable elements of Being-in-the-world in general, and this has the reassuring consequence that we may be helped with some of the unclarities in the above account by parts of the following development. Moreover, the preceding is open to a certain natural misinterpretation: roughly, the tempting reading of this notion of an a priori familiarity with the world in too cognitive or intellectual (or thoroughly Kantian) a way. In much of his explication of Being-in, i.e. of the nature of this familiarity, Heidegger has this likely misinterpretation in view. Again, his general intent is to offer a 'pragmatic' reading of that familiarity, one that more aptly accounts for the character of our everyday experience. He distinguishes four aspects of this Being-in, each of which will be important in what follows.

A first of these aspects is called "**understanding**" [Verstehen], a term that I have already used in the account of world and that might, if unclarified, tend to reinforce the mentioned misinterpretation. But the discussion should also have prepared us for the rather special meaning Heidegger assigns to this term:

When we are talking ontically we sometimes use the expression "understanding something" with the signification of "being able to manage something", "being a match for it", "being competent to do something". In understanding, as an [essential structure of Dasein], that which we have such competence over is not a 'what', but Being as existing. (*BT* 183; cf. also *BPP* 276).

Such understanding, in other words, is a competence not for some specific task, or over some specific tool, but for the whole system of involvements which constitutes our world. Heidegger claims that we always most basically understand ourselves in terms of some possible way for us to be—a 'for-the-sake-of-which'. And this understanding is precisely a capacity and disposition to achieve this possibility, for along with this end we also understand the rest of the involvement structure as, roughly, the possible ways and means by which our own possibility may be 'realized'. We may think of this system of involvements as an intricate network of pathways, oriented towards some ultimate goal or goals; our understanding of our world is then our ability to manoeuvre along these routes, and our directedness through them towards that goal. Most importantly, our understanding of these pathways is not a theoretical grasp of resources available, but a capacity for effectively manipulating these resources. Understanding a hammer's involvements, for example, includes most importantly not a knowing-that hammers are for driving in nails, but a knowing-how to carry this out. And in its most basic and full-fledged form, this know-how will be more in the nature of an implicit bodily competence, than of an ability to follow explicitly some series of operations; where understanding has the latter, more articulable character, it most typically depends on the former sort of mastery over the constitutive operations themselves. We may follow explicit directions to locate some shop in our city, but not in performing those countless little tactical manoeuvres involved in each stage of this procedure.

Our Being-in the world by way of understanding it involves, therefore, our being always directed ahead towards some for-the-sake-of-which, as a way we may be, and our being competently acquainted with those pathways through the involvement structure which lead ahead to that end. We must continue to bear in mind, however, that this end need not be some future state that we are seeking to actualize; it lies 'ahead' not (always) in this ordinary chronological sense, but inasmuch as we do what we do for its sake. Thus this possibility need not be distinct from that competence itself—as I have noted in the case of that carpenter. This explains Heidegger's surprising readiness to use the terms "for-the-sake-of-which" and "possibility" interchangeably with the expression "**potentiality-for-Being**" [Seinkönnen—for which a better translation might be "ability-to-be"]; we would otherwise have expected the latter to refer to a capacity distinct from the states it might realize. But consider this passage, for example: 'In understanding a context of relations such as we have mentioned, Dasein has assigned itself to an 'in-order-to', and it has done so in terms of a potentiality-for-Being for the sake of which it itself is . . .' (*BT* 119). The ends towards which a ballplayer aims, and that allow him to see and use a bat with its defining function, will include not merely such extrinsic possibilities as earning his salary or winning the game, but also the rôle of ballplayer itself, which is constituted precisely by a competence over the relevant equipment. Such a role can be, paradoxically, both the end an ability points towards, and that ability itself. Complementarily, this explains too Heidegger's assertion that Dasein *is* its possibilities: 'The kind of Being which Dasein has, as potentiality-for-Being, lies existentially in understanding. Dasein is not something [concrete] which possesses its competence for something by way of an extra; it is primarily Being-possible. Dasein is in every case what it can be, and in the way in which it is its possibility' (*BT* 183). If the end we strive towards is not genuinely distinct from the activity of striving itself, then it is easier to see how we might be identified with that end. Later, I shall consider why Heidegger makes these statements so baldly, suggesting that our ends are always intrinsic to our competent striving.

We have seen then that understanding is a mastery of the means to an end, and to an end we are striving to achieve. Because it thus resembles not merely a capacity but a disposition, understanding reflects our essential tendency to 'press forward into possibilities', a characteristic that Heidegger refers to as our "**projection**" [Entwurf] (cf. *BT* 184–5). We are not just familiar with that network of routes through the involvement structure, we are always also impelled along them in pursuit of some end they lead towards. We thrust or project ourselves towards this end, through these pathways. But as an understanding of the for-the-sake-of-which reciprocally involves an understanding of the equipmental assignments oriented towards it, "projection" takes on a related sense we shall also be encountering frequently: in projecting towards some end, we simultaneously 'project' the modes of Being of entities within-the-world, in the sense of laying out the possible types to which equipment may then belong. That is, involvements—as the Being of equipment—are projected (disclosed) precisely in our projection (directedness) towards certain possibilities, and in our capacity for achieving them. It is our competent striving towards the ends that may be 'realized' with hammers, for example, that lays out what it is for something to be a hammer.

Now this first aspect of our Being-in, our understanding, plays a privileged role in Heidegger's account, for reasons that will not become apparent until we meet the authentic alternative to everydayness, in my third chapter. But this priority is responsible for the two different senses Heidegger gives to another important term. He refers to our characteristic of understanding ourselves in terms of possibilities as our "**existence**" [Existenz], but he also broadens this term's application, and uses it more generally for that kind of Being belonging to us alone (cf. *BT* 32 f., 274). Heidegger chooses this word for its etymological suggestion of the way we '*stand outside*' ourselves, by projecting ahead towards ways for us to be. But because this feature of understanding ourselves in terms of possibilities is so crucially distinctive of us, it is also appropriate for that broader reference to our Being in general. Heidegger will thus say that stones, hammers, and horses *are*, but that only we '*exist*'. (Note that neither of these Heideggerian uses of "exist" makes a point we would ordinarily call "existentialist"; the term is more closely related to what I have been calling "pragmatic" elements in *Being and Time*. Later, we shall meet themes much more obviously 'existentialist'—and I shall sometimes speak of them so—but should bear in mind that this is in a common but un-Heideggerian sense of that word.) Either the broader or the narrower use of "exist" may be more prominent in the several terms derived from it. Thus "**existentiale**" [Existenzial] is applied quite generally to any constituent of our Being (so including not only understanding but also the other three aspects of Being-in)—and is contrasted with "**category**" [Kategorie], which refers to any aspect of the Being of entities other than ourselves (cf. *BT* 70). And similarly, Heidegger calls the task of describing our Being, in general, "existential analysis". On the other hand, "**existentiality**" [Existenzialität] is used more narrowly, for that aspect of our Being-in our world which I have just been describing: our projective understanding.

Finally, there is a pair of terms in which these broader and narrower uses are complexly and importantly merged. Heidegger distinguishes between two different levels to Dasein's understanding: this understanding is '**existentiell**' [existenziell] insofar as it projects towards particular possibilities, for example Being-a-carpenter, which will be common to some Dasein but not others; this understanding is '**existential**' [existenzial] insofar as it projects towards possibility as such, which belongs to the essential structure of any Dasein. That is, Dasein on the one hand always understands itself by reference to some specific and idiosyncratic end. But, as we shall see, it is also possible for it to understand itself more deeply and essentially, by recognizing its more basic character of projecting towards some end or other; in recognizing this, it will have grasped itself by reference to a genuine existentiale. Having referred to the understanding in general as Dasein's 'sight', Heidegger adopts the term "**transparency**" [Durchsichtigkeit] for that existential understanding in which Dasein '*looks into*' its own Being (cf. *BT* 186–7). We need not untangle this distinction any further for purposes of the passages in which we shall soon encounter it. But it will later assume a particular importance, and so will have to be reapproached.

Now we have seen that Dasein's understanding is an understanding (disclosing) of the Being of entities, and that it grounds any encountering (discovering) of those entities themselves. When we encounter some entity, we do so in the light of certain involvements that we have understood beforehand. Such encountering makes these involvements explicit in a certain way: as belonging to some particular entity within-the-world. Heidegger calls this way in which the involvements already grasped in an a priori understanding can be made explicit as applying to some definite entity, "**interpretation**" [Auslegung]; the latter is thus an ontical instantiation of an ontological understanding. Such application is related to that original understanding, roughly as the exercise of a capacity is to that capacity itself. Thus Heidegger can affirm: 'In interpretation, understanding does not become something different. It becomes itself.' (*BT* 188). Interpretation may be verbal, but need not be; we interpret a hammer as a hammer, i.e. as possessing certain assignments, in merely picking it up and using it to drive nails, and even in that circumspection which just sees it as available for this task.

That which is disclosed in understanding—that which is understood—is already accessible in such a way that its 'as which' can be made to stand out explicitly.... In dealing with what is environmentally ready-to-hand by interpreting it circumspectively, we 'see' it *as* a table, a door, a carriage, or a bridge; but what we have thus interpreted need not necessarily be also taken apart by making an assertion which definitely characterizes it. (*BT* 189).

Those implicit and unarticulated dealings with equipment, which make up the bulk of our everyday relations to the entities about us, thus involve interpretations of those entities, in the 'pragmatic' sense Heidegger assigns to that term.

Such everyday dealings need not be inarticulate, however. And where an '**assertion**' [Aussage] is made, interpretation takes on a distinct form, showing certain new features that will be important later in our discussion; here too Heidegger offers an explanatory structure that will have radical implications. He distinguishes three aspects to this special form of interpreting. First and most basic: assertion is an interpreting that 'points out', in the sense of holding up for view, or of drawing attention to. In this aspect, assertion is linked by Heidegger to two Greek words we shall be meeting again: 'The primary signification of "assertion" is "*pointing out*". In this we adhere to the primordial meaning of *logos* as *apophansis*—letting an entity be seen from itself.' (*BT* 196; cf. also *BPP* 209). Assertion, then, calls the attention, either one's own or another's, to some interpretation, i.e. to the applicability of an involvement to some entity within-the-world. But second, an assertion accomplishes this task in a particular way: by explicitly *predicating* some definite feature of that specified entity. There are, after all, other ways in which an involvement may be pointed out: signs (for example turn signals) in general play this role. In an assertion, however, our sights are explicitly narrowed to some distinct entity, and to an involvement distinguished by some definite predicate: 'In 'setting down the subject', we dim entities down to focus in 'that hammer there', so that by thus dimming them down we may let that which is manifest be seen *in* its own definite character as a character that can be determined.' (*BT* 197). And third, assertion is a pointing-out-by-predicating that *communicates*, i.e. that shares with another Dasein the interpretation it involves. Most basically, this sharing of an interpretation induces that other individual to apply the same involvement to this entity, and this means that it induces the other to adopt the same concernful relationship towards that entity (cf. *BPP* 210). Bringing these three features together, '. . . we may define "*assertion*" as "*a pointing-out which gives something a definite character and which communicates*".' (*BT* 199). In asserting that a light bulb has burned out, we point out this entity as possessing a certain involvement (as unusable), we do so by predicating a concrete property of it, and we seek thereby to induce another individual to share our concernful attitude towards this unusable bulb—to give it that role in his world which it already has within ours.

This Heideggerian schema for assertion may seem innocuous or empty, but will turn out to have important consequences. Before leaving the topic, and the more general phenomenon of understanding, we may quickly anticipate one of these. Because an assertion communicates an involvement by means of a concrete predication, it is always possible for the hearer to retain and repeat this formula without himself ever sharing that relationship. Thus we may speak of the horrors of war because we have heard others do so. This way in which we may 'pass the word along', without a genuine involvement in what is said, thus arises from the basic character of assertion. We shall see that Heidegger treats it as a crucial sort of 'untruth'. And it is untruth even in cases in which the predicate does indeed apply to that entity, and in which the speaker believes it to do so; still, his disengagement from the concern that the assertion intends implies that he has not fully grasped the truth it can convey, and that his use of it is therefore importantly deficient. Heidegger's emphasis on *this* sort of failure to be 'in the truth', rather than on a failure to produce statements that objectively correspond to the facts, will be a pivotal divergence from the traditional point of view.

Let us turn now to the second basic aspect of Dasein's Being-in, one that still more clearly excludes the cognitive misreading of our a priori familiarity with the world; this is '**state-of-mind**' [Be-findlichkeit]. (Although here too I shall adhere to my policy of retaining the translation by Macquarrie and Robinson, it is worth noting the inadequacy of "state-of-mind" as a translation of "Be-findlichkeit". For its implication that Dasein is best viewed as a mind with states reinforces precisely that traditional misinterpreta-tion of this entity which Heidegger is so concerned to contradict. We must avoid this suggestion, and grasp the notion solely from the following explication of it.) We have already seen that Dasein assigns itself to an end towards which the rest of the involvement structure is ultimately oriented. This involvement of Dasein itself in its world prepares the possibility that particular entities encoun-tered within-the-world can matter to it in particular ways, parallel-ling the ways their involvements stand related to that end. One's projection towards the goal of getting across town, and one's ability to use the subway system to do so, make it possible for this train's arrival to come as a welcome event. But such understanding is not the only factor that determines how particular entities will matter to us. With state-of-mind as a further aspect of our Being-in the world, Heidegger adds another condition for entities so mattering:

The fact that this sort of thing can 'matter' to [Dasein] is grounded in one's state-of-mind; and *as* a state-of-mind it has already disclosed the world—as something by which it can be threatened, for instance. Only something which is in the state-of-mind of fearing (or fearlessness) can discover that what is environmentally ready-to-hand is threatening. (*BT* 176).

We see here, first of all, that our a priori familiarity with the world involves not merely a familiarity with the types of equipment avail-able for the realization of our ends, but also a familiarity with possible hindrances or threats to these ends. And this leads on to a more general point. Any particular entity can be interpreted with respect to a variety of involvements, because any entity will impinge in different ways on different ends that we project towards. That same train may be dangerous or ugly or noisy, and not particularly welcome, if it is primarily encountered with respect to some other end. Our state-of-mind will then help to determine which of the involvements available in our understanding will be used in our interpretation of this entity. If one is in a fearful state-of-mind, that train may 'matter' primarily as something dangerous and threatening, whether for its speed or for its riders; if by contrast one feels eager for an appointment, the speed of the train's arrival will be encountered quite differently. That first aspect to our way of Being-in our world—our understanding—needs to be supplemented by another, then, if it is to make possible our ontical experience of entities within-the-world. And so we see that this ontological familiarity or Being-in is non-theoretical not merely in being a capacity for manipulating, but also in crucially involving some **'mood'** [Stimmung], as a preparedness to be affected in some particular way by an entity encountered on the basis of this familiarity. Only because we are 'attuned' in some particular manner, can the entities we encounter matter to us in the definite ways they do—and because it is only as mattering to us that we encounter these entities in our everyday way, such attunement is a further 'condition of the possibility' for our everyday experience. Heidegger's divergence from Kant's precedent is thus particularly striking here.

But there is another side to state-of-mind that will prove equally important in what follows; it arises from a reciprocity like that discovered in Dasein's understanding. As with that first aspect of Being-in, so state-of-mind discloses not only our world—in some definite way for entities to matter to us—but also ourselves—as 'delivered over' to this mood that guides our current experience of those entities. What or who we are just now is partly constituted by this mood we are in. But more generally, state-of-mind reveals about us that we are always delivered over to some mood or other, and so always find ourselves in the midst of some particular mode of encountering, and one that is importantly beyond our responsibility. Moods overcome us, are not chosen by us, and to a great extent are out of our control. We can assume or affect them to only a very limited degree, and this means in turn that we cannot altogether determine the way we will encounter or interpret the entities around us. One finds oneself thrust into a fearful mood, never having chosen to enter it, and now wrapped within it so thoroughly that one is compelled to see all one's surroundings in a definite light. As such, moods reveal that more general predicament of Dasein which Heidegger refers to as "**thrownness**" [Geworfenheit]: we have always already been thrown into our world, and are indeed always 'in the throw', which we can never get back behind. Not only our moods, but even our understanding, is something we find ourselves already in, with no possibility of originally producing it. At every moment we find ourselves already in the midst of a certain style of concern or involvement in our world; all of our striving or projecting proceeds on the basis of this given situation, and cannot turn back behind it to serve as its prior source.

This thrownness revealed by state-of-mind—as, roughly, our rootedness in our past—may thus be viewed as a sort of countervailing accompaniment to the projection connected with understanding—as our pressing ahead into our future. I have already presented this projection as a thrust or directedness along those pathways making up our world, and have shown that it is just this pursuit of ends that makes up our understanding of ourselves. And now Heidegger claims that this thrust towards ends proceeds from a momentum we have not produced, so that while it defines who we are, this is not ultimately a *self*-definition. That way of projecting which constitutes our understanding of ourselves and our world, is one we have been thrown into; we can never fully generate our momentum for ourselves. Heidegger will also refer to this way our Being-in is 'fixed' and settled, impervious to our projecting, as our "**facticity**" [Faktizität]. (This is to be contrasted with that very different type of settledness, or '**factuality**' [Tatsächlichkeit], belonging to entities within-the-world (cf. *BT* 174); in the senses I have distinguished, the latter is a category, the former an existentiale.) And he will pair "facticity" with "existentiality", as he does "thrownness" with "projection".

Now as complementary to one another in this way, understanding and state-of-mind are the two main aspects to our Being-in our world. Together, they constitute that background disclosure of the referential pathways making up our world, which makes possible all our ontical encountering of entities. It is because we understand these pathways, in the sense of knowing our way about them, and because we are always in some mood which reveals these pathways in a definite light, that we can encounter entities as belonging to particular types, and as mattering to us in particular ways. In the absence of any such understanding, hammers could not be hammers for us—could not even be 'unidentified equipment' of the sort we may encounter in the remains of very distant cultures. There would not be available to us even such a generalized role to interpret these entities within. And in the absence of any mood or state-of-mind, hammers could not matter to us in that richness of ways in which they (and more obviously some other equipment) can do. It is these first two aspects of Being-in, then, that give the core to Heidegger's 'pragmatic' account of everydayness. This account attempts to do justice to that involved and unreflective attitude in which we ordinarily see and handle the entities about us—better justice than that offered by the traditional account which treats us as encountering these entities via our concepts and beliefs. It may be easier to feel the radical character of this pragmatic account when I introduce the contrasting theoretical attitude, beginning in the next part.

Let us proceed now to the final two aspects of Being-in. With these Heidegger introduces two further, secondary dimensions to our relation to this world, quite different in type from the preceding. The one refers, we shall see, to the possibility of sharing elements of this world, the other to a tendency we have to turn away from or to avoid the disclosure of this world. Both involve a constituent in the world to which I have as yet paid little attention, and that I must consequently now pause to treat. We must, then, notice that Heidegger's account of everydayness by no means holds that the only entities encountered within-the-world in this everyday manner are tools, nor that our only relation to entities is manipulative. Other Dasein are also encountered there, and such encountering depends upon a familiarity with them that is also prefigured in our ontological understanding. 'Thus Dasein's world frees entities which not only are quite distinct from equipment and Things, but which also—in accordance with their kind of Being *as Dasein* themselves—are 'in' the world in which they are at the same time encountered within-the-world, and are 'in' it by way of Being-in-the-world.' (*BT* 154). We earlier glimpsed this constituent in our world, when we noticed that equipment possesses an assignment to the other Dasein that has produced it; I may add now that these others are in fact indicated in a great variety of such assignments: as other users of that public equipment we employ, as consumers of the goods we produce, even as competitors in the role of supplying those goods. Our understanding of these assignments does not free others as mere ready-to-hand equipment, but as entities each likewise directing and disposing of tools. We view others as each 'in' a world by projecting towards ends—and indeed as Being-in more or less the same world, by pursuing ends largely the same, through similar means. Heidegger calls the a priori familiarity with such assignments, which grounds the encountering of others, our "**Being-with**" [Mitsein], and the Being of those others, which this familiarity is with, their "**Dasein-with**" [Mitdasein]: '. . . the world is always the one that I share with Others. The world of Dasein is a *with-world*. Being-in is *Being-with* Others. Their Being-in-themselves within-the-world is *Dasein-with*.' (*BT* 155; cf. also *ER* 131, mistranslated).

With this expansion in hand we may now turn to the third aspect of Being-in. This is '**discourse**' [Rede], and it has an obvious relevance to Heidegger's relationship to ordinary language philosophers. His discussion of this notion is more than usually obscure, but the point seems generally to be that while the involvement structure or world is always disclosed as well to the others within one's world, it can on particular occasions be explicitly shared with or 'lit up' for these others. We have noted that the Dasein-with disclosed in the system of assignments is disclosed not as ready-to-hand but as likewise projecting towards ends; more than this, the worlds of these others are not detached and distinct, but are largely overlapping with one another and with the world in which their Dasein-with is disclosed. To a greater or lesser extent, in other words, we are projecting along the same pathways towards the same very general ends, with a competence over similar means towards those ends. And Heidegger's point now is that portions of this system of involvements can be 'called to the attention' of others, and the commonage of these sectors made explicit.

To see more clearly just what this involves, we may recall the case of 'assertion' introduced earlier: a speaker points out to another that a light bulb has burned out. He thus induces the other to join in his own interpretation of that tool—i.e. to apply the same involvement (unusability) to it, in the full existential sense of adopting the same concernful attitude towards it. He points out that involvement through the predicate "burned out", and so communicates that concern to his hearer. But in accomplishing this, the speaker also makes explicit to himself and to the other that this part of their world is understood in common. They are alike in sharing a (trivial) concern with this type of equipment—in caring about the ends this equipment is usable for, and in possessing a like competence over this route to achieving those ends. (In other cases, of course, such a shared understanding of a world may be more striking or important.) As the assertion communicates the ontical interpretation of that entity, it at the same time reveals the shared ontological understanding that grounds the interpretation. This activity of 'lighting up' aspects of the world for other Dasein, and of making explicit a common understanding of that world, is what Heidegger calls "discourse": 'Dasein-with is already essentially manifest in a co-state-of-mind and a co-understanding. In discourse Being-with becomes 'explicitly' *shared*; that is to say, it *is* already, but it is unshared as something that has not been taken hold of and appropriated.' (*BT* 205). In our current example, that revelation occurs only incidentally, but in other cases it may be more largely the point of the assertion itself; we shall see later that this is the case in phenomenology's claims.

Heidegger sharply distinguishes between discourse, so defined, and '**language**' [Sprache], which unlike the former is not an aspect of our relation to the world (i.e. to the Being of entities), but is itself an entity within-the-world by means of which that discursive sharing may be accomplished. 'The way in which discourse gets expressed is language. Language is a totality of words—a totality in which discourse has a 'worldly' Being of its own; and as an entity within-the-world, this totality thus becomes something which we may come across as ready-to-hand.' (*BT* 204). Language, in other words, is equipment ready-to-hand within-the-world, that can be used to accomplish this discursive sharing. But we must keep in mind that it is not the only means by which our common world can be made explicit among us. Obviously, this role can also be played by gestures and by the way in which one acts within-the-world. Thus, our understanding of a hammer's involvements might be 'lit up' by witnessing the ease and intimacy with which it is manipulated by an experienced carpenter. And Heidegger will sometimes say that keeping silent is, for some important purposes, the most satisfactory means of discourse. Most important to us, however, will be the sense in which *Being and Time* itself is an instance of discourse, and when we approach this topic in the third chapter's treatment of the phenomenological method we shall consider in more detail how its words, as entities within-the-world, can take on this special function.

The fourth and final aspect of Being-in is '**falling**' [Verfallen]; it is here that we begin to meet the 'existential' themes (in the more popular sense of the word) that will be woven across the 'pragmatic' account we have so far reviewed. As this 'falling' has a very special importance for my inquiry, figuring prominently in Heidegger's diagnosis of epistemology, I must treat it in particular detail. Indeed, we have already implicitly met this phenomenon, for it is this that Heidegger blames for those natural and traditional interpretations of ourselves that his own analysis is always at such pains to rule out. This 'falling' is thus the central villain in my piece, and I shall return to examine its responsibility both for those traditional accounts of Dasein, and for the epistemological project. (It will play this role for us, even though Heidegger emphasizes that the term does not imply a negative valuation (cf. for example *BT* 220); it would be inappropriate to take this at face value, and not view falling as a tendency we should struggle to overcome as far as possible. Only much later shall we be in a position to understand the sense in which Heidegger's warning is intended.) As responsible for these philosophical missteps, falling is similar to—or perhaps the same as—the condition of inauthenticity (cf. again *BT* 220), and thus is opposed to that 'authenticity' towards which Heidegger will be urging us. Here I merely prepare for these later diagnoses, by observing this falling in our ordinary, pre-theoretical everydayness.

Generally, then, "falling" refers to an essential tendency in us to flee or avoid the disclosure of our own Being, and of the Being of entities within-the-world. That is, we attempt to forget or ignore our ontological familiarity with the world or system of assignments, as this is provided by our projection towards ends and by our thrownness into moods. Now Heidegger will claim that we possess this mysterious tendency to flee the disclosure of Being because of a way in which that Being is inherently dissatisfying or troubling to us. When our world, and the way we are Being-in it, are explicit or transparent to us, there is something disturbing about them, which we prefer not to face. This point will be of crucial importance when we reach the third chapter, for there it will turn out that both the epistemological and phenomenological enterprises are at their roots responses to this dissatisfaction, and that the essential contrast between these consists in the difference between them as such responses. Here, however, we are interested not in the 'motives' for this falling tendency, but in its manifestations or consequences—that is, in the activities into which we typically fall, in order to avoid that disclosure. These are of two abstract types: (1) we fall into an absorption in entities within-the-world—and tend to (mis)interpret ourselves and our world in terms of them—and (2) we fall into a particular mode of Being-with—in which we accept uncritically the prevailing public interpretation of ourselves and our world. The former route involves a preoccupation with the ontical to the exclusion of the ontological, while the latter lies at the root of that dependence on 'tradition' to which I have often referred. Heidegger distinguishes between these routes very early on:

Our preparatory Interpretation . . . will make manifest, however, not only that Dasein is inclined to fall back upon its world (the world in which it is) and to interpret itself in terms of that world by its reflected light, but also that Dasein simultaneously falls prey to the tradition of which it has more or less explicitly taken hold. (*BT* 42).

In effect, however, these two routes in falling come to much the same thing, for the public, traditional interpretations will themselves be crucially biased towards the ontical and away from the ontological. But we must see more specifically what these routes amount to, by looking at some concrete features of our everyday lives, that Heidegger attributes to them.

We may begin with that falling into a public interpretation. A key term here, though one difficult to define, is **the 'they'** [das Man]. (Here again, however, I must note a dissatisfaction with the translation. "The 'they'" is an inappropriate rendering of Heidegger's "das Man" for at least two reasons: its plural number suggests that he is speaking of a collection of individuals, and its third person suggests that this is a collection of others. As we shall see, both suggestions are misleading and must be resisted.) Roughly, Heidegger refers with this term to Dasein in its anonymity, in that aspect in which one is arbitrarily interchangeable with any other. Within the involvement structure, for example, such equipment as public transport and newspapers have assignments to the 'they': they are intended for use by *anyone* (cf. *BT* 164). But we are not just familiar with the 'they' as an element of our world; in everydayness it is the anonymous 'anyone' that is responsible for the very structure of this world: 'We take pleasure and enjoy ourselves as *they* take pleasure; we read, see, and judge about literature and art as *they* see and judge. . . . The 'they', which is nothing definite, and which all are, though not as the sum, prescribes the kind of Being of everydayness.' (*BT* 164). We take over from our community our understanding of what we are (i.e. the end towards which we project), and so also our understanding of the rest of the system of assignments (as what entities within-the-world are): '. . . the 'they' itself prescribes that way of interpreting the world and Being-in-the-world which lies closest. . . . When entities are encountered, Dasein's world frees them for a totality of involvements with which the 'they' is familiar. . . .' (*BT* 167).

We have already noted that the world in which we find ourselves is one into which we have been thrown: we grow up into a particular system of assignments, only in terms of which can we then encounter equipment. And we have also seen that this world is held in common with others, and so can be explicitly shared with them, in discourse. Heidegger's further point now is that for the most part we have accepted this system of assignments, and continue to operate within it, precisely because it is so generally and typically adhered to by the others about us. The ends towards which we project are ordinarily selected and validated for us by the very fact that this is 'what one does' in the community to which we belong— that is, they are what anyone values and strives for, regardless of who or what he might more particularly be. And in accepting these ends and assignments as confirmed in this way, we ourselves then belong to this 'they', we ourselves are this 'anyone'. Heidegger characterizes such fallenness into the 'they's' understanding in a striking way: as involving a loss or transformation of our own self: 'The Self of everyday Dasein is the *they-self*, which we distinguish from the *authentic Self*—that is, from the Self which has been taken hold of in its own way.' (*BT* 167). This claim is based upon his presentation of the self as not a thing, substance, or subject, but a *way* in which Dasein exists (cf. *BT* 312); because there are these two fundamental modes of existence, either of two selves is possible for Dasein. In falling, we have embraced an understanding of ourselves and our world merely because it is publicly accepted, and have thus merged or receded into the 'anyone' or 'they'; authenticity, the contrasting possibility of separating ourselves off as individuals, will be a central topic of the third chapter.

Now this public understanding is not established as such by any statistical survey of our neighbours; we do not study the extent to which varying ends are pursued, and then follow along with a majority. Rather, the 'they's' understanding of the world is immediately conveyed and acquired in a certain mode of discourse in which we commonly engage. This is '**idle talk**' [Gerede], the mode of discourse Heidegger claims to be typical of our everydayness. Most basically, such idle talk is a form of communicating in which one is concerned not with the subject-matter itself, but with one's intercourse with the other . An assertion is offered and received not as lighting up some involvement for an entity, but as a move in one's current interaction with that other. We are mainly intent on carrying through that interaction smoothly and effectively, and say what we do not out of a genuine concern for our topics, but with an eye to the conversational situation. In developing our ability to manage such interaction, we naturally acquire a facility at speaking in ways accepted as appropriate there; we learn conversational moves that are welcome and effective among our partners in such intercourse. In idle talk, then, we align ourselves with a common way in which things are spoken of, and acquire a facility at speaking of them so ourselves. And this talk embodies a particular understanding of ends and world, which we inevitably take on in the course of such interaction. But because this understanding is acquired in this indirect and artificial way, it is characterized by a certain detachment from its subject-matter. Thus even the speaker may not stand in that concernful relationship towards his topic, which his assertion implies. Indeed, if he has himself grasped the entity and the involvement only in such idle talk, he does not, in Heidegger's sense, genuinely understand this segment of the world at all; he understands, i.e. has a mastery over, only the procedure for speaking of these involvements to others, and not over the involvements themselves. When we speak of the miseries of poverty, or of the pressures on a test pilot, we typically do so without any direct experience of such lives—without ever having pursued their ends, or been competently acquainted with the means towards them. The structure and the quality of their concerns are thus understood only indirectly, or artificially.

Heidegger claims that it is through such idle talk that we acquire our only familiarity with broad sectors of our world, so that for the most part everyday Dasein understands only 'at second hand', and with an 'average intelligibility':

> And because this discoursing has lost its primary relationship-of-Being towards the entity talked about, or else has never achieved such a relationship, it does not communicate in such a way as to let this entity be appropriated in a primordial manner, but communicates rather by following the route of *gossiping* and *passing the word along*. (*BT* 212).

Now it is because idle talk thus shares with others an understanding that is indirect or second-hand, that Heidegger also describes it as a mode of discourse in which Being is not 'lit up' but rather concealed: 'Discourse . . . has the possibility of becoming idle talk. And when it does so, it serves not so much to keep Being-in-the-world open for us in an articulated understanding, as rather to close it off, and cover up the entities within-the-world.' (*BT* 213). In this sense, then, idle talk is a mode of discourse that falls away from the latter's proper role; as indicated above, its assertions will thus be 'untrue' in Heidegger's preferred sense, even where they objectively correspond to the facts. That public understanding which idle talk conveys is not a genuine familiarity or mastery of its subject-matter, and hence not a genuine disclosure of the world or system of assignments. And it is in this way that falling into idle talk and into the 'they's' understanding of the world enables us to avoid the disclosure of Being. Again, our motives for this avoidance, and what a contrasting acknowledgement would involve, must be postponed to the third chapter.

Let us turn quickly now to the second main route by which we may flee this disclosedness. This consists in a preoccupation with the ontical to the exclusion of the ontological; in other words, we throw ourselves into our concern for entities in such a way as to ignore the familiarity with Being that grounds such concern. In order to distract ourselves in this way, we shall naturally seek out involvements that are as gripping and vivid as possible, and that thus most tenaciously hold our attention. And one way of entering such vivid involvements is by discovering new and exotic entities, with which we can stand in fresh relationships. Thus this general falling tendency will encourage what Heidegger calls "**curiosity**" [Neugier]. I must backtrack a moment to explain this more fully.

We have seen that our everyday relation to entities consists in our dealings with equipment, in an attitude of concern. Further, the way of seeing that belongs to such concern is circumspection, which typically desevers (or brings close) that upon which it is directed. Now when one finishes or rests from one's task, '. . . concern does not disappear; circumspection, however, becomes free and is no longer bound to the world of work' (*BT* 216). Its desevering no longer operates upon the equipment with which one was engaged, but

. . . circumspection provides itself with new possibilities of de-severing. This means that it tends away from what is most closely ready-to-hand, and into a far and alien world. Care becomes concern with the possibilities of seeing the 'world' merely as it *looks* while one tarries and takes a rest. Dasein seeks what is far away simply in order to bring it close to itself in the way it looks. (*BT* 216).

We may rest from our work in the evening, but our striving to 'bring close', to master and organize our surroundings, may still persist, though in different form: we might now pay attention to the stars, for example, and try to make them more accessible to us by noticing new aspects to them. It is this rampant desevering that results when circumspection is disengaged from any task, that Heidegger calls "curiosity". And he argues that such curiosity is typically a way of diverting ourselves by attending to unfamiliar entities, and that this in turn is a way of maintaining our immersion in ontical experience, and avoiding an acknowledgement of Being. In thus turning our attention to these entities distant from our concernful involvements, and encountering them independently of such involvements, in the way they 'look', we are also interpreting these entities in isolation from the system of assignments, in a new and 'theoretical' way. This route by which our falling tendency may lead us to a theoretical interpretation of entities will be a key topic for us later on. For now, however, this introduction of curiosity and idle talk may suffice as my opening presentation of falling.

Now as I did at the end of the discussion of the concept of world, I shall pause here to consider how much of the above account of Being-in describes structures essential to Dasein as such, and how much rather presents the modes taken by these structures in the state of everydayness. For my purposes it is most vital to pose this question with respect to the last of the four aspects of Being-in: is this falling essential to us, or is it merely a feature of our every-dayness? Does it continue to characterize us in any state we may be in, or does it hold only in this one, though primary, condition? Now there are certainly passages that favour the former alternative—for example: '*The 'they' is an existentiale; and as a primordial pheno-menon, it belongs to Dasein's positive constitution.*' (*BT* 167). But as has been hinted already, and will be further developed in the third chapter, Heidegger's considered position is that we need not be falling or inauthentic, but can escape these into the position of authenticity: 'Inauthenticity characterizes a kind of Being into which Dasein can divert itself and has for the most part always diverted itself; but Dasein does not necessarily and constantly have to divert itself into this kind of Being.' (*BT* 303). Moreover, Heidegger will even take back the suggestion that authenticity is merely a modified or derivative form of a more basic falling con-dition, a suggestion occurring often in the first Division, for example here: '*Authentic Being-one's-Self* does not rest upon an exceptional condition of the subject, a condition that has been detached from the 'they'; *it is rather an existentiell modification of the 'they'—of the 'they' as an essential existentiale.*' (*BT* 168; cf. also *BPP* 171). As we shall see, Heidegger later reverses this priority, and refers to authenticity as the 'more primordial' phenomenon. Thus we may best view falling and authenticity as two positions along an axis that is itself the fourth essential aspect of our Being-in; it is along this dimension that Heidegger will locate the best life for us, and the life in which we are 'in the truth'. What is essential to us is that we occupy some position or other along this continuum, while falling is the position we take in everydayness. On the other hand, Heidegger does believe the tendency or temptation towards falling to be essential to us (cf. *BT* 299, and also *BT* 229, where falling is described as Dasein's 'ownmost inertia'); we may capture this point by imagining that continuum to have an inherent tilt, so that we tend to slide from the position of authenticity towards that of inauthenticity.

Heidegger does indeed make it fairly clear that in passing from Being-in's first three aspects to the topic of falling, he is narrowing his focus from Dasein as such to its everyday condition; he remarks after his discussion of understanding, state-of-mind, and discourse:

In going back to the existential structures of the disclosedness of Being-in-the-world, our Interpretation has, in a way, lost sight of Dasein's everydayness. . . . The question now arises: what are the existential characteristics of the disclosedness of Being-in-the-world, so far as the latter, as something which is everyday, maintains itself in the kind of Being of the 'they'? (*BT* 210).

He then proceeds to the discussion of falling, and it therefore appears that everydayness will be constituted precisely by the falling modes of each of those first three aspects—as idle talk, for example, is the falling and everyday mode of discourse. This picture is a useful approximation, but must be qualified in two ways. First, even that original discussion of understanding, state-of-mind, and discourse has not characterized these quite generally enough to encompass indifferently the authentic and falling modes of them. Thus for example the discussion of the first aspect presents us as understanding ourselves in terms of the end lying at the apex of the involvement structure, and as we noticed in the qualifications to the discussion of world, there is a sense in which this is not true of authenticity. And second, we shall see in the next chapter that everydayness is not the only position into which we can fall—for that 'theoretical' position mentioned earlier will turn out to involve a slightly different form of falling. But once again, full clarification of these points can only come when we have been properly introduced to the alternatives to everydayness.

d. Being-in-the-world as care. This concludes my summary of Being-in-the-world—Heidegger's opening account of our structure as this is revealed in the condition of everydayness. We may briefly review its main points. Heidegger claims that our everyday encountering of the entities about us, which is typically a manipulating of equipment, is made possible by the a priori disclosure to us of the world as a whole—that is, of the system of assignments. This disclosure represents a familiarity both with our own Being and with that of entities within-the-world. But this familiarity is neither theoretical in type, nor necessarily explicit to us, being constituted first by the way we project ourselves towards possible ways for us to be, and understand how these ends may be realized, and second by our having been thrown into a mood which we have not chosen and which involves the world's mattering to us in ways beyond our control. Moreover, this familiarity with the world is already shared with others, and this sharing can be articulated by discourse. And finally, this familiarity is not only not usually explicit to us, but is also disquieting in such a way that we tend to turn away from it and to fall into an absorption in those entities discovered on the basis of it.

In the last chapter of Division I Heidegger attempts to pull these apparently disparate elements together into a unified account of the structure of Being-in-the-world—or rather, as he prefers to put it, he attempts to 'look all the way *through* this whole *to a single* primordially unitary phenomenon which is already in this whole in such a way that it provides the ontological foundation for each structural item in its structural possibility.' (*BT* 226). He begins with a recapitulation of the elements of this structure, and then, in the light of a privileged state-of-mind called "anxiety", discussion of which is best postponed until the third chapter, he argues that the unity underlying this structure consists in the way in which our existentiality, facticity, and Being-fallen (three of the four aspects to Being-in; discourse is omitted) are 'woven together'. He redescribes Dasein's existing (i.e. its projecting towards possible ways for it to be) as its 'Being-ahead-of-itself', its facticity (i.e. its thrownness into a world that matters to it in ways beyond its control) as its 'Being-already-in-a-world', and its falling (i.e. its fleeing the disclosure of Being into an absorption in entities) as its 'Being-alongside entities within-the-world'. Later, we shall see that these new formulations refer to the three dimensions of our 'temporality'. Now, Heidegger joins them into an expression for the unity of our ontological structure: ' . . . the Being of Dasein means ahead-of-itself-Being-already-in-(the-world) as Being-alongside (entities encountered within-the-world).' (*BT* 237). He gives to this structure the title "**care**" [Sorge], which thus becomes the name for our distinctive manner of Being, as this has been uncovered through the study of our everydayness.

2. *Everydayness serves as a standard for evaluating Epistemology*

a. Initial account of the theoretical attitude, and of epistemology. We may turn now to take a first look at the general way in which everydayness, so characterized, is used by Heidegger as a standard against which to judge the epistemologist's claims. That is, we may consider what it is in everydayness that is used as such a standard. Before we can do so, however, we need a first look at Heidegger's account of the epistemological project and its roots, as that to which this standard is applied. My main interest here is in the manner of application, and the account of epistemology will be only a preview of the more detailed treatment to follow in the next chapter.

Now Heidegger finds at the root of the epistemological enterprise a certain special attitude or relation to entities, which may be adopted secondarily, on the basis of our concernful Being-in-the-world. In this attitude—the '*theoretical*' attitude—we *know* these entities, and encounter them not as the ready-to-hand, but 'the **present-at-hand**' [das Vorhandene]. An entity that had been equipment, is now discovered quite differently, as an '**object**' [Objekt]. And so it is also natural to speak of this attitude as "objective", although Heidegger himself will not do so. He gives a rough sense of the transition to this attitude here:

Being-in-the-world, as concern, is *fascinated by* the world with which it is concerned. If knowing is to be possible as a way of determining the nature of the present-at-hand by observing it, then there must first be a *deficiency* in our having-to-do with the world concernfully. When concern holds back from any kind of producing, manipulating, and the like, it puts itself into what is now the sole remaining mode of Being-in, the mode of just tarrying alongside. . . . This kind of Being towards the world is one which lets us encounter entities within-the-world purely in the *way they look (eidos)*, just that . . . (*BT* 88).

While I must postpone a full and careful account of this transition, some preliminary remarks will be helpful not only as a preparation for the upcoming discussion of epistemology, but also as a further clarification, by contrast, of the preceding Heideggerian account of everydayness. For we can best appreciate the radical nature of this account by seeing now what it has implicitly denied: that we are ordinarily related to the entities around us in about the same way the theorist is related to objects.

We may begin with a minor qualification. Heidegger in fact uses "the present-at-hand" in two senses, a wider and a narrower one: either for all entities other than Dasein ('. . . any entity is either a '*who*' (existence) or a '*what*' (presence-at-hand in the broadest sense)' (*BT* 71)), or only for those that are the objects of the theoretical attitude. *Being and Time* usually supposes the former, broader class to consist solely of the present-at-hand in the narrower sense, plus the ready-to-hand (though some obscure remarks, e.g. at *BT* 100, have been interpreted as providing for further sub-classes; these are certainly introduced in later writings). But in any case the narrower use of "present-at-hand" is by far the more common, and I shall restrict myself to it in the following. There will thus be, in this Heideggerian ontology, three fundamentally different types of entities: the ready-to-hand, the present-at-hand, and Dasein.

Now roughly, present-at-hand objects are those determinate and isolable entities of the sort treated by science. Or as I shall usually put it, an entity is treated *as* present-at-hand when it is viewed by us as determinate and isolable in this way. For it is important to bear in mind about Heidegger's distinction that what we would ordinarily consider the *same* entity may nevertheless fall into both classes; that is, it may be either ready-to-hand or present-at-hand, depending upon the attitude in which it is encountered. The hammer in use, transparent in the swing of the carpenter intent on driving the nail, is ready-to-hand, though 'this same hammer' in the product-tester's laboratory, being weighed and scrutinized for flaws, is present-at-hand (cf. for example *BT* 412). Although there may be entities that are only encounterable in one of these contrasting attitudes (as electrons might be encounterable only within the physicist's theorizing), for the most part it is best not to think of equipment and objects as forming distinct classes of entities; rather, it is our own relationship to an entity that assigns it, for that moment, to one type or the other. (But although I shall present Heidegger's position in this way, it must be recognized that this involves a certain simplification, or avoids a certain puzzle. For the Being of tools and objects is different, and this implies that they must be different entities. To show my usage to be strictly correct, a more complex story would have to be told, explaining in what sense 'the same entity' can have both modes of Being, and so fall under both of these types. Without this story, my way of presenting these points must remain a simplifying short-hand, adopted for convenience.)

I shall postpone to the following chapter a more careful account of what is involved, in treating objects as 'determinate and isolable' in this way. For current purposes it is more relevant to notice some general, background features of this manner of encountering entities, and particularly in its comparison with the everyday manner. Most importantly, each of these contrasting attitudes or relationships in which we may stand to an entity depends upon a way the Being of that entity has been previously projected. We have already seen, at some length, how this is so for the everyday, concernful attitude in which the ready-to-hand is met: this depends on a prior disclosure of the Being of the ready-to-hand, through a prior understanding of the world as the system of assignments equipment can have. But neither is the theoretical attitude an unmediated relationship in which we encounter bare facts; it depends on a special projection all its own, in which we sketch in advance the Being of the entities we then go on to discover. So Heidegger asserts: 'All ontical experience of entities—both circumspective calculation of the ready-to-hand, and positive scientific cognition of the present-at-hand—is based upon projections of the Being of the corresponding entities . . . .'(*BT* 371; cf. also *ER* 23–5). And again: 'Only 'in the light' of a Nature which has been projected in this fashion can anything like a 'fact' be found and set up for an experiment regulated and delimited in terms of this projection. . . . [I]n principle there are no 'bare facts'.' (*BT* 414). Heidegger calls this projection of Being as presence-at-hand "**thematizing**" [Thematisierung] (cf. *BT* 414). Thematizing thus plays an analogous role to that concernful understanding which discloses the Being of equipment. But this secondary projection is accomplished in a quite different way than that everyday understanding. Thematizing proceeds by way of *basic concepts*, which lay out more or less precisely and explicitly the most essential character of the entities the theorist goes on to investigate. By contrast, we have seen that the everyday understanding is roughly an ability to do: a capacity and indeed a disposition to manipulate types of equipment in pursuit of certain ends; it is not aligned by reference to any concepts or principles.

Now as we have been prepared to see, Heidegger takes Kant to have uncovered the general character of this projection of Being as presence-at-hand. Scientists, philosophers, and others had of course entered into the theoretical attitude, and discovered entities as present-at-hand, but it was only with Kant that the a priori understanding that grounds such discovery, came to be explicitly recognized and described. Kant presented, in the categories and the forms of intuition, precisely that thematization of Being which makes possible discovery of the objects of natural science:

'Similarly the positive outcome of Kant's *Critique of Pure Reason*
lies in what it has contributed towards the working out of what
belongs to any Nature whatsoever, not in a 'theory' of knowledge.
His transcendental logic is an a priori logic for the subject-matter of
that area of Being called "Nature".' (*BT* 31). But Heidegger's
claim, as I have hinted already and shall show more fully in the next
chapter, is that this projection of presence-at-hand is secondary or
internal in character, being based upon that 'pragmatic' understanding of the world which it is the task of *Being and Time*'s first
Division to describe. In this respect, then, Heidegger's general
intent is to appropriate Kant's transcendental method and apply it
(as he thinks) at a deeper level, and with respect to a broader field of
entities, than had been done by Kant himself:

> The question of Being aims therefore at ascertaining the *a priori* conditions
> not only for the possibility of the sciences which examine entities as entities
> of such and such a type, and, in so doing, already operate with an under-
> standing of Being, but also for the possibility of those ontologies themselves
> which are prior to the ontical sciences and which provide their foundations.
> (*BT* 31).

The theoretical discovery of the present-at-hand is based, then, not
only upon the thematization which Kant describes, but also upon
our Being-in-the-world, that understanding involved in our striving
towards ends and in our capacity to use equipment to achieve them.

The precise sense in which Heidegger claims our 'pragmatic'
understanding to be prior and more basic will be a crucial issue in
the following. Most clearly but trivially, he argues that our concernful attitude is prior in that we are first engaged in it, and only
later pass it into a detached, theoretical perspective. But the claims
he will be making require a logical and not merely temporal priority
for the pre-theoretical understanding. We can see this by noting
how Heidegger disputes a conception that is natural to us: that the
hammer 'really is' as the theoretical attitude discovers it, while its
use and the other involvements encountered in it from a position of
everyday concern are external relationships added secondarily,
'subjectively', to that bare, present-at-hand subsistence. Both
modes of Being possible for the hammer originate in our own
understanding. But what is more, if priority is to be allotted it must
be done by reference to the respective projections of Being, and
because the disclosure of readiness-to-hand involved in our Being-

in-the-world is (in some sense) more fundamental than the thematization of presence-at-hand through basic concepts, the hammer is, according to Heidegger, more fundamentally a tool than an object. And this priority applies even to entities whose equipmental character may be less obvious to us: 'The wood is a forest of timber, the mountain a quarry of rock; the river is water-power, the wind is wind 'in the sails'.' (*BT* 100). And so readiness-to-hand

... is not to be understood as merely a way of taking them, as if we were talking such 'aspects' into the 'entities' which we proximally encounter, or as if some world-stuff which is proximally present-at-hand in itself were 'given subjective coloring' in this way.... To lay bare what is just present-at-hand and no more, cognition must first penetrate *beyond* what is ready-to-hand in our concern. *Readiness-to-hand is the way in which entities as they are 'in themselves' are defined ontologico-categorially.* (*BT* 101).

Not only, then, is an entity's mode of Being determined by the way this Being has been projected by the Dasein currently encountering it, but its more basic mode of Being is determined by the relative priority in these types of projection. It is only a logical priority to our concernful understanding that can justify such claims. And these claims, as we can now see in a preliminary way, play a central role in Heidegger's argument against epistemology.

Now Heidegger has no quarrel with the theoretical attitude in itself. But he thinks that it naturally tends to generalize itself in a certain way, and to take all Being as presence-at-hand, or to claim that this is the fundamental way in which entities 'really' are. Indeed, we shall see that the intent that leads into the theoretical attitude in the first place, encourages just this extended application of it. Generalizing in this way, we view equipment, and even ourselves, as *essentially* present-at-hand; we take a nail, for example, to be really only a piece of metal of a certain shape, size, chemical composition, and so on, and its use and other involvements to be relations with only a secondary status. Moreover, this over-extension of the theoretical attitude leads to, or already involves, a certain interpretation of itself and its own ontological status. In taking all entities to be really present-at-hand objects, this theoretical attitude either overlooks the projections on which it is based, believing that it really does encounter bare and unmediated facts, or else it supposes that those projections can themselves be explained in its own present-at-hand terms. In either case, Heidegger will claim, this over-generalized theoretical attitude misinterprets itself, and must inevitably do so on account of its limitation to the present-at-hand.

It is a version of this latter mistake that the epistemologist is guilty of, according to Heidegger. For the epistemological project is precisely the attempt to ground the knowing attitude in itself—an attempt following directly from the generalizing of this attitude, from its effort to show itself complete and self-sufficient, capable of explaining everything in its own present-at-hand terms. As a natural part of this broader effort, the epistemologist attempts to explain how knowing can arise in an entity that itself has the kind of Being this knowing encounters; he attempts to explain how knowing is possible for us, but for us interpreted as present-at-hand. In epistemology the theoretical attitude turns about upon itself, and attempts to describe itself in the present-at-hand terms alone available to it. We shall see that it is this present-at-hand interpretation of us—or more especially of our knowing—that is the main focus of Heidegger's attack on the epistemological project.

b. How everydayness is used in criticism of epistemology. This very sketchy summary of Heidegger's account of the epistemological project is a sufficient basis for me now to characterize the way in which everydayness is turned against this project. Heidegger takes the epistemologist's interpretation of us knowers as present-at-hand to be a mistake; now what role does everydayness play in his argument that this is a mistake? First, the claim is not that this interpretation of us contradicts characterizations we tend to make of ourselves in everydayness. Indeed, it rather corresponds to them. For as we have already glimpsed in the opening outline, our everydayness is pervaded by a falling tendency which inclines us to absorb ourselves in entities within-the-world, so that we may avoid the disclosure of their Being. And we shall later see that this absorption in the ontical at the expense of the ontological further inclines us to misinterpret ourselves as entities within-the-world, too nearly on a par with the equipment we encounter there. This mistake is a close relative of that of which Heidegger accuses the epistemologist: interpreting Dasein as a present-at-hand object of the type discovered in his theorizing. And indeed, we shall also see that the latter mistake is likewise due to our everyday falling tendency. In both cases, Heidegger will argue, our effort to avoid facing the disturbing character of our own Being leads us to misinterpret ourselves as entities of a fundamentally different sort, merely 'within' the world in the manner of tools or objects, rather than 'in' it by way of disclosing it, or originally opening it up. So if we were to appeal to our everyday characterizations of ourselves as our standard of comparison for a philosopher's interpretation, the present-at-hand reading which Heidegger claims to be misguided would rather tend to be corroborated. But Heidegger is very far from wishing to use everydayness as a standard in this most straightforward sense, as we can see from the following:

> Dasein's *kind of Being* thus *demands* that any ontological Interpretation which sets itself the goal of exhibiting the phenomena in their primordiality, *should capture the Being of this entity, in spite of this entity's own tendency to cover things up*. Existential analysis, therefore, constantly has the character of *doing violence*, whether to the claims of the everyday interpretation, or to its complacency and its tranquillized obviousness. (*BT* 359).

Diagnosis of traditional problems and positions will not proceed by comparing these with the views we explicitly assert or accept in everydayness; presumably, these latter make up the 'common sense' that Heidegger warns the philosopher not to rely upon (cf. for example *BPP* 14). It is not this aspect of our everyday condition that serves Heidegger as a standard.

But on the other hand, it is not simply that Heidegger's account of everydayness, as an external description of that state, is demonstrably incompatible with the epistemologist's interpretation of us as present-at-hand. If this were all his use of everydayness amounted to, his similarity to commonsensical and ordinary language philosophers would be quite thin and tenuous. It would not be anything we believe, say, or have access to *in* everydayness that was used as a standard for philosophy, but a condition discovered *about* it, from without. The epistemological project would be undermined by being shown to involve a mischaracterization of our everydayness, but the truth about everydayness would not also be a truth in everydayness, and there would be no intent to return us from the philosophical to our everyday condition.

Now although Heidegger does hold that in everydayness we are guilty of the same type of misinterpretation of ourselves as is the epistemologist, he yet manages a route that allows this missed truth about everydayness to be available within it. I have indeed already suggested this route. While in everydayness we are falling and so tend to misinterpret our own Being, still this falling is a fleeing from this same Being, as something disquieting to us, and such fleeing is only possible because that Being has already been disclosed to us in Being-in-the-world: 'Only to the extent that Dasein has been brought before itself in an ontologically essential manner through whatever disclosedness belongs to it, *can* it flee *in the face of* that in the face of which it flees.' (*BT* 229). And so there is after all a way in which everyday Dasein is familiar with its own Being and with that of entities within-the-world: these are disclosed to it by way of understanding and state-of-mind. And it is only on the basis of this disclosure that any explicit interpretations of Being are possible, including the falling everyday and philosophical misinterpretations. It is this disclosure of Being that is the truth *in and about* everydayness, and that is used by Heidegger as a standard against which the philosopher's claims are judged and found wanting.

We may still ask, however, whether it is everydayness as everydayness that serves Heidegger as a standard in this way. For in noting that the projection of Being as presence-at-hand itself depends upon our more basic concernful understanding, I have implied—and correctly—that the scientist or philosopher who carries out this projection does so on the basis of that same deeper understanding which is at work in everydayness. And because it is this understanding that Heidegger adopts as his standard, it might seem to be merely incidental that he focuses on its everyday manifestation, and not rather on its presence behind the theorist's special attitude. If Heidegger could equally well sketch this understanding by reference to that latter context, it seems that his use of everydayness would not be dictated by any genuine priority he grants to that condition; his choice of this condition as starting-point would be shown to be harmless but unnecessary. And if so, his use of everydayness would again turn out to bear only a surface similarity to that by commonsensical philosophers.

Against this, however, I must note two further points. First, even if that understanding which serves as true standard is not unique to everydayness, it may still be far more accessible there, so that the choice of this context for describing it would not be merely arbitrary. Our everyday activities of physically manipulating and arranging equipment may reflect in an especially direct and obvious way that basic concernful understanding. With the theorist this understanding is covered over by a competing projection and by a secondary way of discovering entities, and may be far more difficult to extract. (This advantage to the study of everydayness is analogous to one Heidegger grants to the study of 'primitive Dasein': 'To orient the analysis of Dasein towards the 'life of primitive peoples' can have positive significance as a method because 'primitive phenomena' are often less concealed and less complicated by extensive self-interpretation on the part of the Dasein in question.' (*BT* 76).) And second, we must not assume that the theorist has passed completely out of everydayness; it may be that the extent to which he does still retain that deeper understanding is precisely the extent to which he is himself still in everydayness, only mounting above it in some few aspects or respects. Later, we shall see that my early presentation of the theoretical attitude as an alternative to everydayness will need to be qualified in some such way.

So much for now, then, on the general character of Heidegger's use of everydayness as a standard. Of course, we still need to see much more clearly just how his arguments here run, and in particular just what misinterpretation the epistemological project is supposed to rest on or involve. In the next chapter I shall enter into the details of these issues, by examining more closely Heidegger's account of the origins and structure of this epistemological project.

3. Everydayness is determined as a starting-point by the nature of Phenomenology

Before leaving this chapter with its two-fold role as treatment of everydayness and introductory exposition of *Being and Time*'s first Division, it will be useful to say a few first words about Heidegger's phenomenological method, a subject that will not move into the foreground until my third chapter. Conveniently, this may be done in such a way as to uncover further his attitude towards everydayness. For his account of this method is related both to his choice of everydayness as a starting-point, and to his use of it as a standard for evaluating philosophical claims. Now Heidegger's conception of phenomenology is developed in two parts, which correspond (typically enough) to the Greek roots to the term, *logos* and *phainomenon*. Phenomenology is to provide a *logos* for *phainomena*, in the (apparently) idiosyncratic senses Heidegger will give to these terms. The first term gives the method's formal character, i.e. the way in which it approaches and treats its

objects, while the second delimits the type of 'objects' that are
properly its own. Each has implications for the other, and for the
role of everydayness in philosophy.

We have already met the first of these Greek words in the
discussion of assertion, where we saw Heidegger introduce it to
explain the sense in which any assertion is a 'pointing out'. As such
pointing-out, *logos* belongs most fundamentally with discourse,
one of the four basic aspects to our Being-in our world; much later
in my discussion, it will be crucial to determine in just what sense
phenomenology must be such discourse, and in doing so we shall
see how this Heideggerian phenomenology is deeply fused with
existentialism. Here, however, we may recall more specifically that
the earlier passage associated *logos* with the further Greek term
apophansis (derived from *apophainesthai*), and clarified both with
the phrase "letting an entity be seen from itself". As providing such
a *logos*, then, phenomenology is in its formal aspect the holding of
something up for view, so that it can show itself to us:

Thus "phenomenology" means *apophainesthai ta phainomena*—to let that
which shows itself be seen from itself in the very way in which it shows itself
from itself. This is the formal meaning of that branch of research which calls
itself "phenomenology". But here we are expressing nothing else than the
maxim formulated above: 'To the things themselves!' (*BT* 58).

And again: 'To have a science 'of' phenomena means to grasp its
objects *in such a way* that everything about them which is up for
discussion must be treated by exhibiting it directly and demonstrat-
ing it directly. The expression "descriptive phenomenology",
which is at bottom tautological, has the same meaning.' (*BT* 59).

These explanations are of course so schematic that very little is
very definitely either included or excluded by them. Later, it will be
important to grasp Heidegger's intent more concretely. But here I
shall only mention several equally schematic relations in which
these explanations stand to themes already uncovered. To begin
with, there is already an implicit rejection of appeal to or reliance
on any prior interpretations of the phenomena, no matter how
obvious, familiar, or long-standing. The phenomenologist is to free
himself from the influence of such interpretations, an influence that
is often subtle and difficult to detect. This rejection is made more
emphatic and pointed with the later introduction of the notion of
falling (which attributes to us an essential tendency to misin-

terpret), but is already suggested here in Heidegger's early explication of his method, and is made explicit a bit later: 'The achieving of phenomenological access to the entities which we encounter, consists rather in thrusting aside our interpretative tendencies, which keep thrusting themselves upon us and running along with us. . . . ' (*BT* 96). Moreover, this formal aspect of phenomenology is also partly responsible for the choice of everydayness as a starting-point for the analysis of Dasein:

To put it negatively, we have no right to resort to dogmatic constructions and to apply just any idea of Being and actuality to this entity, no matter how 'self-evident' that idea may be. . . . We must rather choose such a way of access and such a kind of interpretation that this entity can show itself in itself and from itself. And this means that it is to be shown as it is *proximally and for the most part*—in its average *everydayness*. (*BT* 37–8).

Thus we see prefigured in the formal aspect of Heidegger's phenomenological method both his orientation towards our everydayness, and his distrust of accepted interpretations of this.

What then of the second aspect, that concerning the proper 'objects' of this method. i.e. phenomena? Heidegger wishes to use "**phenomenon**" [Phänomen] not just for anything that can show itself, but (oddly enough) for what for the most part does *not* show itself, but lies as the 'hidden ground' for what does:

What is it that must be called a "phenomenon" in a distinctive sense? . . . [I]t is something that proximally and for the most part does *not* show itself at all: it is something that lies *hidden*, in contrast to that which proximally and for the most part does show itself; but at the same time it is something that belongs to what thus shows itself, and it belongs to it so essentially as to constitute its meaning and its ground. (*BT* 59).

This is then identified by Heidegger as the *Being* of entities, so that phenomenology, it turns out, amounts to ontology: 'With regard to its subject-matter, phenomenology is the science of the Being of entities—ontology.' (*BT* 61). Heidegger's intention here is clarified by his remark (at *BT* 54–5) that in the Kantian system it is the forms of intuition—space and time—that play the role of phenomena in the distinctively phenomenological sense. Notice of this affinity with Kant is a useful antidote to the popular conception of phenomenology as involved in the description of our 'experience', a conception that suggests strong links to the epistemologist's attention to sense-data, as that which we are immediately given, prior to any theoretical construction. While phenomenology's first, formal aspect, in its intent to begin before all familiar interpretations, might encourage this conception, the identification of phenomena with Being, as the ground for all ontical experience of entities, should sufficiently discourage it—in Heidegger's case at least. (We must of course bear in mind that Heidegger's conception of phenomenology diverges considerably from Husserl's precedent.)

We may note further that with this identification of Being as phenomenon, in the sense of that which 'proximally and for the most part' lies hidden but can be brought to show itself, we again see foreshadowed that notion of falling which at first seemed to preclude any appeal from philosophy to everydayness. Being lies hidden, for the most part, because in everydayness we evade recognition of it, and fall into a preoccupation with entities. And yet as the hidden ground for the encountering of entities, Being must nevertheless be already familiar and available to us:

This phenomenological interpretation ... is rather a determination of the structure of the Being which entities possess. But as an investigation of Being, it brings to completion, autonomously and explicitly, that understanding of Being which belongs already to Dasein and which 'comes alive' in any of its dealings with entities. (*BT* 95–6).

We have already seen a large part of the way in which Heidegger develops the character of this grounding understanding of Being: involvements, as the Being of equipment, are understood by us in advance of particular manipulations of that equipment; our understanding of the structure of these involvements consists in projection towards some for-the-sake-of-which and in the capacity for achieving this end through use of the available types of equipment. This understanding of the involvement structure is one aspect of the disclosures of Being to everyday Dasein. In identifying Being, so understood, as the subject-matter of phenomenology, Heidegger therefore builds into his conception of that method the task of remaining faithful to, while bringing explicitly to light, a familiarity already found in our everydayness, but neglected and covered over in traditional theorizing, and indeed in our everyday interpretations themselves. And the work of phenomenology will run counter to that falling tendency which characterizes our everydayness and is at the root of these misinterpretations.

The bare interest in everydayness, which I took as my opening clue that there might be illuminating connections between Heidegger's treatment of traditional problems and those by commonsensical and ordinary language philosophers, has now been shown to reach down even into Heidegger's conception of his own method, which we have seen to involve a requirement of faithfulness to an understanding present in everydayness. This further reinforces my background hope, by showing these parallels at least not completely superficial. Nevertheless, we are still very much at the surface of Heidegger, and of our problem. We must see in much more detail just how he conceives of the traditional epistemologist's undertaking, and just why he rejects it. And, ultimately, we must return to his conception of phenomenology as the proper philosophical method, and consider, for example, in precisely what sense it is supposed to 'make explicit' that understanding of Being which we have now seen to be implicit in everydayness.

II

EPISTEMOLOGY

IN the last chapter we acquainted ourselves with the principal features of Heidegger's account of our everyday condition, and saw the general way in which this everydayness is to be used as a standard for judging the epistemologist's claims. *En route* to this latter topic it was necessary to look briefly at Heidegger's conception of the nature and origins of epistemology, and we saw that he views this project as rooted in a special theoretical attitude we may adopt as an exception to the concernful involvements typical of our everydayness. In this chapter we now focus in on epistemology, developing in more detail Heidegger's conception of it and his arguments against it. More fundamentally, we thus improve our grasp of his position on traditional philosophy in general: his account of the way this enterprise attempts to improve upon our everyday condition, and his reasons for thinking this direction of effort misguided. As in the account of everydayness, so too in this diagnosis of epistemology we may expect Heidegger's discussion to bear interesting comparison to the treatments by commonsensical and ordinary language philosophers, for many of these share in his general strategy of undermining the traditional project, rather than straightforwardly answering it. Does Heidegger think this project misguided for reasons like those cited by these analytic philosophers? What account does he give of our persistent attraction to a problem that is thus misdirected? And how does he use this originating error to explain the typical course of this project—in particular, its constant difficulty in avoiding a sceptical conclusion? Although, once again, I shall not address any comparisons on these topics, an interest in such relationships has helped to guide my selection of the topics themselves.

Now in focusing upon the epistemologist's project it may seem I have chosen an unpromising site for examining Heidegger's general stance towards the philosophical tradition. For he is unsympathetic to the epistemological undertaking nearly to the point of being uninterested in it, and even the one discussion that confronts this project at any length (section 43 of *Being and Time*) offers only the broadest outline of an attack. But the neighbouring regions of the Heideggerian system bear the potential for a much fuller and more sympathetic treatment of the field, a treatment that not only reveals a special appropriateness to the choice of *this* representative of the philosophical tradition, but that is more consistent with his insistence, in other contexts, that phenomenology is not simply to cast aside and then ignore this tradition, but must rather attempt to uncover and develop the 'positive possibilities' it contains. As we shall see in the next chapter, not only can such 'positive possibilities' be discovered within epistemology, consistently with Heidegger's fuller perspective, but phenomenology itself, as his recommended, post-traditional philosophical method, can be plausibly interpreted as having the task to develop these possibilities. In this chapter, though, my attention will rather be on the limited and misdirected form that Heidegger claims the epistemological inquiry has taken so far—a misdirection that consists, as we shall see, in its choice of a natural but inappropriate route as its exit from everydayness.

Even my development of this more negative aspect will require considerable supplementation, or extrapolation beyond the account explicit in the texts, so that here I already leave behind the more purely summary intent of the previous chapter. Still, this chapter will also add to my exposition of Heidegger's system, by beginning to introduce material from *Being and Time*'s second Division. In particular, the key concept of temporality now has a part to play in our argument, and at a quite crucial stage. We here meet one of the most exciting and puzzling of Heidegger's notions, though still only in a preliminary way. The details to his account of temporality, as well as the other main ingredient to that second Division, its existential themes, may still be postponed until my last chapter.

My discussion is again broken into three parts, corresponding to the topics of the three chapters. I shall look first at the way in which the forerunner to epistemology, that special theoretical attitude, arises out of everydayness. My purposes here are to explain what is most crucial to that attitude's projection of Being as presence-at-hand, and to motivate the transition to this from the everyday understanding of Being as readiness-to-hand. What factors or tendencies within everydayness are responsible for the adoption of this attitude, and how do they help to determine the way it encounters its objects? In explaining this theoretical attitude, it will be helpful to orient the discussion towards Descartes, as a paradigm occupant of that position. Second, I shall treat the key pair of issues concerning traditional epistemology itself: the precise way in which Heidegger views this as developing out of that theoretical attitude, and the arguments he presents against it. For of course not all theorizing is epistemology, and not all is subject to the objections Heidegger raises against that latter project. Epistemology is a particular application of the theoretical attitude—one that is misguided in special ways, but that is also especially revealing about the general status of that attitude itself. As mentioned, I here focus on the negative, critical side to the Heideggerian diagnosis of this project, the side that is indeed more prominent in the text, though still developed only in outline. Here, my major constructive work is in filling the steps in this outline, and it is in doing so that I shall make central use of the concept of temporality. Third, as a way of once more preparing for the discussions of the last chapter, I shall again consider Heidegger's phenomenological method, this time in its contrast with the general method implicit in the traditional project.

1. Epistemology arises out of tendencies within Everydayness

a. Review of relevant points; summary of this part's argument. We may begin by reminding ourselves of certain points introduced in the previous chapter, in which we had a first glimpse of the topics now to be examined. Heidegger claims that our everyday manner of encountering entities is in seeing and using them as equipment, or as ready-to-hand. Now first, as we saw in that chapter's opening part, such everyday dealings typically serve to desever the equipment they operate upon, in that they tend to bring this equipment close to us, in the sense of putting it in order and in place so that it is maximally functional and accessible; once keys have been used to make the equipmental totality of one's apartment available, they go back to the pocket in which they are handiest. And we noted in connection with this that during interruptions in our dealings this desevering could operate autonomously—and so generate that falling curiosity which looks at or thinks about entity after entity, bringing each close in turn, and setting it in order by assigning it some place within an alternative framework. Second, as we saw in the next part, in our everyday dealings we do not explicitly notice or focus our attention on the entities we are manipulating, but rather through or ahead of them to our purposes, so that in our use equipment typically withdraws, or 'holds itself in'; when eyeglasses are properly in place, one attends not to them but to that which is visible through them. But we saw that during those interruptions in our dealings we may pay explicit attention to entities 'merely in the way they look', and so no longer encounter them only by the way, and only in relation to other means and to ends. Our curiosity, once disengaged from particular concerns, thus leads us to discover entities in a rather different fashion.

In such cases we obviously witness a transition from an everyday concernful attitude to a theoretical or knowing one. And as we have also noticed, this involves for Heidegger a change too in the types of entities encountered, from ready-to-hand tools to present-at-hand objects—a change that itself depends on a different way of understanding the Being of the entities to be met. But many questions arise about this important transition. Just what is the relationship between that desevering curiosity and that detached attention to the 'look' of things? How and why might disengagement from our projects tend to place us in the theoretical attitude, and how might it be responsible for the character of the objects we then go on to discover? And what is the fundamental way in which these objects differ from the equipment encountered in everydayness?

My aim in this part is to describe and explain this transition more comprehensively than was possible in the previous chapter. Because the theoretical attitude is viewed by Heidegger as a crucial root to the epistemological enterprise, it is obviously vital that I make clear the precise character of these moves that lead to that attitude. To explain them, as above, solely by reference to an interruption in concernful dealings with equipment is obviously unsatisfying, but fortunately Heidegger both admits this (cf. *BT* 409), and offers us much more. Still, this 'more' that he offers comes mostly in the form of suggestions rather scattered through the text. And so here, as often in the discussions to follow, it is necessary to build a continuous theory for Heidegger out of these suggestions, and out of his more sustained treatment of related issues. Most importantly for this part, for example, Heidegger gives no clear and unifying statement of the nature of presence-at-hand, seeming instead to rely on an intuitive sense that does indeed develop fairly quickly in us, but that cannot by itself suffice in the arguments to follow. I must, then, piece together and extrapolate, if I am to arrive at a satisfactory account of the present-at-hand, and of the theoretical attitude which discovers it and which lies at the root of epistemology.

In proceeding towards such an account, I shall look first at the aim or intention that motivates Dasein to pass out of everyday concern and into the theoretical attitude. As we shall see, Dasein thereby seeks to improve its position in a couple of related ways, by dealing with certain aspects of its everyday position that are disturbing or dissatisfying to it. This unsatisfactoriness intrinsic to everydayness will be a central topic in the third chapter, and I shall develop it there to a deeper level (and in a different, 'existential' direction) than is appropriate here. My interest now is in that level of description which will explain most directly the general manner of encountering entities that Dasein seeks in the theoretical attitude, and for this the 'pragmatic' materials introduced in the previous chapter will prove sufficient. This part's second stage, then, will be an account of how our motive for departing from everydayness dictates the general character of present-at-hand objects, and of that special attitude in which we discover them.

But my treatment cannot stop at this level of generality. For the theorist always discovers his objects as present-at-hand in some definite way. That is, he always interprets these objects in terms of some particular properties that have been singled out as essential to them—as Descartes singles out extension as essential to corporeal substance, for example. This specification of certain basic properties for objects is accomplished through 'thematization', i.e. through the theorist's adoption of some particular set of basic concepts. The general intent to encounter entities as present-at-hand imposes broad limits on the range of possible thematizations—only some properties are suited to be essential to *objects*. But within these limits different theorists, working in different disciplines or in different historical periods, may project the basic properties of their objects quite differently. Heidegger took an interest in the historical evolution of these thematizations; while we need not consider his account of this development, it will be useful to focus on some one stage in the historical sequence, in order to bring the discussion of the present-at-hand down to a more concrete level. Thus the third stage of this part's argument will treat Descartes' conception of corporeal substance as an instance of the theoretical discovery of the present-at-hand. More generally, I shall discuss a group of properties that have tended to assume a special importance—not only for Descartes but for many other scientists and philosophers—in the discovery of present-at-hand objects; these are the so-called 'primary qualities'. Where entities have been viewed as objects, it has been very commonly supposed that such qualities constitute what they most fundamentally are. I shall attempt to explain the privileged status these properties so often have had within theorizing, by referring back to that original motive which attracts us into this special attitude from out of our everyday concern. If I can show not only how this motive might lead us to discover the present-at-hand in general, but also why these primary qualities are well suited for the role of basic properties within such discovering, I may be the more confident of having grasped what is most crucial to the theoretical attitude which underlies epistemology.

b. Why we move from everyday concern into the theoretical attitude. Now because the underlying intent of this attitude is to make a particular improvement upon our everyday way of encountering entities, it is best to turn aside first to review the understanding that grounds such encountering, paying special attention to those aspects that the theoretical projection aims to surmount. The disclosure of the Being of ready-to-hand entities lies in our familiarity with the system of assignments that such entities essentially have. This familiarity is not theoretical in type, but has as its two main aspects: (1) understanding, which consists in our projection towards certain ends and in our 'knowing how' to make use of equipment to achieve them, and (2) state-of-mind or mood, which discloses the world as now mattering to us in definite ways. (For current purposes I shall leave aside the remaining two aspects, discourse and falling. These will have important parts to play later, however.) To take a familiar example, Heidegger claims that in order for us to see and use a hammer as a hammer we must already be familiar with such assignments as those to its towards-which (driving in nails) and to the other equipment associated with it (nails, wood, workbench). This familiarity does not lie in a cognitive mastery of some theory, but consists in our pressing ahead towards ends that may be realized with hammers, and in our ability to manipulate them and associated equipment so as to achieve those ends. But hammers, like any equipment, can impinge on different ends, and in different ways; our understanding of the system of assignments prepares for a great many roles within which any given hammer might be interpreted. What will help to determine the particular assignments that hammer will be encountered with respect to, is the state-of-mind or mood one happens to be in. This helps to specify the way in which this particular hammer will now matter to us: in a fearful state-of-mind, we may find a hammer threatening. Only, then, on the basis of the disclosure of the world in such ways is it possible—Heidegger claims—to discover a ready-to-hand entity within-the-world. And this disclosure is a familiarity with the Being of such entities.

Let us now recall two distinctive features of our consequent discovery of the ready-to-hand, features that are dictated by this founding disclosure of the Being of equipment. The first belongs to the attitude in which we encounter those entities, the second to the entities themselves; the two are to some extent just sides to a single phenomenon. First, our everyday experience of equipment has a certain '*implicitness*' to it. We typically encounter a tool in such a way that it 'withdraws', in that our attention passes through it and focuses ahead on the ends for which it is used. The carpenter, when his hammer is most thoroughly ready-to-hand, pays it no explicit attention at all, attending rather to the placement of his nails, or to some similar next step. Moreover, to the extent that attention *is* paid to current means, it is spread across a whole system of tools, and not focused on any one member. The carpenter does not experience his hammer in isolation, but in conjunction with the nails and wood and other interconnected equipment without which it would not be in use at all. While he is most absorbed in his work, these parts do not stand out from one another, but smoothly intermesh in an organic whole—and indeed are 'organic' in the further sense of being inconspicuous extensions to his own body. In our everyday dealings, this implicitness is lost only when something goes wrong: the hammer is noticed when it seems too heavy in the hand, or when its head is loose (cf. *BT* 102 ff.); the explicitness produced by such breakdowns will be a topic in the next chapter.

Second, these features of our everyday attitude have complements on the side of the entity that is an 'object' of this attitude. A particular tool is not encountered in and by itself, but in relation to our purposes and to the other equipment it is used with. As we might put it, it is encountered '*contextually*': in terms of a role it plays within some much broader context of means and ends. A ready-to-hand entity is never grasped in its own right, as it is in itself, but always in its relative position within the structure of our involvements. Its very identity or 'essence' is given by this role, or by these relations—it is always something 'for this' or 'with that'.

Both of these features of our everyday encountering are prepared for in the structure of the world, a familiarity with which makes such encountering possible. In particular, it is because we assign our-selves first to a for-the-sake-of-which, and understand equipment only in terms of this end, that such equipment is typically encoun-tered so as to 'hold itself in'. And this encountering has another dimension of contextual dependence, resulting from its reliance not only on understanding but on state-of-mind. The way a tool is interpreted in part depends on the mood one is in at the moment, since this mood helps determine which involvement it is encoun-tered with respect to. The combination of these types of depen-dence suggests that different individuals, or the same individual at different moments, will interpret the same entity in quite different ways.

These two features of our everyday dealings with equipment may be illustrated in Heidegger's treatment of a more complex example—that of the turn signal of a car:

The sign is *not* authentically 'grasped' if we just stare at it and identify it as an indicator-Thing which occurs. Even if we turn our glance in the direction which the arrow indicates, and look at something present-at-hand in the region indicated, even then the sign is not authentically encountered. Such a sign addresses itself to the circumspection of our concernful dealings, and it does so in such a way that the circumspection which goes along with it, following where it points, brings into an explicit 'survey' whatever around-ness the environment may have at the time. This circumspective survey does not *grasp* the ready-to-hand; what it achieves is rather an orientation within our environment. (*BT* 110).

This example reveals more concretely both the implicitness of our everyday attitude, and the context-embeddedness of its 'objects'. To be sure, the sign's peculiar way of being equipment affects the first aspect: a sign functions precisely by attracting our attention, by becoming conspicuous in this sense—but only in order that we may immediately attend elsewhere, and pass through the sign to those assignments it picks out. If our attention dwells on the sign we are not encountering it as a sign in the typical and primary way; this requires that we immediately take account of the specified feature of our current situation (the turning of this car)—and we take account of this feature not by dwelling on it either, but by aligning ourselves within that full situation in an appropriate way (by revising our course to account for the car). Thus even this discovery of equipment involves an indirectness, a lack of focus. And the second aspect is still more straightforwardly present in the case of this sign. For clearly, to encounter it as a sign we must notice not so much any properties intrinsic to it, which determine what this entity might be 'in its own right', but relations in which it stands to other entities, and to our purposes. We must notice where and when this car will turn, and how we shall keep out of its way. Our concernful attention is spread across the range of interlocking involvements constituting our current situation, and the sign is encountered only in the subsidiary role it plays within this wider context.

Now I am trying to explain why we try to move out of this original position of everyday concern and into the theoretical attitude. Of course, different types of explanations can be given here, explanations that are not incompatible with one another. For example, the occupations or roles that many people are involved in may themselves require the adoption of that special attitude—as do roles as diverse as those of product-tester and philosopher. And we are obviously educated and habituated into this attitude, as we grow up. But I am after that dimension of explanation which will account not merely for some individual's adoption of this attitude on some occasion, but for the general character of that attitude itself. And my suggestion will be that it is the attempt to overcome the implicitness and contextuality of everyday encountering, that constitutes this essential motivation. So taking as my clue these two features of this everyday way of discovering entities, I may restate the problem as follows: what tendencies in our everydayness might incline us to encounter entities explicitly and in their own right? Why might we be dissatisfied by the implicit and contextual character of our everyday dealings, so that we should seek to eliminate these aspects by adopting some other attitude or stance? What other feature of our everydayness might dispose us to overcome these two aspects?

The beginning of an answer is to be found in a notion introduced in the last chapter and recalled at the start of this part. Our everyday relation to equipment is permeated by desevering, i.e. by our tendency to set these tools in order, to make them maximally accessible and serviceable to ourselves. In its primary form, such desevering occurs as we physically operate upon our environment so as to produce and arrange equipment to be most conveniently 'ready-to-hand', i.e. most handy and available for the uses for which it will be required. I have cited such familiar examples as the shelving of books by some system, and the returning of keys to a customary pocket. But second, we also desever in that concernful sight, or 'circumspection', which surveys the environment and notes its possibilities, by assigning to the available equipment involvements it may find within some one or another of our projects. Such circumspective desevering—or '**deliberating**' [Überlegung] (cf. *BT* 410)—desevers without concretely manipulating entities; it 'brings close' and makes tools more accessible by uncovering additional uses or involvements they may have. Thus one desevers a chair just by recognizing that one may stand upon it to twist in a lightbulb; by interpreting it with respect to this new involvement, one heightens at once both its usefulness and one's mastery over it.

Now in the previous chapter, and again at the beginning of this part, we noted still a third form this desevering may take—one in which the relation to concrete manipulation becomes still more remote. When we pause from our equipmental dealings, and pause even from the planning associated with them, our desevering tendency may still seek material to operate upon, beyond the range of our current involvements. And so it may 'bring close' a succession of entities, independently of such involvements; this is the mode of discovering called "curiosity". What persists in this third form of desevering is the intent to make entities more accessible and available, but this is no longer accomplished with respect to particular projects one is engaged in. Rather, we now achieve a more generalized mastery or grasp over entities, by discovering to ourselves new details to the ways these entities are. We improve our general familiarity with the entities in our world, and thus help ourselves to feel more at home and at ease in this world, more capable of coping with unexpected contingencies that might arise and break in on our projects. Curiosity involves a 'deficiency in concern', then, only in the sense that it does not proceed from a concern for particular enterprises and their results—indeed, it permits a refreshing distraction from the dealings with which we have most recently been occupied. But it is in fact a sort of more generalized concern, arising when a mechanism at the heart of these concernful dealings—our desevering tendency—is released from its subordination to some particular project, and seeks to improve control outside that project's limited scope.

I have already expressed a dissatisfaction with this reference to 'deficiencies in concern': as an explanation for the theoretical attitude, it is so simple as to beg the question, and seems to do nothing to explain the nature of this special attitude, or of its contrast with concern. But we are now in a position to see how our desevering, as it operates through a period in which we are thus at rest from our given projects, might be responsible not merely for some specific occasion of entry upon theoretical discovering, but even for the general character of this discovering, as of present-at-hand objects. In those periods of rest from manipulation and deliberation, this desevering will no longer bring entities close by interpreting them with respect to the involvement structure, since our projective drive towards its ends is precisely what we are at rest from. But this does not preclude its working to bring these entities more fully within our control in less direct a fashion, by interpreting or placing them with respect to some other system.

Our effort to desever, to order and organize the entities about us, when no longer committed to definite projects and goals, will naturally try to place these entities with respect to a system other than that given by the context of these projects and goals. Which such system might it prefer? If the projection of Being as presence-at-hand should permit us to encounter entities as they are 'in themselves', it would provide a system that is especially suited to this attempt at a more generalized control. In discovering entities with respect to this system, we would then be grasping them as they intrinsically are, for themselves and independently of the projects in which we are now but perhaps not later involved. By placing them within this system we would have fixed them at a site where they will always be available to us again, regardless of what projects might occupy us at some later moment. And so this desevering that operates in independence from our particular projects, will naturally attempt to overcome the contextuality of the 'objects' of our everyday concern. And correlatively, it will try to avoid the implicitness of our everyday dealings—to achieve an attitude that is focused upon its 'objects', and not pressing beyond them towards ends, or diffused around them across a broader situation. Such desevering will aim, in other words, at an explicit discovery of decontextualized objects. In pursuit of this goal, dissatisfaction with the 'subjectivity' of everydayness may be expressed by *doubts* over its interpretations of entities.

As mentioned already, this 'pragmatic' account of the rise of the theoretical attitude will be 'deepened' in the next chapter, when the 'existential' machinery of *Being and Time*'s second Division is available. In particular, I shall there consider further why desevering might come to be disengaged from our accepted concerns, and might try to place entities in independence from them. Heidegger will suggest an 'existential' root to our dissatisfaction with the 'subjective' or relative aspects of everydayness, one that tempts us towards the theoretical attitude, with its explicit focus on objects. We shall also see that this explicitness typical of that attitude stands in contrast with another explicitness belonging to 'authenticity', and that it is the latter that is his recommended response to that root dissatisfaction. Moreover, these types of explicitness, as well as the implicitness of everyday concern, will be given the temporal development that Heidegger thinks shows them most deeply. None of these elaborations, however, is needed for the critique of epistemology that this chapter will present.

We can see our adoption of the theoretical attitude as rooted, then, in the desevering tendency which permeates everyday concern. It is the persisting operation of this desevering, on occasions when we put aside our efforts on behalf of our more immediate involvements, that makes us attempt to overcome the implicitness and context-dependence of our everyday discovery of equipment. Our adoption of the theoretical attitude might express this intent, even if we do not actually 'look ahead' to some use this more generalized grasp will allow us to make of the entity. And we proceed on this attempt by projecting a *new* system, other than that of assignments or involvements, within which to locate or interpret the entities about us—a system in terms of which we can grasp these entities explicitly and in their own right. Our projection of this alternative system is the thematization of Being as presence-at-hand.

c. How this attitude's motivating intent determines its general character. This account seems to fit some rather obvious general features of the theoretical attitude itself: most generally, it does seek to discover entities explicitly and in their own right. It attends single-mindedly to the objects it studies, and attempts to grasp them in isolation from one another and from ourselves (cf. *BPP* 320). In these two ways, it intends to encounter entities differently than is the case in the everyday—and indeed, to improve (as it thinks) on such everyday encountering, to correct an inadequacy it senses there. Presence-at-hand, as the general mode of Being of the objects of this attitude, is best understood by reference to this intent: that which is suited to being discovered as present-at-hand is that which is explicitly encounterable in entities independently of the relations in which they stand to other entities and to our own ends. An entity is to be fixed and held in a scrutiny that surveys it directly and single-mindedly, leaving no aspects or parts outside the beam of this explicit attention, which itself is confined to the entity and not allowed to leap elsewhere. And whenever one returns to the entity—whenever *any* ('competent') observer approaches it—in whatever situation, within the scope of whatever projects, possessed by whatever moods, its present-at-hand properties must again be discoverable in it. An entity grasped in this way is an 'object'.

The 'decontextualization' of the present-at-hand expresses itself, among other ways, spatially:

> ... we *overlook* not only the tool-character of the entity we encounter, but also something that belongs to any ready-to-hand equipment: its place. Its place becomes a matter of indifference.... This implies not only that the multiplicity of places of equipment ready-to-hand within the confines of the environment becomes modified to a pure multiplicity of positions, but that the entities of the environment are altogether *released from such confinement.* (*BT* 413).

They are released, that is, from those intersecting assignments to purposes and other equipment, and to the regions proper to them, and thus are stripped of the spatiality characterizing everydayness. The hammer as the scientist views it is not located by its accessibility for use, nor by reference to an equipmental context. Its 'real' position is not specified as 'at arm's length' or 'on the workbench', for such expressions can fix it only with respect to a situation or a project or a world that may not be shared by others, or by the same individual at later moments. And more generally, this removal from context will require that the 'real properties' of the hammer include none of those involvements that give it its role in our everyday concern: it is not 'too heavy' or 'good for pulling out nails'—nor 'a gift from my father'. The theoretical attitude attempts to desever this entity in a more general way, so that the control achieved is confined to no particular projects or worlds, but adaptable to any among them.

These guiding aims of the theoretical attitude are thus realized, first of all, by abstracting from all such contextual involvements, and allowing them no role in any account of that entity 'itself'. But second, these aims of explicitness and independence from context require in addition a more positive step: the selection of some particular concepts to replace the sense-giving role of our everyday involvements. So for example the framework of Cartesian co-ordinates replaces the regions of everyday space, and gives a new setting within which entities can occupy definite positions. Without such basic concepts, with respect to which the properties of entities can be 'located', it would not be possible to arrive at any content for a characterization of what these entities are 'in themselves'. As I put it above, while entities are no longer interpreted with respect to involvements, they must still be 'placed' in terms of some other 'system'. Heidegger calls this adoption of some such basic concepts "thematization". It plays the role of projecting the Being of objects, just as our concernful understanding projects the Being of equipment. And it is such thematization that gives to theoretical encountering 'a *definiteness* of its own' (*BT* 110), once it has lost that provided by a context of concern. Descartes' 'extension' is one way in which presence-at-hand may be projected, and the aims guiding the theoretical attitude realized.

Thus this special attitude does not discover its objects in independence from every context, but only from that of any projects or involvements. The thematization underlying this attitude must lay out a different type of context, and present-at-hand objects will be discovered only in relation to it. Still, this new context is special in type: it is one that can be 'carried along' or 'entered into' by any 'competent observer' (what makes an observer competent, of course, is precisely his ability to do so)—no matter what enterprises he might be involved in at the moment. Thus the Cartesian co-ordinate system can be adopted as the context within which to give an entity's spatial location, no matter what regions of equipment within an individual's environment might be significant to him. While the carpenter may identify a particular hammer for his assistant as 'that one we use for the small nails', someone not sharing a familiarity with their situations and projects will have to be addressed in more 'objective' terms.

The most prominent thematizations are of course those providing such a grounding for the sciences; only on such a basis, according to Heidegger, can any positive research begin: 'Every science is constituted primarily by thematizing.' (*BT* 445). And again: 'Basic concepts determine the way in which we get an understanding beforehand of the area of subject-matter underlying all the objects a science takes as its theme, and all positive investigation is guided by this understanding.' (*BT* 30). Thus thematizing occurs in a variety of specific forms, corresponding to the different sciences. In each of these cases, the guiding concepts pick out the properties that are to be used in essential descriptions of the entities within that restricted realm—as extension, we shall see, serves Descartes for the realm of corporeal substance. It is these concepts that then allow and determine the particular content of the consequent 'pure discovering'—that determine, for example, that the biologist's intent to encounter his entities explicitly and in themselves will lead to the treatment of them as 'organisms'.

The 'movement of the sciences' will consist in replacement of one such set of concepts by another. Presumably, such development will itself be guided by the general motives to thematization itself, and so will be in the direction of still further freeing it from any explicit reliance on involvements, and of broadening the realm of entities to which it is applied. Among these sciences, it was in physics that this prior projection was first developed to a high level, and this has been responsible for its leading role:

Thus the paradigmatic character of mathematical natural science does not lie in its exactitude or in the fact that it is binding for 'Everyman'; it consists rather in the fact that the entities which it takes as its theme are discovered in it in the only way in which entities can be discovered—by the prior projection of their state of Being. (*BT* 414).

It is the general character of this projection grounding physics that Heidegger takes Kant to have recognized. But of course it was the physicists themselves who had already accomplished this thematization, though not in such a way that its role was transparent to them. They had thematized the Being of their entities more precisely, and had more thoroughly subordinated their positive researches under this projection, than had been managed for the other sciences. But doing so did not require that they notice explicitly this thematization itself, or the essential work being done by it.

d. An example of theorizing: Descartes on corporeal substance. I have attempted to motivate the transition from everyday concern to the theoretical attitude, and to show how the general character of this attitude might be explained through that motivation. It remains to describe this attitude more concretely, in final preparation for the discussion of epistemology in the next part. I shall attempt this concreteness by focusing on one particular way in which Being may be thematized—that found in Descartes' notion of corporeal substance.

Now if Kant represents for Heidegger the discovery of the way the Being of the present-at-hand is projected, it is Descartes' system that stands as the most decisive modern statement of the properties basic to entities, insofar as they are conceived of as present-at-hand:

When Descartes was so radical as to set up the *extensio* as the *praesuppositum* for every definite characteristic of the *res corporea*, he prepared the way for the understanding of something *a priori* whose content Kant was to establish with greater penetration. Within certain limits the analysis of the *extensio* remains independent of his neglecting to provide an explicit interpretation for the Being of extended entities. (*BT* 134).

Descartes of course does not invent the theoretical attitude. He provides only one among the many possible understandings of presence-at-hand congenial to the motive that impels to this attitude. But it is one with enormous influence on the thematizations by scientists and philosophers since. Moreover, this Cartesian ontology is an especially clear product of those motives to the theoretical attitude; in developing it so, my Heideggerian account casts interesting light on some over-familiar features of it. And later, we shall see how this ontology guides or underlies Descartes' epistemology, which will also serve us as an example. For all these reasons it is appropriate to round out my discussion of the present-at-hand by reviewing Heidegger's treatment of Descartes, presented in sections 19–21 of *Being and Time*. As we shall see, Heidegger's dispute with Descartes is not over the internal details of his description of the present-at-hand, but with his claim to be uncovering all entities as they really are—just as Heidegger's objection to Kant has been, roughly, that he misrepresents the projection he describes in taking it to be unique or fundamental. The content of each account is incorporated into our Heideggerian position.

Entities are, then—for Descartes—'*substances*', and the Being of entities is substantiality. Substances are of three basic kinds: God, the *res cogitans*, and the *res corporea*. Descartes acknowledges that the term "substance" does not apply to these univocally, but he does not, according to Heidegger, succeed in explaining the principle that grounds its use 'by analogy' (cf. *BT* 126). A clue is offered, however, by Descartes' clarification that substances are self-sufficient—i.e. do not depend for their existence on any other entities (or on none other than God). As such, a substance should be fully comprehensible in its own right; to understand why it is as it is, one need not introduce references to any other entities, nor speak of its relations to such entities. This defining feature of the Cartesian concept of substance thus fits nicely with one of the motivations we have seen leading towards the present-at-hand: the intent to discover entities in themselves, apart from any context. In claiming that such substances are what there most basically are, and in attempting to bring all his explanations down to ground in just these, Descartes already displays that guiding feature of the theoretical attitude.

Now it will turn out that for my purposes the interpretation of human beings as (present-at-hand) thinking substances is of central importance, but as Heidegger's treatment of Descartes focuses instead on the characteristics of corporeal substance, I shall begin with this. Corporeal substance will also be a more straightforward case with which to complete this introduction to presence-at-hand. In the next part's discussion of epistemology, Descartes' conception of thinking substance will be more relevant, and I shall there try to bridge the 'analogy'.

Descartes holds, then, that for each type of substance there is one property defining its kind of substantiality, and that for corporeal substance this '*attribute*' is extension in length, breadth, and thickness. While the concept of substance revealed Descartes' guiding theoretical intent, this specification of an attribute is the particular thematization by which he carries through this intent. It is here, in other words, that we meet those 'basic concepts' with which he lays out a new system for 'placing' or describing entities. Such extension, he asserts, is presupposed by, though not presupposing, all other characteristics that can be assigned to bodies, such as shape, motion, hardness, weight, and colour; each of these indeed turns out to be only a '*mode*' of extension (cf. *BT* 124–5). But Descartes does not merely single out one property already there among others, he also grasps this 'extension' in a distinctive way. We can see this by recalling the type of spatiality we operate with in everydayness: equipment has a closeness to us that is determined, roughly, by its accessibility ('a ten minute walk'), and is in a direction from us that is fixed by reference to certain regions to which whole contexts of equipment belong ('towards town'). In the extension in length, breadth, and thickness that Descartes makes basic to corporeal substance we also find a spatiality, but one quite different in kind. We find instead a space laid out along and measurable in terms of the Cartesian co-ordinate system: a space of three pure, equivalent dimensions. Corporeal substances occur indifferently at positions that may be determined by reference to these co-ordinates, and the position of one thing with respect to another can be expressed mathematically by giving a distance in a certain direction. The extension of a corporeal substance consists in its occupation of a certain volume of such space, and it is this extension that constitutes what that substance most fundamentally is, according to Descartes' manner of conceiving it as present-at-hand.

Given that this Cartesian conception of an entity as a corporeal substance is dependent upon this thematic projection of its Being, we may now ask how it might have happened that this projection should have specified just such extension in length, breadth, and thickness as essential to the objects whose encountering it makes possible. Can our account of the theoretical attitude help to explain why its discovery of objects should pick out this particular content? The move to the theoretical attitude would not, ordinarily, be thought to dictate any such content. Why should just these basic concepts be chosen? Such extension is especially suited to mathematical determination, and this might initially suggest that it was a personal fondness for mathematics that led Descartes to understand Being as substantiality in just this manner. Some of those other properties that are allowed only a secondary status, such as colour and hardness, are less easily expressible in mathematical terms, and we might think this the reason he assigns them that status in his guiding thematization. But instead, it was the manner in which extension *persists* through changes in shape, colour, and the other 'secondary' properties that led Descartes to assign priority to it. 'In any corporeal Thing the real entity is what is suited for thus *remaining constant*, so much so, indeed that this is how the substantiality of such a substance gets characterized.' (*BT* 125). But what is this persistence or constancy? This too can be plausibly explained by reference to the theoretical intent.

The properties that are basic to a substance, that serve as its attributes, must be those it can always be discovered to possess, whatever the circumstances in which it occurs, and whatever the situation of the person observing. The particular context of discovery cannot be responsible for properties that are genuinely essential. This condition is not satisfied, however, by any of the properties our perception discovers in entities; these do not strictly belong to the entity itself, but reflect the interaction between it and some particular perceiver. When the situation or capacities of the perceiver change, these properties are no longer discoverable in the entity; thus hardness is not discovered by a hand moving at the same speed with the entity (cf. *BT* 124). It is only through the intellect, rather, that we can discover properties that have the required constancy or persistence: substances can and must be thought of as extended through the dimensions defined by a co-ordinate system, whatever the relations in which those substances stand. And those merely relational properties, which lack this required persistence, will in the end be explained in terms of that extension most basically constitutive of the objects themselves. This is also of course the reason for Descartes' 'improvement' on our everyday spatiality. By contrast with the distances and directions of everyday concern, in the Cartesian system we and our projects play no special, determining role. (And yet, although Descartes does not acknowledge it, there remains something relational—and hence variable—in the intellectual discovery of substances as extended, for it is only a person who has mastered the system of Cartesian co-ordinates who can conceive of entities as extended in that fashion. As we have noticed, this dependence is less disturbing than that on perceptual perspectives and abilities, because that system can apparently be mastered by anyone, and applied with identical results from any position. But this dependence will be important for the Heideggerian critique of epistemology.)

We saw that the goal of decontextualized objects has as its complement a goal of explicitness or focus on the side of the attitude that views these objects. And this too is nicely illustrated in Descartes. His familiar notion of 'clear and distinct perception' has obvious affinities to that intent. We get an adequate grasp of corporeal substances only in those mental states that show them clearly and distinctly. But this is so only in our intellectual grasp of them as extended, and not in those sensory experiences that show them, for example, as coloured. Once again, this is precisely because that intellectual view can fasten upon them as they are in themselves, and is not dispersed over the relation between these substances and our own bodies.

So Heidegger claims that Descartes employs his criterion of persistence or constancy because he is implicitly operating with a more general understanding of Being as 'constant presence-at-hand'. Indeed, it is really this basic understanding that leads him to assign so favoured a role to mathematics:

Thus his ontology of the world is not primarily determined by his leaning towards mathematics, [as if this were merely] a science which he chances to esteem very highly, but rather by his ontological orientation in principle towards Being as constant presence-at-hand, which mathematical knowledge is exceptionally well suited to grasp. (*BT* 129).

To project Being as presence-at-hand is, most generally, to undertake to discover entities directly and in themselves, in a way that can be reproduced in any later position, and that thereby provides a most satisfying sort of mastery of them. This aim stands obviously behind Descartes' insistence that basic properties be such as to 'persist'; it helps to clarify what such persistence amounts to, and why it should be important to him. It is responsible for his more specific projection of extension as the essential property of corporeal substance, and it even underlies the three-fold application of "substance" 'by analogy'—although Descartes is not able to make this or its other roles explicit to himself. Moreover, it is this same general understanding, according to Heidegger, that grounds modern mathematical science, and the somewhat different thematizations that it depends upon: 'In this projection something constantly present-at-hand (matter) is uncovered beforehand, and the horizon is opened so that one may be guided by looking at those constitutive items in it which are quantitatively determinable (motion, force, location, and time).' (*BT* 414). And finally, as we must now go on to see in the next part, this understanding lies also at the roots of the traditional epistemological undertaking. And this will give us the beginnings of Heidegger's reply to that project.

2. *Epistemology: a critique of the traditional philosophical project*

a. Summary of this part's argument. Having characterized the special theoretical attitude which discovers present-at-hand objects, and shown how it is related to everyday concern, I turn now to my Heideggerian diagnosis of the way epistemology develops out of that attitude, and then to the objections to this project. It is here that the contrast between Heidegger's few explicit remarks and my own elaborate construction upon them is greatest. I shall try to make clear where the evidence ends and extrapolation begins. But my claim is not just that the following is consistent with what Heidegger says—it seems to me, in its broad lines, a quite natural and continuous extension of his system, in application to a network of problems he neglects to address. And so, for example, I shall rest heaviest weight on the concept to which Heidegger himself gives priority: our 'temporality'.

We may begin by anticipating, first quickly and then more fully, the main steps in this argument. Generally, then, epistemology represents the attempt by this theoretical or knowing attitude to turn upon itself and to validate itself in its own terms—that is, to explain, with reference solely to present-at-hand objects, how such knowing can be the transparent access to things in themselves, that it claims. Such self-confirmation is a task that this attitude's own motives will challenge it to perform. And so this attitude tries to account for itself as the activity of a present-at-hand entity, or as the occurrence of a sequence of present-at-hand events. But such efforts are doomed to fail, and epistemology to slide towards a sceptical conclusion, because as Being-in-the-world we are essentially antithetical to such present-at-hand accounts. Thus Heidegger's most common criticism of epistemology argues the illegitimacy of this present-at-hand interpretation of ourselves, which that enterprise essentially involves. And my main challenge in this part will be to present this general criticism in such a way that we can see it to apply—and in as convincing a way as possible—to recognizable versions of epistemological inquiry.

More particularly now, I shall begin (in the next section) by presenting the epistemological project as a quite natural development of the theoretical attitude. The guiding motivation towards that attitude makes it claim to confront its objects as they are in themselves, independently of any relations, or any special context. But can it show that it does so? To be secure in its image of itself this attitude must turn about on itself, to show that its own relation to its objects has not 'relativized' the content of its accounts of them. Thus the theoretical attitude, when it does not just take its objectivity for granted, is driven to interpret itself—its knowing—in its own present-at-hand terms. It tries to show in these terms that it really does have the status it claims for itself. In order to make this account of epistemology more concrete and plausible, I shall then (in this part's third section) show how it applies to the case of Descartes. In particular, we shall see how the earlier analysis of the present-at-hand character of corporeal substance can be extended to explain his conception of thinking substance as well, and then how this latter conception is bound up with the epistemological aim to validate the theoretical attitude.

Given this rendering of epistemology, I shall then present my Heideggerian criticism of it; as mentioned, this will be a development of Heidegger's main claim that any such present-at-hand interpretation of us is illegitimate. The argument will proceed in two stages: first (in the fourth section) by seeing why no such interpretation can succeed in grasping our concernful understanding or Being-in-the-world, and second (in the fifth section) by exploring the sense in which this understanding is 'basic' or 'fundamental' to us. It will turn out to be basic in such a way that the impossibility of grasping it as present-at-hand undermines as well any similar account of such secondary or 'founded' activities as theorizing; because theory is unable to grasp its own dependence on that concernful understanding, it is unable to explain itself in its own terms.

So stated, the argument lies close to Heidegger, but rather far from the motive and the route of concrete epistemological inquiries. But each of these stages bears a second aspect, or companion point, that is more apt in this way—each reflects a point more immediately relevant to the question whether theory could ever achieve the transparency it seeks. For the very feature of our concernful understanding that prevents it from being captured as present-at-hand, at the same time makes it implicit and relativizing in the way theory attempts not to be. And the fact that such understanding is basic to our theorizing, means that these same paired points apply to theory as well: it too is immune to capture as present-at-hand, and at the same time it too is inescapably infected with these same 'defects' of implicitness and contextuality. It is precisely because we are basically such that theory cannot capture our nature, that our knowing, as incapable of rising free out of this nature, is denied a transparent access to objects.

These points will be clearer as they are developed at more length, in these fourth and fifth sections below. And to make them more plausible as a critique of epistemology, I shall then next (in the sixth) apply them concretely, to a familiar version of epistemological inquiry: one that hunts for a sum of evidence to establish the priority of some beliefs over all others. The Heideggerian diagnosis explains why this version falls short in this attempt to confirm our knowing. This immediately raises the question, however, whether Heidegger is not then a sceptic. So I shall conclude (in this part's final section) by addressing this issue, and by showing how it opens up topics we must pursue in the following chapter.

b. Epistemology is the theoretical attitude's interpretation of itself as present-at-hand. We have seen that we may, as an exception to our concernful absorption in the ready-to-hand, put ourselves into a special theoretical attitude in which we instead encounter entities as present-at-hand. This attitude, with the aid of basic concepts determining the more specific mode of presence-at-hand for objects within some limited realm, is that operating in the various branches of science. Now Heidegger's quarrel is not with such restricted applications of the knowing attitude; as we shall see in the next chapter, he allows the possibility of 'authentic' science, which will be, roughly, science that recognizes its own 'embedded' status. But we tend to extend this attitude beyond such limitations, in a couple of interconnected (and perhaps not really distinct) ways. We tend, that is. to universalize this attitude, and to extend its application to all entities; or, we tend to take presence-at-hand as the way in which entities, including ourselves, really or most basically are:

Thereby the Being of what is proximally ready-to-hand gets passed over, and entities are first conceived as a context of Things (*res*) which are present-at-hand. "*Being*" acquires the meaning of "*Reality*". Substantiality becomes the basic characteristic of Being. Corresponding to this way in which the understanding of Being has been diverted, even the ontological understanding of Dasein moves into the horizon of this conception of Being. (*BT* 245).

Indeed, the tendency to generalize the application of the theoretical attitude in such ways is to be explained by the very factors that motivate that attitude itself. As we have seen, it is the intent to circumvent all contextual dependence and to arrive at the way in which entities are in and by themselves that makes the theoretical attitude so attractive a route for desevering Dasein. Discovering an entity in this way, we can be most confident of having fit it securely into a place at which it can later be rediscovered and most effectively used. This intent to allow an encountering freed from the implicitness and contextual dependence of our concernful relations to equipment in turn guides, as we saw, the choice of those basic concepts by which Being is thematized as presence-at-hand. Interpreting entities in terms of these concepts, the theorist believes he has arrived at the way in which these entities essentially or fundamentally are. For must this not be the result, when the 'relativity' of everydayness has been stripped away? In the next chapter we shall see that this motive implicit in our desevering has a still deeper, and 'existential', root. But here it is enough to note that its effort to make entities maximally accessible and controllable by 'locating' them in some privileged way will itself tend towards that generalization of the conception of Being as presence-at-hand.

Such generalization imposes a great range of tasks on the theorist: he must try to show that entities of all different types can be interpreted in his present-at-hand terms. For this reason already, he and his theorizing will be targets for a present-at-hand account, just because these are entities among others, all equally in need of accounts. So the goal of completeness in his explanations will already require that the theorist explain himself, and show in his own present-at-hand terms what his knowing is.

But such self-explanation is more specifically and emphatically required by theory's need to confirm its own status. A theorist proceeding within some thematization may of course simply take it for granted that his interpretations of entities match them as they really are. But a more self-reflective and responsible theorist might continue to worry whether he has genuinely succeeded in meeting this goal of his special attitude. He might, that is, entertain doubts whether this attitude is encountering its objects as they are in themselves, apart even from their relation to that attitude itself. These doubts would parallel those raised against interpretations in everyday concern: the latter are quite obviously 'subjective', describing entities only in context, only in relation to our projects; doubts that reveal them as such have in fact helped to inspire his own thematizations, to replace the relativizing structure of everyday concern. For the theorist to be legitimately satisfied that his own interpretations have overcome these defects, he must be able to turn back similar doubts, directed against his own attitude, and against the system within which it places its objects. A theorist faithful to his original motive will thus be on guard against the status of his own theories, and anxious to validate that status, once and for all.

The threat or challenge that confronts this attitude, is that it too presents its objects only in their relation to it—that its descriptions show them not as they are in themselves, but as they are in this context provided by that attitude itself. Perhaps it too is 'merely subjective', so that some other attitude must be adopted to explain these descriptions as a product of the interaction between theorist and objects. How can this attitude validate itself, in response to this challenge? In the first place, the theorist must perform the task mentioned above: he must interpret himself and his theorizing in purely present-at-hand terms, must show that he and it can themselves also serve as objects for this attitude. By accounting for itself in this way, this theoretical attitude would suggest that it is able to stand by itself, and is not in need of supplementation in terms other than its own. It would confront the threat that its own terms might not be adequate for a complete account, and confront it where this threat seems most a danger: in its own case. But in the second place, and more positively, the attitude must try to show in these present-at-hand terms that it has the very status it claims for itself. It must explain in these terms how it can give the explicit or transparent access to things, that its motive intends. It must not merely interpret itself as something present-at-hand, but as a present-at-hand *access* to the present-at-hand. While the first task is as broad as psychology, the latter is more distinctively epistemological. But they also affect or guide one another, as we shall see in the case of Descartes.

This account of the motives towards epistemology thus makes that project especially significant for theorizing in general. The epistemologist attempts to confirm that the objectives that generate the theoretical attitude have indeed been achieved by it. (I here present the epistemologist as essentially constructive and optimistic, rather than critical and pessimistic: he raises objections to theory which may trouble him, but which he hopes or expects will be beaten back, so that theory can be confirmed as objective. The other, critical epistemologist seems a relative of the sceptic, who will be treated near the end of this part.) Should this project of validation be fated to fail, as Heidegger will argue, this will have repercussions for the status of that attitude quite generally. Once again, these diagnoses of epistemology and theory will be deepened in the next chapter, by being developed along an 'existential' dimension. And we shall see that the self-understanding that epistemology has been shown to intend, can only genuinely be had along this different dimension, which is where phenomenology goes. But these points will supplement the current accounts, and not supersede them.

c. *An instance of such self-interpretation: Descartes on thinking substance.* As the attempt by this theoretical attitude to explain and to validate itself in its own terms, epistemology involves—intrinsically, and not merely as a by-product—an interpretation of ourselves as present-at-hand. I have already mentioned, and shall soon show in detail, that Heidegger's criticisms of epistemology most commonly focus on this aspect, and argue the illegitimacy of any such interpretation. Before turning to these criticisms, however, I must try to explain what it means, to interpret ourselves as present-at-hand, and must try to make more plausible the claim that epistemology inevitably involves such a self-interpretation. To do so, I shall again focus on the example of Descartes, trying first to show that the above diagnosis of epistemology is plausible for his case, and then to see how the resulting effort at a present-at-hand account of himself is expressed in his conception of thinking substance. Later, once the Heideggerian argument against this effort has been presented, I shall try to show that Descartes is not here an isolated case, and that such self-interpretation is involved even in epistemologies with far less obvious metaphysical roots.

The above account of the epistemological project seems consistent with its most famous instance: Descartes' beginning in his *Meditations*. Descartes officially supposes that his ontology (of substances) emerges out of his epistemological doubt as a conclusion, not as something guiding it in advance. And this reading might seem reinforced by the fact that later epistemologists have taken over that project in epistemology while quite completely dispensing, as it seems, with the Cartesian metaphysics. But we can at least see those more general motivations towards the present-at-hand already at work, and affecting both the way Descartes' doubts are raised, and his later presentation of substances as complete in themselves.

Descartes' focus, of course, is on his theories or beliefs. And in judging their adequacy, he pretty obviously applies just those standards I have attributed to the theoretical attitude: his beliefs are to give him a transparent access to things as they are in themselves. Descartes is already operating, then, with an intent to discover entities as present-at-hand. It is because he intends this goal, that his concerns and activities in the world are so immediately put aside; they are not to affect his investigations, since they so obviously interpret entities only relatively to his ends. Descartes thinks it proper and possible to make a beginning within the theoretical attitude by itself, purified of any dependence on everyday concern. Thus his project presupposes that this attitude is capable of a certain self-sufficiency, and can proceed in independence from his worldly concerns. Indeed, the results of this project will later be used to re-establish these concerns—they will then be directed along better lines, from within that prior and privileged stance.

But what of Descartes' theories and beliefs as they stand so far— have they achieved access to things in themselves? Does his theoretical attitude have the explicit or transparent character it needs, if it is to provide such access? Consideration shows that it does not, at least as theory has proceeded so far, for it has relied on the senses for its evidence, and sensation does not give such undistorting access. Rather, it merely reflects the interaction between things and ourselves (our bodies). Theory therefore requires some other way to its objects, one it can be confident displays them transparently as they are by themselves. It is in the context of this self-scrutiny that Descartes' theorizing leads into his account of himself; his conception of thinking substance thus occurs as a crucial stage in the self-validation of his theoretical attitude. And so it is that this account has the two main goals we distinguished above: more generally, it attempts to show him to be a present-at-hand substance, and more specifically, to be a medium through which other substances can be explicitly revealed. Pursuit of the first goal guides his presentation of thinking, or the mental, in general, while pursuit of the latter results in identification of certain privileged thoughts, his clear and distinct perceptions. We may consider these two efforts in turn, although we shall also see that they are intimately related.

I have already noted how Descartes' identification of extension as the essential attribute of corporeal substance, and his explication of such extension as graspable in terms of a system of co-ordinates in three equivalent dimensions, result from his pursuit of the present-at-hand, and so are due to his founding intent to encounter entities explicitly and in themselves. Such 'pure' extension can be determined and fixed in isolation from any of those projects or involvements that an entity might participate in at one moment but not another, or for one but not another Dasein. How now might this same intent be responsible for that way in which Descartes explains thinking substance, i.e. for the particular way he grasps us as present-at-hand? Here his theoretical intent has an extra dimension: he must not just explain us as present-at-hand, but do so in such a way that our theorizing, as one of our states or activities, can give transparent access to its objects. Perhaps this latter, epistemological aim is partly responsible for the more general account of these states and activities as all essentially conscious, and for the very division between thinking and corporeal substance.

Even on its own, that first goal has a somewhat different form than it did in the account of corporeal substance. For a thinking substance is not something that a range of observers can have access to, and encounter in an identical manner despite their different points of view— that substance alone has immediate access to itself. So it is not the intent to encounter an entity in some way that is available to all others as well, that is most operative in determining the conception of thinking substance. But this recapturability is only one of the types of decontextualization that the theoretical attitude attempts to achieve. More generally, the intent to meet entities as they are in themselves is the attempt to discover them independently of any relations in which they may stand. As we might also put it, it is the attempt to get a grasp on something complete, which is not what it is because of other entities not now in view. Thus corporeal substances are not really coloured, because colour is not a fact just about them, but about their relations to perceivers; when one speaks of the redness of an apple, one does not bring in view a property complete in itself, but something that ramifies beyond this entity itself.

When this general intent is directed towards us, only what is capable of standing in focus in the foreground will show itself in this attitude's gaze. Only what can stand complete in itself in the moment, with no sides or fringes lying by necessity beyond the spotlight, is suited to appear as present-at-hand. It is in this way that the thoughts of a true thinking *substance* must be independent of context. But—to take an example that will be important for us later—a *disposition* is the sort of entity that might offer some resistance to this intent. A disposition may *express* itself at some particular moment, may 'realize' itself in an action of the type it is a tendency to perform, but the disposition is not exhausted by this realization. While that action may stand, as a sharply bounded event, under the direct and explicit scrutiny of the theorist's attitude, and so achieve the title "real" from that attitude, the disposition itself might lie inevitably largely behind such realizations, and so avoid placement within the class of the present-at-hand.

I shall return soon to consider at more length such resistance to the theoretical attitude, and to see whether such difficult cases might perhaps be capturable in that attitude's terms after all. Here my interest is rather in those types of entities that would apparently offer themselves up to that attitude most eagerly, and be most easily treatable as present-at-hand. Among these will clearly be those concrete events of thinking that Descartes identifies as the essential attribute of his thinking substance. A Cartesian thought, whether it be a belief, a doubt, a feeling, or a sensation, is to be an episode completely present within some restricted interval of time, and fully accessible to the explicit examination of the thinker himself. It has no content that is not or cannot become transparent to this thinker, and that he cannot fix in a permanent way with a description. Although some such thoughts, for example expectations, may point in various ways beyond themselves, they can be quite completely grasped—according to Descartes—without pursuing such references beyond the boundaries of the thoughts themselves. And so an expectation may be exhaustively studied while it itself stands within the attention's focus, and it is not necessary to follow the expectation's reference beyond itself, while the event itself recedes into the background. Whether the present-at-hand view is adequate even here, will be an issue for us shortly, but for now it is enough to have seen why Descartes might be led to present thinking substance in such terms. He notices the various modes of thinking, and he treats them as well-bounded events in the way that he does, because this permits that explicit and focused discovery of objects, which the theoretical attitude aims for.

But we must remember the second goal in this epistemological self-interpretation. The theorist must not only account for himself in present-at-hand terms, but do so in a way that confirms his own special attitude's access to its objects. Descartes must discover among his present-at-hand thoughts, some that themselves give him access to the present-at-hand, by explicitly and transparently revealing such objects. Descartes has recognized that not all his thoughts play this role, and this point helped to spur his inquiry. Eventually, of course, he claims that those thoughts that are *'clear and distinct'* allow him such access. By a route we need not recall, he tries to argue that such thoughts must show entities as they really are in themselves; in the attitude that clearly and distinctly perceives, we overcome the implicit and subjective quality of everyday encountering, and achieve an explicit focus on substances complete in themselves. And how do we achieve such clarity and distinctness? Precisely by narrowing or sharpening the focus of our thoughts, and by confining our judgments to what is immediately given in them. Thus Descartes shows an early reluctance to trust even chains of reasoning, where these are too complex to be held all at once in a present survey.

The complementary relation between a substance, as something complete in itself, and that clear and distinct perception which grasps it as such, is interestingly revealed in Descartes' argument for the 'real distinction' between his mind and his body. This argument hinges on the claim that he can clearly and distinctly conceive of himself as just thinking; from this he infers that as thinking he is complete, not depending for his existence on anything further (God excepted), hence not on his body. Thus Descartes links the character of his attitude with that of its objects in a particularly emphatic way: a certain explicitness in the former *entails* that the latter are 'in themselves'. And more even than this, such thinking is complete in each moment: from the fact that he thinks now, Descartes cannot infer that he has existed in the past, or will exist in the future. As we shall see in the next chapter, this means that the goal of explicitness in the attitude implies a certain account of the way objects are in time.

It may still seem, however, that the connection between the epistemological project and this present-at-hand interpretation of us is idiosyncratic with Descartes. Perhaps the latter is just a medieval remnant, as separable from the project as is Descartes' peculiar notion of degrees of reality. Is such a present-at-hand acount common elsewhere as well, and is it in particular present in more recent versions of epistemological inquiry? More needs to be done, to make this Heideggerian diagnosis plausible for the great variety of forms epistemology may take. I shall postpone this work for a couple more sections, until after I have also laid out the Heideggerian critique of epistemology. That done, we can test both diagnosis and critique against a less overtly metaphysical attempt on that project.

d. Being-in-the-world cannot be grasped as present-at-hand. We have seen, first generally and then with respect to Descartes, that the theorist's attempt to confirm his attitude's status has two main aspects. First, he tries to interpret himself and his knowing in this attitude's present-at-hand terms; second, he tries to show in these terms that this knowing gives transparent access to its objects. It is the latter task that is more specifically epistemological, and yet Heidegger's attacks on epistemology all focus on the former. He tries to show that project to be basically misguided, by arguing that the present-at-hand interpretation of Dasein, which it involves, is illegitimate. In this section, I shall consider Heidegger's rejection of all such accounts of ourselves (cf. for example *BT* 68, 82, 168, 292, 419). Why must these be illegitimate? Why can the intent of the theoretical attitude, to discover entities as they are in themselves, not be properly realized in an account of us as present-at-hand? To answer these questions we must focus on a claim that is central to *Being and Time,* that indeed is implicitly defended through most of the published length of the book: we are most basically Being-in-the-world, and such present-at-hand accounts of us as Descartes' are distortions of this essential nature.

By itself, however, this argument may seem beside the point. It is more obviously relevant to psychology, or to the attempt to state our 'essence', than it is to epistemology. Heidegger rests all his case against the epistemological project on this one claim, but if this claim is not further developed, it makes that case look quite artificial. In particular, we need to see what it implies about that more narrowly epistemological goal of showing that our theories give us transparent access to objects. Why should the point that our Being-in-the-world cannot be captured as present-at-hand, imply that this goal cannot be reached? The epistemologist's interest is after all in our knowing, and not in our everyday concern— so why should he be disturbed by difficulties in explaining the latter? A part of the argument here will be the point that our concernful understanding is essential to us in precisely the sense that it underlies or supports all our secondary activities, our knowing included. Thus the impossibility of a present-at-hand account extends from our Being-in-the-world to the 'founded' activity of knowing. This impinges more directly on the epistemologist's project, but still does not seem to affect his ultimate hope that our knowing should reveal things as they are in themselves. And yet, really, it does: we shall see that the foundedness of knowing on concern implies not only that the former can never be captured as present-at-hand, but also that it must still be subject to the implicitness and contextuality of the latter.

I have already paid considerable attention to some early parts of this overall argument: the previous chapter introduced Heidegger's alternative account of Dasein as Being-in-the-world, and the previous part described how the theoretical attitude develops derivatively out of that concernful understanding. But now I must confront a cluster of further steps and problems. What is it about our Being-in-the-world that makes it immune to description in present-at-hand terms? And in what sense is this Being-in-the-world 'more basic' than our knowing? Heidegger must show—or I must show in his terms—that this priority in attitudes is more than merely genetic, so that the theoretical attitude is 'based upon' our concernful understanding in more than the sense that we are first in the one and then, later, in the other. This priority to concern must be such as to imply that our knowing cannot be explained as present-at-hand, either. And most important, it must be such as to imply that this knowing cannot give us access to things in themselves.

I shall present this Heideggerian critique in two parts, considering first (in this section) what obstacles might prevent a present-at-hand account of our Being-in-the-world, and then (in the next) how the founding role of the latter might prevent that secondary activity of theorizing from attaining the transparency it intends. I shall argue that our very access to entities—our ability to intend or encounter them—depends on our concernful understanding, so that this access can never reach things as they are in themselves. Eventually, I shall also try to illustrate these arguments by applying them more concretely to a version of the epistemological project: even in a non-metaphysical instance of this project, we can find an ontological bias towards the present-at-hand, and can see this as responsible for the enormous difficulty of the attempt to 'win back the world' from Cartesian doubt. Although the difficulty in accomplishing the epistemologist's project, or its sceptical upshot, are not Heidegger's grounds for criticizing it, we may see them as results and hence symptoms of the failing he does attribute to it. They reveal, that is, how the theoretical attitude here overreaches itself—and not accidentally, but in attempting to carry through what its originating motive intends.

Let us consider first, then, the question why our concernful understanding cannot be grasped in present-at-hand terms. In fact, I touched on the beginnings of my Heideggerian answer in the discussion of Descartes' account of thinking substance. For we saw there that the theoretical attitude's intent to discover objects that are so determinate and narrowly bounded that they can be held all at once in a momentary gaze, might have difficulty accounting for such intentional phenomena as dispositions. A disposition, it seemed, cannot be completely and explicitly present in a theorist's scrutiny of himself. Such a theorist, prepared to encounter only entities that can be thus present, may notice 'within' himself such things as wishes, desires, urges, and impulses to act in some way, and will more easily treat these as well-bounded events which may indeed possess a reference into the future, but which can be fully comprehended by a study confined within their own definite limits. I shall return later to question the adequacy of such an interpretation even of these phenomena. But the dispersed and implicit quality of dispositions makes them much more resistant to such treatment as present-at-hand.

We may take as an example our disposition to use chairs for such interconnected purposes as resting, working at desks, and dining at tables. This disposition may realize itself on particular occasions, when we 'actually' use a chair for one or another of these purposes. And it may achieve another type of explicit expression in cases in which a special urgency of the purpose and unavailability of the means combine to produce a desire for a chair: having been out walking all day, the disposition to sit to rest may not be able to realize itself as smoothly and implicitly as it normally does, and may receive a certain 'heightening' as a result. Such events are explicitly present within well-bounded intervals, and will easily show up as the theorist catalogues his 'mental states'. The disposition, by contrast, lies 'behind' them, and encompasses them all in its much greater temporal breadth. And, according to Heidegger, it is not reducible to those states that express it, nor to any others we might momentarily be in.

To see this, we must enter a short way into Heidegger's discussion of **'temporality'** [Zeitlichkeit], the topic that serves as the keystone for (the published part of) *Being and Time*. In addition to playing a crucial role in the present argument, this concept begins a more general modulation in my Heideggerian position; it will serve as a new point of reference in all my accounts. For in his second Division, Heidegger claims that with this new phenomenon he has uncovered the deeper source of all those structures to our existence that he has laid out so far. And he undertakes to re-explain these structures in terms of temporality, claiming that by doing so he is arriving at the most fundamental level of description possible for them:

But the primordial ontological basis for Dasein's existentiality is *temporality*. In terms of temporality, the articulated structural totality of Dasein's Being as care first becomes existentially intelligible. . . . We must go back and lay bare in their temporal meaning the ontological structures of Dasein which we have previously obtained. (*BT* 277; cf. also *BPP* 228).

Given such claims, it is appropriate to resort to this notion at this crucial point in the argument against the epistemological project. We shall see that the theoretical attitude which discovers the present-at-hand is most basically a particular mode of our temporality, one that (to speak roughly) gives a certain priority to the present, at the expense of past and future. (The resemblance

between the terms "present-at-hand" and "present" is not reflected in the German [vorhanden; Gegenwart]; still, Heidegger
intends to connect the concepts.) And it is this temporal orientation that is then responsible for the inevitable failure by this
theoretical attitude to account for that 'fuller' temporality which
characterizes our Being-in-the-world. I shall confine this introduction of temporality to such points of application to the problem
now in view; in the next chapter it will be appropriate to bring in
further aspects of this important concept.

To begin with, this concept can help us to see the sense in which
Being-in-the-world, as something like a disposition, has a 'temporal
stretch' to it. We are in our world by virtue of the way we project
towards ends, have been thrown into moods, and absorb ourselves
in the entities about us. In the first Division of *Being and Time* these
three aspects of Being-in are referred to as existentiality, facticity,
and falling. In the second Division they are identified as the three
dimensions of our temporality, being correlated respectively with
the future, the past, and the present. Heidegger calls these dimension "**the ecstases**" [die Ekstasen] of temporality (cf. *BT* 377; *BPP*
267; *MFL* 205), meaning by this that they are the ways in which we
'stand outside' ourselves. And they also constitute the sense in
which we are 'stretched along' temporally. As fundamentally
'ecstatic' in this temporal way, we reach ahead towards our ends,
from out of a rootedness in what we have been, and through (or by
means of) the entities with which we are preoccupied. Our future,
grasped at this fundamental level, does not consist in some span of
moments that have not yet become present and that therefore have
no relevance to the way in which we currently exist; our future is
given as the 'horizon' towards which we are already projecting, and
only because the future is given in this way is any present experience
of entities possible. Similarly, the past of our temporality is not that
sequence of nows which we have left irrevocably behind, but that
which we understood ourselves to have been, and out of which all
our current projects and actions arise. And the present, finally, is
not some detached instant of internal experience, but an encountering of entities 'outside' ourselves, held within the context of those
ecstases into past and future.

Let me illustrate these interlocking dimensions to our temporality with an example. Consider a Dasein preparing an evening
meal. While the dinner itself will not always be explicitly in mind, all

the individual's activity is directed towards this result, and takes its course and significance by its reference to it. The individual is *en route* upon a familiar pathway which issues in this end, and his attention stretches out across this route and provides an overall orientation, whether or not any explicit thoughts or pictures of the various stages happen to occur. Along with this self-propulsion into the future, the individual's activity is also guided by his attunement from out of his past. Perhaps it has been a productive day at work, and the developing meal appears as an earned reward, while his hands seem to manipulate the kitchen appliances as skilfully as they had that other equipment during the day. Or perhaps the contrary: he has been ineffective and frustrated in his work, and this current enterprise seems an unwelcome labour, the appliances reluctant and unfriendly to his hands, the meal itself a mere necessity. Again, in his thrownness into some such mood he reaches back to his past and encounters present things from out of it, whether or not he explicitly dwells on this past in his thoughts. In general, then, this cooking Dasein is 'stretched out' into or towards a past and future, and all its current manipulations and encounterings of the entities present to it occur within the scope or context of this temporal spread.

It is in this sense, then, that we must understand the temporal 'stretch' or dispersal I attributed to dispositions—at least, we must do so if dispositions are to be enough like Being-in-the-world to play this role I have assigned them. We shall then be 'disposed' to sit in chairs in the sense that we reach or project towards the ends that can be realized with chairs, and encompass the pathways towards those ends with an implicit familiarity or know-how. These dispositions are thus quite unlike such properties as the brittleness of glass, which might be called by the same name. Glass does not stretch itself out towards the state that we say it is disposed to—that state is not a goal it intends. Heidegger would prefer not to describe this difference in the way that is probably most obvious and plausible to us—it is not that we are conscious, the glass not. To describe our projection towards ends in this way would attribute to it an explicitness, a clarity to itself, that it typically lacks. Although we intend these ends, and although our activities and experiences are oriented towards them, we are typically not reflecting upon them, or fully aware of our directedness there.

Now it is precisely this temporal stretch lying behind all our everyday experience, that is responsible for those two features of this experience that theory attempts to overcome. When we see or use some particular chair as a chair, this encounter has the implicit and contextual character it does, precisely because of this goal-directed temporality of the concernful familiarity it depends on. The encounter is guided by our stretch towards ends, and by our moody envelopment in the past, and this is why we encounter the chair in a subordinate role within a subjectively organized situation. The theoretical attitude, attempting to overcome these 'defects', and to achieve an explicit grasp of a decontextualized object, attempts to eliminate such temporal stretch in its own discovery of entities—it tries to contract this stretch to a momentary, self-contained view that no longer grasps the entity in context. It tries, we might say, to encounter its objects in a purified present, one that has severed its links with past and future. Only so, it seems, can it encounter the thing in itself, and not by reference to personal projects and moods.

Such a momentary view might do reasonable justice to such entities as chairs. And it might also work for the quasi-dispositional properties these entities have: it is plausible to suppose that the brittleness of glass can be captured in an account of its molecular structure, which makes it such that a blow would shatter it. But this present-at-hand view must fail when directed back upon attitudes that are essentially stretched out towards ends. How could something purely momentary and goal-less—as the theorist attempts to become, for the purpose of discovering objects—understand something essentially stretched ahead in that way? And how could such a temporally directed entity be adequately analysed into a sequence of self-contained nows? Any appearance of success such analyses might have, must be due to an illicit reliance by the theorist on his own temporal stretch: it must be this that links together these nows, and adds the thrust through time that is lacking from the materials of the analysis itself.

The theoretical attitude is thus intrinsically limited by its attempt to treat entities as reducible to a sequence of moments or nows, each self-contained and susceptible to a complete description within its own narrow bounds. For such an analysis cannot be extended to Dasein itself, as Being-in-the-world, since the ecstatic temporality that characterizes this Being-in-the-world resists any such reduction. Our projection towards future ends cannot be reduced to such purely present and momentary events as thoughts about those ends, and our moody envelopment in our past cannot be captured by referring to explicit recollections. But it is only such self-contained events that the theoretical attitude is prepared to discover, because only these satisfy its standards for presence-at-hand: only they can be grasped completely explicitly, and independently of any context.

It will turn out that the theoretical attitude's pursuit of these defining goals, as well as its fixation within a certain 'mode' of the present ecstasis, have a still further, 'existential' root. In the next chapter I shall pursue Heidegger's diagnosis of the theoretical attitude to this deeper level. But at the level of diagnosis now before us, we should note an important irony: it is precisely the features of our everydayness responsible for the theoretical attitude's dissatisfaction with it, that also prevent that attitude from grasping this everydayness in its present-at-hand terms. For it is the ecstatic temporality of our concernful understanding that is both the source of the implicit and contextual character of everyday encountering, and to blame for theory's inability to accommodate this understanding within the present-at-hand. What makes everyday concern not a transparent access to things in themselves, is what also makes it immune to capture by the theoretical attitude. A parallel point will be crucial in the next section.

e. Being-in-the-world is basic in a way that prevents the theoretical attitude from achieving the transparency it seeks. But *is* this Being-in-the-world, characterized by such ecstatic temporality, truly basic to us? And is it basic in such a way that the theoretical attitude's inherent incapacity to describe it must undermine also its account of itself, and its claim to be a transparent access? I here return to the second main stage in the argument Heidegger needs, a stage temporarily shelved above. For given what has been argued—that our concernful understanding is such that it cannot be grasped as present-at-hand—it might still seem legitimate and feasible for the epistemologist to attempt to explain (and to validate) our *knowing* in his present-at-hand terms. The epistemologist's project does not (by intent) require that he offer a comprehensive account of us, with all our levels of activity, but only that he explain that specialized activity in which we theorize and know. It might yet be that this knowing is in some way detached from that Being-in-the-world, so that the attempt to treat the former as present-at-hand is not infected by the misguidedness and infeasibility of any such attempt on the latter. And it might be that such treatment can show knowing to be an undistorting access to its objects. The case so far, in other words, seems not enough to the point of the epistemological project; even if correct, it would seem to have argued against it only accidentally, and not to have addressed its true motive.

Heidegger must show that Being-in-the-world is fundamental to us, and underlies or supports our theoretical activity, in just such a way that this activity cannot have the status it claims for itself. He must show that the theorist cannot escape his dependence on the concernful understanding, and that this inability prevents him from achieving a grasp of things in themselves. In treating this question, I shall begin by looking at some of those passages in which Heidegger explicitly maintains or argues for the priority of Being-in-the-world. But we shall see that these discussions are over-general, and not immediately relevant to the epistemological intent; they seem un-apt or artificial, as does the claim in the previous section, if left undeveloped. So once again I shall try to extrapolate from the text to a more concrete argument, and one more directly engaged with familiar epistemological moves.

The line of reply to epistemology that is most common in *Being and Time,* but also most distressingly abstract, begins by pointing out that in any present-at-hand self-interpretation Dasein attempts to treat itself as an entity within-the-world, along with and on a par with other entities there. But in doing so it must fail to do justice to the phenomenon of the world as such, and to the special relation in which it itself stands to this world. For it is only because the world has been disclosed by way of Dasein's understanding and state-of-mind, that entities can be discovered within-the-world; in fact, only so can such entities even be at all: '. . . [A]*ll* the modes of Being of entities within-the-world are founded ontologically upon the worldhood of the world, and accordingly upon the phenomenon of Being-in-the-world.' (*BT* 254). It can never be legitimate, then, to treat Dasein as merely one type of entity among others. And this is all the more so because Dasein is the only entity capable of this special role: 'Dasein is an entity which does not just occur among other entities. . . . It is peculiar to this entity that with and through its Being, this Being is disclosed to it. *Understanding of Being is itself a definite characteristic of Dasein's Being.* Dasein is ontically distinctive in that it *is* ontological.' (*BT* 32).

The founding status of this role we play, and that we are distinctive in playing it, are taken by Heidegger to indicate that this is what we essentially are. But the epistemologist's project, directed by his narrowed ontological conception, forces him either to ignore this founding understanding of the world, or to attempt to explain it in his present-at-hand terms. 'The question of the 'Reality' of the 'external world' gets raised without any previous clarification of the *phenomenon of the world* as such.' (*BT* 247). And so the epistemologist fails to do justice to a phenomenon that is a condition of the possibility for any discovery of entities whatsoever. And this failure undermines in turn his accounts of activities that are founded upon this phenomenon: 'But in any of the numerous varieties which this [epistemological] approach may take, the question of the kind of Being which belongs to this knowing subject is left entirely unasked, though whenever its knowing gets handled, its way of Being is already included tacitly in one's theme.' (*BT* 87).

We must try to make concrete sense of this doctrine that we are 'essentially' or basically' Being-in-the-world. And among the various claims encompassed within this general pronouncement, we must especially try to clarify the claim of dependence by the theoretical attitude on this basic state. Heidegger asserts this foundedness of the theoretical stance in passages such as these: '. . . knowing is grounded beforehand in a Being-already-alongside-the-world, which is essentially constitutive for Dasein's Being' (*BT* 88). And again: '. . . the thematizing of entities within-the-world presupposes Being-in-the-world as the basic state of Dasein . . .' (*BT* 415; cf. also *BPP* 208). I shall put aside such other claims as (the very radical one) that entities can only be at all, given our existence as Being-in-the-world. How does Heidegger describe and argue the foundedness of the theoretical attitude in particular upon our concernful understanding? And why is this foundedness such that in any account of that attitude, Being-in-the-world is 'included tacitly in one's theme'?

In the previous part we saw in some detail one prominent type of argument that seems used to support his claim: Heidegger tries to show how we pass into the theoretical position from a prior condition of everyday concern. But clearly this is not by itself enough. Unsupplemented, such accounts can have very little force, as we can see from the fact that the opposite transition, from theorizing to everyday concern, obviously occurs as well—yet a description of this other transition would not be allowed to show that concern is 'founded upon' the theoretical stance. Heidegger considers these transitions asymmetrical, because he takes these knowing and concernful attitudes not to be simply on a par, so that they merely alternate with or replace one another. Rather, our concernful understanding encompasses the theoretical attitude within its scope, in that it is persistingly present 'beneath' that attitude. The theorist does not remove himself from the position of everyday concern, and his knowing is in fact only possible because of the persisting (though submerged) operation of that concern. 'If I 'merely' know about some way in which the Being of entities is interconnected, if I 'only' represent them, if I 'do no more' than 'think' about them, I am no less alongside the entities outside in the world than when I *originally* grasp them.' (*BT* 89–90). Similarly: 'When we ascertain something present-at-hand by merely beholding it, this activity has the character of care just as much as does a 'political action' or taking a rest and enjoying oneself. 'Theory' and 'practice' are possibilities of Being for an entity whose Being must be defined as "care".' (*BT* 238). By contrast, and despite the tradition's tendency to hold otherwise, the theoretical attitude does not underlie or support our concernful activities in any such way; our manipulations of a hammer, for example, need not be guided by any explicit or implicit thoughts or beliefs about it.

Let us now try to see more clearly and concretely just how the theoretical attitude might persist in depending upon our Being-in-the-world. I shall begin by looking at what might be called "manifestations" of this dependence: evidence that the theoretical stance does indeed occur within a context of concern. Later, I shall argue that it *must* so occur. These manifestations can be presented in either of two complementary ways, by now well familiar: there are ways the theorist's self-interpretation occurs within the scope of a concernful self-understanding, and ways his interpretation of objects as present-at-hand is underlain by a familiarity with ready-to-hand equipment.

I have noted more than once how our understanding of the world, and of the Being of entities there, is at the same time an understanding of ourselves. For we understand the system of assignments precisely by projecting competently towards some end, as a possible way for us to be. And as we must now notice, such projection encompasses not only such obvious cases as the equipmental manipulations of a carpenter, but even the theorizing of a scientist or philosopher. When we enter the theoretical attitude by thematizing Being as presence-at-hand, and thereby set the stage for discovering ourselves as mere objects, the adoption of this special attitude is itself an expression of our concernful pursuit of a possible way to be. Thus even apart from the momentum of our desevering tendency, whose contribution I have already described, the level of our everyday concern determines our thematizing because the latter belongs within roles towards which we project. Such thematizing, and so also our discovery of ourselves as present-at-hand, are encompassed, for example, within the scope of our projection towards ends such as being-a-scientist or professor or intellectual. Different such roles will require the adoption of different thematizations: a mathematician's basic concepts will differ from a philosopher's, an anthropologist's from a physicist's. And it is only because we have come to understand ourselves in terms of some such way to be, and because a particular thematization is understood to belong to the route by which this possibility may be realized, that the theoretical interpretation of ourselves as present-at-hand comes about. To become a physicist, for example, one must accept a certain system of basic concepts, and recognize an overall current situation structured by settled facts, open problems, and accepted techniques for attacking the latter on the basis of the former. Being-a-physicist is precisely to have acquired a familiarity with this situation, and an ability to manoeuvre within it. These manoeuvres will include particular ways of interpreting entities as present-at-hand objects. Such interpretations thus depend upon a competence acquired as part of a concernful projection towards the role of physicist—the theorist understands himself by reference to the latter role, at a level deeper than that of his self-interpretations in terms of basic particles.

This situatedness of thematizing and knowing may also be expressed at the level of our temporality, even within the narrow limits to which I have so far introduced that notion. Adoption of the knowing attitude in which the present-at-hand is discovered takes place within the texture of a day or other cycle across which the theorist is, as Heidegger puts it, 'stretched along' in his concerned familiarity with his projects and accustomed routine. Even while an epistemologist discovers, for example, that all there is to his self is a sequence of impressions and ideas, he is implicitly understanding himself as occupied with philosophy in the interval before dinner and billiards and social engagements—and not in the sense that any ideas of these need be occurring, but in a preparedness that in effect contextualizes or encloses his current reasonings. This way in which the theorist is stretched along constitutes an understanding of his ends or roles which underlies even that contrasting interpretation of himself as a mere series of momentary events.

The nesting of the theorist's thoughts and discoveries within this context of concern, and their continuing dependence on the understanding that belongs to this concern, are evident also in his complementary relationship to the entities he encounters in pursuing his projects. Even while interpreting objects as present-at-hand, the theorist is typically engaged in concernful manipulations, often of those same entities. To be sure, some of these may seem quite accidental, and detachable from a purer activity that is the theorizing alone. Thus Descartes' manipulations of the wax, as he turns it about in his hands with an ease engendered by long familiarity with objects of similar size and weight, might seem quite peripheral in his investigation of the properties it essentially possesses. For could he not, after all, have uncovered the changeableness of all its sensory properties without actually handling the lump? And Descartes himself, of course, wishes to hold that he can comprehend its underlying and essential corporeality even without any sensory perceptions of it, much less such gross physical manipulations. I shall consider in a moment the possibility of abstraction or detachment of this sort, but for now shall simply continue to note the situatedness in which theorizing typically and familiarly does occur. And besides such handlings of the entities the theorist directly treats, there will be such incidental and not-so-incidental related manipulations as those of cigarette, glass, chair, book, pen, and paper. The philosopher is able to attend 'single-mindedly' to his researches only because an intricate network of such and other equipment is functioning smoothly—and that means, being employed by him with an ease that owes to his concernful understanding of their equipmentality. Such supporting equipmental dealings, we may note, have come to play an especially crucial role in the theoretical discoveries of the modern scientist. The experiments these discoveries depend on often cannot be imagined without a complex apparatus constructed and handled for that purpose. The entities this science considers basic can only be discovered by means of this apparatus; that *it* is efficiently employed as ready-to-hand is a pre-condition for the discovery of other entities as present-at-hand.

But of course the self-sufficiency of the theoretical attitude could be defended against these points, and in rather obvious ways. It might be pointed out, for example, that a physicist need not himself either build or handle this experimental apparatus: he may simply take the findings of those others who do, and develop his theories accordingly. Moreover, it might even seem possible to dispense with those equipmental dealings apparently needed for the theorist to sustain his existence 'in a body'. Without going to the extreme and favourite fantasy of a brain in a vat, we can imagine our theorist paralysed, with all his physical needs seen to not through any activity of his own, but by attendants; could we not indicate by such an example the possibility of a theorizing not 'encompassed within' a persisting discovery of the ready-to-hand? And finally, it must be noted that it is still not clear what the nature of this claimed dependence on a concernful understanding might be, and without this it will in any case be impossible to evaluate the implications of this dependence for the epistemological project.

It is because such replies are available that I have introduced the above points as mere 'manifestations' of the theorist's dependence on everyday concern. As they stand, they remind too much of such commonsensical rebuttals to the sceptic as those by Johnson and Moore. Yet I think we also sense a strength to such moves—some legitimate point they are struggling to express. Now, I shall try to offer such a point, which avoids the previous paragraph's objections all at once, in this way: by focusing on a type of equipment (if that is what it is) that the theorist *must* still employ even in the most extreme cases—this is language—and by asking whether and in what sense this use must depend upon Being-in-the-world. This focus on language is appropriate for two reasons, presumably inter-related. First, the use of language is obviously and inextricably bound into the activity of theorizing. No matter how thoroughly we might imagine our theorist stripped of (other) equipment dealings, we cannot remove his use of language without eliminating that theorizing itself. If it should turn out that the traditional account of that use is misguided, and that it can only be adequately explained in quite other terms, these points could be plausibly extended to

that theorizing itself. And second, it is to language that recent
analytic critics of the tradition have most typically directed their
attention. We might anticipate that they have done so for reasons
similar to those that have moved Heidegger, and that the relationships between these two anti-traditional approaches may be particularly conspicuous at this point.

I shall argue that our use of language depends upon our concernful understanding: it is only by virtue of the latter that our
words can mean or intend their referents. Even in more purely
theoretical moments, our words have sense only because we are
'stretched along' temporally. When the theorist attempts to explain
such meaning solely in his present-at-hand terms, by analysing it
into momentary states, these terms' inability to grasp that understanding makes this meaning escape his account. All such a theorist's elaborations and additions leave him just as far short of an
adequate explanation, because his terms are essentially inadequate
to the work he wants them to do. This failure runs parallel to the
epistemologist's inability to account for his knowing in these
present-at-hand terms. For it implies that our access to entities
—our ability to think or intend them—depends on a concernful
understanding, and so is inevitably relative or subjective. And this
implies that even our knowing, as one such way of access, can never
be that transparent insight into things in themselves, which it
wishes to be; it is ultimately unable to escape the relativizing
impact of our concernful understanding. The rest of this section,
and the next, will try to argue these points.

Let us begin by recalling, at an extremely general level, some
typical ways in which language has been explained by the philosophical tradition, and by noting how these accounts reflect the
attempt to capture this phenomenon as something present-at-hand.
The most obvious such interpretation would reduce language to
those concrete signs—spoken sounds and written shapes—that
could be discovered and described according to the same criteria as
any other present-at-hand sounds and shapes. But the inadequacy
of such an account is equally obvious: it is also necessary to explain
what makes these sounds signs, while others are not—in other
words, to explain their meaningfulness. This problem is typically
translated into the problem of explaining how these signs can refer
to other entities, and the theorist hunts about for some intermediary that can help bridge the gap between sign and referent. This

intermediary must apparently be something mental, since the sound is meaningful not in itself, but only for people, so that it is natural to seek 'in' people the explanation for its relation to its referent. And it is the theoretical attitudes's drive towards explicitness and determinateness that again helps settle the type of 'thing' that is discovered there. A familiar attempt in this direction is to view each of these sounds as associated, in the minds of speakers and hearers, with some *idea* that provides the meaning of that sign. And this idea, typically, is presented as an image or picture, i.e. as something as determinately and definitely present-at-hand as the pictures we hang on walls, but occurring instead 'within' some mind. This idea provides the sense or meaning of the sound by virtue of being an image *of* something, and this consists in turn in its resembling that thing.

But we are familiar too with the difficulties that arise at this point. When the notion of resemblance is examined more closely, it is noticed that the range of entities that must be picked out by any abstract term cannot permit this resemblance between the idea and each of these entities to be exact: there must instead be considerable leeway, and entities resembling the idea to some degree must be allowed to be selected by it. But to determine this necessary degree, the speaker must apparently refer to some standard or *rule*, which he must also hold 'in mind' when he uses a sound meaningfully—and the hearer must then apply that same rule to the same idea, if he is to understand the sound in the same way. When the need for some rule is recognized, it may even come to seem superfluous to continue to speak of ideas or images, and all the labour here may be assigned to the rule itself. Conformably with his present-at-hand orientation, the theorist will attempt to explain this rule as something as completely and distinctly present to the speaker as the idea itself had been; an individual will be considered to grasp the rule, for example, when there is 'present to his consciousness' a certain formula. But once again difficulties have arisen with this improved version, and it begins to look doubtful whether it really represents an advance at all. For as Wittgenstein famously noticed, the same questions apply to this formula as were raised with respect to the original sound: what does its meaningfulness consist in? What is it to understand it correctly? The mere occurrence of this formula in the speaker's mind is no more sufficient to determine his comprehension of the original sound, than was the

hypothesized idea. In both cases the criterion for comprehension—
what it is to understand it correctly—lies in an *ability* to go on to *use*
that idea or formula appropriately, i.e. in ways legitimized by their
conformity to the general practice. And this same criterion can be
applied directly to the original sound itself, obviating the need for
any reference to a mental intermediary. The meaningfulness of that
sound is to be explained by reference to a capacity to join in a shared
practice of using that sound in certain ways in certain contexts.

This familiar sequence of attempts to explain the phenomenon of
language suggests a lesson I shall now try to state in Heideggerian
fashion. The meaningfulness of language resists any attempt at
capture in present-at-hand terms. In particular, the 'act' of understanding some unit of language cannot consist in the occurrence,
within a sharply bounded present interval, of any event such as an
idea or definitional formula; when understanding or meaning is
analysed into such present-at-hand terms, it evaporates. It must
rather amount to something like a purposive ability to use that unit
appropriately in a range of different contexts. Only given this more
broadly stretching ability does any such determinate event as the
articulation of some sound or the mental reference to some rule
have meaning or significance. Considered in isolation from this
background ability, such present mental events or contents fall
short of specifying a determinate sense.

This ability is in fact a part of our concernful understanding, and
has the temporal structure whose immunity from present-at-hand
treatment I have argued. It is the ability to employ a special type of
equipment for a special purpose: to use ready-to-hand signs in order
to 'light-up' portions of their world for others. As such, the ability
that grounds the meaningfulness of language is a peculiarly 'second-
order' part of that concernful understanding. For it is only given a
shared familiarity with the involvements belonging to more ordinary equipment, that signs can be used by someone to make explicit
to another the application of an involvement to an entity. Understanding the use of such signs depends on a prior understanding of
the 'Being' of the signified entities, since if two individuals were not
already in the same world they could have no ability to light up
aspects of that world for one another. Nevertheless, this second-
order status to the linguistic understanding does not diminish its
basic affinity to the more obvious level of equipmental know-how.
Like the latter, our understanding of the use of some linguistic

expression rests in the way we are stretched out towards certain ends, and familiar with the routes or means leading towards them. It depends, therefore, on that peculiar temporal stretch we have seen to characterize Being-in-the-world in general, a stretch that cannot be reduced to the present-at-hand.

Let me bring out these points more concretely by considering some examples. Let us think first of Heidegger's carpenter announcing to his assistant "Too heavy", as he hands back one hammer and reaches for another. In what does the meaningfulness of these sounds consist? The carpenter is in the midst of a certain project—but not simply in the sense that he is making a door now and will be making it still five minutes from now, and not even in the sense that he now thinks to himself what steps will come next. Rather, he holds himself stretched out all along the course of this project with an implicit familiarity with what came before and what will come after, and with how his current manipulations fit within this overall sequence. He is engaged in this project by way of projecting towards a certain (low-level) end, and knowing his way all along the path that leads to this end. Moreover, his assistant is engaged in the project in a similar way (though perhaps with less competence over its route); this places them both in the same 'situation', involves them both in the same little sector of the same world.

Now the carpenter's assertion comes out in the midst of this shared project, is in fact an employment of one more tool within that project. It aims at a particular adjustment—access to a hammer better suited to the current task—and seeks this adjustment by a rather complicated route: given the assistant's general familiarity with the situation, it aims to 'light up' for him another, more specific detail to this situation, the application of a particular involvement (overheaviness, a species of unsuitability) to an entity encountered within this situation (the hammer). And in a strong sense, the assertion will in turn only be 'meaningful' to his assistant, he will only 'understand' it, if it induces him to apply the same involvement to that same entity, i.e. if he comes to stand in the same concernful relationship to that entity as the carpenter already does. And this will be possible only because he is set within the same general project as the carpenter, and is similarly familiar with the assertion as one among other moves possible there. Of course, the assertion "Too heavy" can be used within the scope of many more projects than this one, and the carpenter and assistant will have a more generalized familiarity with it, which comes into play in a particularized manner here. But this holds as well for the other equipment they employ—the hammer itself, for example—and does not detract from this 'pragmatic' account of the linguistic understanding. The meaningfulness of this assertion for a speaker or hearer can only be adequately explained, then, by reference to the way he is 'stretched along' in his familiarity with the route through a particular project, for the significance of the assertion consists in the adjustment it is to make in an individual's progress along this route. This use of language depends upon the concernful understanding of Being-in-the-world, in that it requires the same temporal structure or spread as that underlying our use of more concrete tools. And this understanding itself, with this peculiar temporality, is—as we have seen—immune to explanation in present-at-hand terms.

Now I entered upon this discussion of language because it seemed a phenomenon inseparable from the theoretical attitude, and I wished to understand in what way this attitude might depend upon everyday concern. Recalling this, one might object that this recent example has been chosen unfairly, since it is a case of concernful rather than theoretical use of language. Perhaps the situation is quite different in the latter type of use, so that there is no such dependence by that special attitude. In investigating this possibility, let us look first at an example that seems midway between the case of the carpenter and a case of more purely theoretical speech. I have already contrasted the carpenter's relationship to his hammer with that of a product-tester who weighs it and checks it for flaws. Let us now compare two assertions expressive of those respective relationships to the entity: the carpenter's "Too heavy" (exchanging it for another), and the product-tester's "This one's five and a half pounds" (refusing to pass it). (Cf. *BT* 200 for a related discussion.)

In the transition to the latter assertion (which is closely related to the transition to an objective empirical judgement in Kant) we find an obvious instance of the thematic intent to confront the entity directly and in its own right: the hammer is to be five and a half pounds not just now and not just for the weigher. Thus the hammer is encountered as present-at-hand, and the resulting assertion is an expression of the knowing attitude. Nevertheless, this assertion, like the other, occurs within a shared context of concern, and displays all the same features uncovered in the previous example:

the tester and his assistant are projecting towards the same (low-level) end, and the assertion occurs at a quite specific site within the scope of this projection. The assertion is again a particular 'move' within this project, and the speaker and hearer can grasp its meaning as such a move, only because they are already set within that project by way of striving towards its end and having a competence over the routes or means that issue in it. The character of this project and its end has even determined that the weight of the hammers will be tested in this relatively 'objective' fashion—this permits a type of consistency and reliability, by eliminating those perspectival factors that would be involved were the tester to judge by 'feel', hefting one hammer after another. But on the other hand this test is only relatively objective, with a degree determined again by the nature of the project: the scales are perhaps only accurate to the quarter pound, or the tester only reports weights to the nearest such unit, because greater precision is not needed. The speaker's meaning will only be grasped, then, by one who interprets his assertion from out of an understanding of the project that serves as its context. And this is still clearer when we acknowledge that a really adequate comprehension involves recognizing that the assertion is classing the hammer as *too* heavy. So here too the assertion is understood only by virtue of an individual's Being-in-the-world.

Once again, however, it might be objected that I have prejudiced the argument by choice of an overly 'practical' assertion. So let us turn now to a use of language that seems as purely 'theoretical' as possible, to see whether even here there is this dependence on concernful understanding. We may imagine a traditional epistemologist choosing this hammer as example of an object in the 'external world', and posing the question whether he can know this object exists. But this question occurs within the context of the epistemological enterprise as a whole, and takes its meaning from its role as move in this larger undertaking. Ordinary language philosophers have made much of the point that this same question (or the formula used to express it) will be understood to have a quite different sense in other contexts—or perhaps no sense at all. And my Heideggerian line will now capture this point by remarking that these different contexts are precisely different projects in which speaker and hearer can be engaged. For the carpenter involved in building a door, that question will be nonsense if raised by his assistant—not just because it is not a step along the path of their project, but because it is inconsistent with the involvement they have shared up to that point. The epistemological use of this question, by contrast, takes its sense from the quite different context it is set within; this is the appropriateness to the expression "epistemological project" I have been using so freely. This sense-giving context for that question consists in the fact that the epistemologist is already 'stretched along' within this enterprise, in that he projects ahead at certain ends (in particular, a solution to that traditional problem) and has an implicit familiarity with the routes leading towards those ends. His grasp of the question arises out of this projection and know-how, and can only be shared by someone who already shares in the latter.

It is not necessary, then, to argue the dependence of such theoretical activity on an individual's handling of concrete tools like pens and books, or on his projection towards such 'external' roles as tenured professor. For the theorist's uses of language are already and inherently dependent upon a concernful understanding with the peculiar temporal spread of Being-in-the-world. When he uses words like "object" and "know" in stating his problems or his answers, they have the meaning they do not by virtue of his momentary state, or any immediate insight he has into them, but because of his implicit and stretched-out competence over these peculiar instruments. In particular, he 'knows how' to use these words in the special context of the theoretical project he is engaged in—they are used to make rather different moves, towards rather different ends, than in more ordinary contexts. Without such an underlying competence, there could be no such use, and no such theorizing. Indeed, that 'thematization' I spoke of as grounding our theories, must ultimately be of this character. When we 'project the Being of entities by way of basic concepts', this must amount to our acquiring such a competence to use these words in a special role: roughly, we are disposed to translate our other descriptions into these terms, when attempting a basic description.

This persisting dependence of theorizing upon the concernful understanding suggests a need to qualify my previous talk about a 'transition' from everydayness to the theoretical attitude. For we should not suppose that by thematizing Being as presence-at-hand, and interpreting entities accordingly, the theorist lifts himself wholly out of that position of everyday concern. Instead, we have now confirmed what was hinted above: the priority of our concernful understanding is not merely genetic; rather, our thematizing is always still 'set within' that understanding of Being as readiness-to-hand, and the theorist is always still Being-in-the-world. Most crucially, he is always still 'stretched along' temporally, and experiencing his present by virtue of an implicit familiarity with past and future. As we shall see in the next chapter, the only genuine alternative to everydayness, because the only other equally fundamental modification of this temporal stretch, is authenticity; the theoretical attitude may be founded upon either of these, with corresponding differences in the way we carry out its thematization.

Now these points apply equally to the many different varieties of more purely theoretical activity; research both in mathematics and in epistemology will be dependent upon their respective contexts of projection and competence. Thus we need not deny, as ordinary language philosophers have so often gone on to do, that the epistemologist's question does get a sense from the special context in which it is raised. This Heideggerian reply will not attempt to return us from epistemology by the very simple manoeuvre of denying that there *is* any epistemological context or epistemological sense for these questions, so that we must immediately revert to an everyday context, an everyday sense, and the everyday answer that results. Indeed, we shall see that there is a definite aptness to the philosopher's distinctive use of "know". Nevertheless, the epistemological project is inherently flawed in a way those in science and mathematics are not, so that there is an illegitimacy and infeasibility to the questions to which it does give sense. And I can now complete my sketch why this is so.

The epistemologist, fixed within the knowing attitude which is prepared to discover only the present-at-hand, attempts to confirm this attitude's claim to objectivity. That is, he tries to show, in purely present-at-hand terms, how it can be an access to things in themselves. But this attitude or relation to entities is only possible on the basis of a concernful understanding which is dispositional in character; the theorist can only mean or intend his objects because he is 'stretched along' temporally. This temporal spread, however, is immune to capture as present-at-hand. Thus the theorist is not only barred from explaining his Being-in-the-world in his present-at-hand terms—the same difficulty is transferred to his meaning, and hence to his knowing, as well.

Now this dependence of meaning on a concernful understanding need not cut short the effort to explain such meaning—it does not undermine the project of explaining how our words have sense. A linguist can acknowledge the role of that background understanding, and can acknowledge that it cannot be analysed into momentary states, without renouncing this guiding task. For this task, unlike epistemology's, is not to validate the theoretical attitude, and so is not essentially limited to that attitude's present-at-hand terms. On the other hand, a linguist might bring to this task an additional expectation: he might suppose that the 'act' of meaning should be something entirely transparent to the speaker himself— he might suppose that the factors that determine a referent, should all be open and available to this speaker. This expectation cannot be satisfied, and its failure may incline him to conclude that then we do not mean or understand anything, after all. And yet because this expectation is not an intrinsic part of the linguist's project, this sceptical conclusion is not necessary there.

By contrast, this point is essentially damaging to the epistemological intent. The epistemologist is trying not merely to explain our knowing, but to validate it in its own present-at-hand terms. But this dependence of knowing on concern simultaneously precludes its capture as present-at-hand, and reveals it to be not the transparent access to its objects, that it intends. Just as the goal-directed and temporally diffused character of our concern prevents that attitude from giving access to things in themselves, so these same features 'infect' the theoretical attitude, and prevent it as well. The temporal spread that underlies our intentional relation to entities, thus has two complementary consequences. On the one hand, because unable to serve as present-at-hand object for theory, it prevents our intentionality from being explained in present-at-hand terms. And on the other it prevents that relation from ever achieving the focus and transparency it seeks. It is precisely because we are inescapably such that a momentary view cannot comprehend us, that knowing can never give us access to things as they are in themselves. And so the epistemological project is doomed from the start—doomed by the impossibility of escaping our dependence on Being-in-the-world, and by the deep incompatibility between this concernful understanding and the goals of the theoretical attitude. This attitude wishes to view itself as no longer pressing ahead through involvements, as 'merely observing' in a present without presuppositions—but it cannot escape the condition of thrown projection. As inescapably rooted in concern, as unavoidably dispersed in our ecstatic temporality, we must always fall short of theory's goals.

f. Epistemology's limitation to the present-at-hand explains its tendency towards a sceptical conclusion. This general diagnosis of the epistemological enterprise—as attempting unrealizable validation of knowing at present-at-hand—may still seem difficult to connect with those attempts on this project that are common today. Contemporary epistemologists may not (as did Descartes) offer any ontological account of human beings in general, and may even avoid speaking of such distinctly present-at-hand 'mental contents' as ideas or sense-data. We need to see that this Heideggerian diagnosis is indeed applicable to current efforts at this project. Moreover, we must consider what implications this diagnosis has for the concrete course of an epistemological inquiry: given that the general project is unrealizable for the reasons I have argued, how will this affect the path of the epistemologist's investigation? In particular, does it help to explain why he has so severe a problem avoiding the sceptical conclusion? For both of these reasons, let us focus now on one such route by which a contemporary epistemologist may more typically proceed, to see how the various elements in my diagnosis apply to this version, and how they help to explain the direction it takes. This diagnosis runs largely in parallel to that given in the last section for present-at-hand theories of meaning.

Attention to particular cases in which someone (in the common sense) 'knows' something, will often reveal that such knowing requires the possession of a certain fund of *evidence* about the fact in question. Someone who claims knowledge may be challenged to justify his claim, and (often at least) his justification will consist in citing such evidence. In other cases the claimer will be challenged by some competing account, and if he is to retain his status as knower must produce evidence that rules out this alternative. Such evidence, then, is offered in the context of a conflict between two or more interpretations, each claiming to give *the* account of the thing itself; it is used to support the claim of a particular interpretation to be the objective account of an entity—either by reinforcing its status directly, or by undercutting its competition. The reference to evidence thus accompanies the theoretical attitude, and its claim to discover things in themselves; it contrasts with the persuasive devices of a pre-objective attitude, aimed merely at inducing another to fall in with one's own, admittedly subjective, stance. (By contrast, the somewhat analogous procedure of offering a 'rule' for the use of a word is not thus tied to the goal of objectivity—it is typically just an aid to acquiring or conveying a competence. This accords with the above distinction between the intrinsic intentions of theories of meaning and knowing.)

The epistemologist, when he attempts to validate his theoretical attitude, will quite naturally take over and develop this strategy for defending claims to objectivity. To show quite decisively that theory has met its own standards, he will try to cite evidence to establish the priority of its interpretation to all others. Beyond this, he typically also supposes that the theorist must himself grasp this evidence in order genuinely to know; we may attribute this back to the theoretical attitude's intent to be entirely explicit and transparent to itself—so that it must not merely grasp things as they are in themselves, but see that it does so. Knowing, then, would require possession of a sum of evidence sufficient to establish the objectivity of the account it supports. And because the epistemologist is himself operating within the thematic projection of Being, when he interprets this knowing and the evidence it surveys he is constrained to view them as present-at-hand—just as understanding and its idea or rule were so viewed by the traditional philosopher of language. And just as the latter's present-at-hand account discovered a gap between idea and referent, so now the epistemologist finds a gap between evidence and fact. It becomes clear that this sum of evidence falls short of guaranteeing that state of affairs, because it is not sufficient to rule out various (often quite imaginative) alternatives possibilities. It now seems questionable whether sufficient evidence could ever be gathered, and so whether knowing is possible after all.

Now what has gone wrong here, according to Heidegger? In developing knowing in his present-at-hand terms, the epistemologist has distorted its true character; he has attempted too thoroughly to 'purify' it, in order that it might live up to a standard he wishes for it. We may remind ourselves of this actual character by recalling the intermediate case described above, of the product-tester telling his assistant a particular hammer weighs five and a half pounds. If he has just read this figure from his scale, he would commonly be said to know the hammer's weight. His assertion depends on a thematization whose ultimate intent is to allow a pure discovery of entities (and in particular of their weights) in and by themselves; this intent bears fruit in the 'intersubjective' measure "five and a half pounds", and in the way this purports to exclude any rival accounts of that hammer's weight. But as we saw in the last section, this thematization is still subordinate to the ends of an encompassing project, and this limits the extent to which that theoretical goal can be approached. Thus the meaning of the assertion is determined by the speaker's position with respect to a system of ends, a system that both individuals have an implicit competence over. Any concrete rules the speaker might employ in using his words, or in clarifying them to another, will only determine a definite sense on the basis of this background competence—they will only be able to rule out alternative interpretations arising from within that competence. And now similarly, the speaker's claim to know what he asserts rests on this same shared competence; it is a claim to be able to rule out competitors arising within this accepted context. Any objection the assistant makes to this assertion must suggest itself from out of the system of involvements both are here operating within: the alternatives he proposes must be generated by his own concernful understanding of this weighing procedure, of what may go wrong with it, and of how this might be put right. The claimer, for his part, will grasp and respond to such objections from within the scope of this shared understanding: the evidence he cites to support his assertion will rule out alternatives only in conjunction with that understanding. And so the 'objectivity' of the assertion is necessarily limited in extent. It means that *some* subjective factors that might affect an interpretation of the hammer's weight, have been barred in this case. But the relativizing effect of the shared projection towards ends has not been—and could not be—altogether overcome.

Attention to the upshot of the epistemologist's inquiry can help to make this dependence on a shared project all the clearer. For when he attempts to explain this knowing in his attitude's own present-at-hand terms, this context of understanding dissolves, or cannot show up for his scrutiny. That background projection towards ends is at once both immune to capture as present-at-hand, and so obviously relativizing that it could not ground an objective interpretation in any case. And so the epistemologist evaluates

evidence independently of it, and tries to exclude alternatives regardless of whether they have presented themselves from out of
that context. His view widens beyond the interpretations that are
competitors within the understanding these testers share—he tries
also to exclude interpretations that treat this understanding itself as
mere subjective perspective. For example, the doubt citing the
dreaming alternative plays this role. But this effort fails in the
same way as the parallel attempt at a theory of meaning: such alternatives multiply ahead of any fresh increment of evidence, and the
knowing attitude thereby undercuts itself, landing the inquirer in
scepticism.

Once again, it is important to see that this attention to a relatively
'practical' case has not prejudiced the argument. The goal-directedness and the reliance on an implicit competence are particularly
obvious here, but they are more subtly or deeply present behind
more narrowly theoretical claims as well. We saw in the previous
section that any use of language rests on such projection towards
ends and mastery of means—so we can make a knowledge-claim
only by virtue of the temporal spread or dispersal this involves.
Such a claim, then, can never have that focus or self-sufficiency the
theoretical attitude intends. It can never, as a circumscribed act,
even mean or intend a state of affairs; to do so, it must be held in the
context of a competent projection. But this means that our overall
relation to the state of affairs is both too cloudy or implicit, and too
relativized, to meet the standards the theoretical attitude has set for
itself.

Such then is the way in which this more general Heideggerian
diagnosis might apply to one particular route the epistemologist
may follow in his inquiry. Although this route does not involve any
explicit present-at-hand characterization either of Dasein or of any
'mental contents', we have seen that it may still be plausible to claim
that the epistemologist relies implicitly but crucially upon a narrowly present-at-hand ontology, and that this is responsible both
for the nature of the problem he poses himself, and for its sceptical
upshot. For it requires him to consider the adequacy of evidence
without reference to that underlying context of concern which
ordinarily determines the alternatives requiring dismissal, and the
evidence adequate for that purpose. This concernful understanding
cannot be grasped as something present-at-hand, and cannot be
allowed a role in support of theory. But in omitting it from his

account the epistemologist is driven inevitably on to the conclusion that we cannot know. Although Heidegger does not use these sceptical consequences in his argument against epistemology, they may still serve to remind us in an especially vivid way of the dependence of that special attitude on the context of everyday concern: when it overlooks this dependence by trying to account for itself solely in its own present-at-hand terms, it undermines its own claim to an access to entities. Despite Heidegger's own relative lack of interest in epistemology, then, the nature of its endeavour, and its results, are particularly suited to substantiate his claims for the founded character of the theoretical attitude. And so this attitude's interpretation of entities, although obviously useful within more restricted contexts, must not be allowed to generalize itself in the way epistemology essentially involves.

g. Does this diagnosis of epistemology imply scepticism? I have presented in some detail this Heideggerian response to epistemology, and yet some key questions remain surprisingly open. In particular, we must now consider whether Heidegger is a sceptic. The response I have sketched provides obvious grounds for supposing so. For after all, it characterizes the epistemological project as attempting to validate the theoretical attitude's claim to a transparent access to things in themselves—and then it shows why this attempt must fail, and why we must always fall short of such access. Our theorizing is inevitably rooted in a concernful understanding whose goal-directedness and temporal diffuseness precludes the explicit and focused grasp of things independent of context, at which theory aims. And is this not simply to conclude that we cannot know?

On the other hand, some of Heidegger's own statements seem to run in the opposite direction. We have seen that his chief objection to the epistemological project is that it involves a distortion of our Being, since it takes this as presence-at-hand. And he sometimes seems to hold that properly interpreting this Being—i.e. recognizing it as Being-in-the-world—implies a *positive* response to the epistemologist's problem. Referring to the latter's task of proving the external world, Heidegger says: 'If Dasein is understood correctly, it defies such proofs, because, in its Being, it already *is* what subsequent proofs deem necessary to demonstrate for it.' (*BT* 249). And again:

To *have faith* in the Reality of the 'external world', whether rightly or wrongly; to '*prove*' this Reality for it, whether adequately or inadequately; to *presuppose* it, whether explicitly or not—attempts such as these which have not mastered their own basis with full transparency, presuppose a subject which is proximally *worldless* or unsure of its world, and which must, at bottom, first assure itself of a world. (*BT* 250).

These passages suggest that the epistemologist is attempting to prove, of a subject, that very thing which Heidegger has uncovered as belonging essentially to Dasein. When we recognize that we are the latter and not the former, we are supposed to see that we need no argument or evidence for that conclusion about the external world—we are essentially 'in the world'. So it now seems that Heidegger is rather saying that we *can* know, though on rather unusual, ontological grounds.

A confusion is pretty obviously at work here, however, over just what epistemology's project or intention is. I have taken this to be the validation of theory's claim to objectivity: a demonstration that in our present-at-hand accounts of things we have achieved access to the way they are in themselves. The previous paragraph, on the other hand, has attributed to epistemology the goal of establishing that there is an external world. But this only belongs to that project of validation if understood a certain way—in particular, if the goal is to establish this external world without any reliance on such obviously 'subjective' views as our concernful understanding. When Heidegger says that such understanding is essential to us, and that recognizing this dissolves the need to establish that world, he cannot be allowing that we do have the objective grasp of this world that the epistemologist is after. Our Being-in-the-world is not a transparent access to things in themselves, within that world.

This returns us to the earlier question, whether Heidegger's claim that this concernful understanding is inescapable, implies that we can never really know, and hence a sceptical answer in epistemology. Such scepticism does indeed seem at odds with what Heidegger says and seems disposed to say—it seems inconsistent both with certain explicit remarks, and with the general tenor of *Being and Time*. And yet I think that it is in fact implied by the system of that book, for the reasons I have already given. Now some of the remarks that seem to exclude this position are those implying a positive solution in epistemology, and I have tried to show that this cannot in fact be their sense: Heidegger's claim that we are always concernfully confident in a 'world' of things about us, can be compatible with the denial we could ever 'know' them as they are in themselves. But it is also necessary to explain those passages in which he instead seems to renounce epistemology altogether, and to suggest that *no* answer to its question could be legitimate. Thus he says, referring to Kant's famous line deploring the lack of any proof of the external world:

The 'scandal of philosophy' is not that this proof has yet to be given, but that *such proofs are expected and attempted again and again.* Such expectations, aims, and demands arise from an ontologically inadequate way of starting with *something* of such a character that independently *of it* and 'outside' *of it* a 'world' is to be proved as present-at-hand. (*BT* 249).

And a page later he again suggests that the epistemologist's faulty ontology undermines his whole project:

The 'problem of Reality' in the sense of the question whether an external world is present-at-hand and whether such a world can be proved, turns out to be an impossible one, not because its consequences lead to inextricable impasses, but because the very entity which serves as its theme, is one which, as it were, repudiates any such formulation of the question. (*BT* 250).

Such passages, and Heidegger's more general dismissive attitude towards epistemology, show the need for qualifications or reservations in attributing scepticism to him. Presenting these will also prepare for my last chapter, and its account of Heidegger's positive phenomenological method.

The first qualification looks minor, and has by now the ring of a cliché: to describe the failure of the epistemological project as implying that we cannot know, involves a choice in our use of the word "know". In our Heideggerian terms, it is to associate that use with the goal of the theoretical attitude—the goal of a grasp of the way things are in themselves. And it is to link it with that goal quite strictly: unless we have achieved such access to things, unless we have overcome all the dispersal and 'subjectivity' of everyday concern, we cannot be said to know. More even than this, it is to require that we have evidence for the objectivity of our grasp—that our attitude transparently reveal not just its objects, but the adequacy of its own grasp of them, by being in a position to exclude all rival accounts.

Now such a use of "know" cannot be dismissed as deprecatingly as some ordinary language critics have done. It is certainly appropriate that this word should be linked with the goal of the attitude it names; presumably, it is this connection we sense, when we feel an appropriateness to that epistemological use. But we need not link it so strictly. We may be satisfied to say (as we do) that we know, if we have managed to overcome *some* of the relativizing features of our everyday concern, or have evidence for this. Thus we may say that our product-tester knows the weight of his hammer, while the carpenter does not, because the former but not the latter can give an account of the weight that eliminates the pronounced subjectivity in judging by 'feel'. Heidegger's willingness to say that we know, and his use of the phrase "knowing attitude", presumably reflect this choice: we 'know' when we have moved towards a position which is itself unattainable. (Parallel points will apply to such related terms as 'real' and 'object'.)

This leads on to a more important rider to my attribution of scepticism to Heidegger. What grounds might there be for adopting one or another of those alternatives—i.e. for associating "know" more or less strictly with that goal of a pure objectivity? We may be the more inclined to deny knowledge, and to call ourselves sceptics, the more seriously we take this goal, whose inevitable failure I have argued. If we suppose it something we want for good reasons, we will be more preoccupied and disturbed by our inability to achieve it. But if, on the other hand, this goal is one we adopt misguidedly—because we suppose it a means to an end that it does not contribute to, or else that itself ought not be pursued—then our inability to achieve it may be worth noting, may indicate an interesting limitation on us, but will be less something we emphasize or dwell on with regret. It is for roughly this reason, I think, that Heidegger is so little occupied with the epistemological project, whose failure is implied by his system.

We can see a hint of this in his frequent announcements that we are always already 'in the world' by way of being concerned with our projects there; Heidegger supposes that it is the style of such concern for the entities about us that is genuinely important, and not whether we can know them as they are in themselves. But his full position here is far more complex than this: it is not merely that the epistemological project stands aside from our true concerns, but that we involve ourselves in it because we mistakenly suppose it will help us with other, 'existential' difficulties. It is the latter that are genuinely important, and when we see this, and that epistemology is an inappropriate way with them, the latter task will diminish for us, and so too our inability to accomplish it. Heidegger's phenomenology tries to uncover these existential sources to the philosophical tradition, and to direct us to more fruitful responses to them. These will be the 'positive possibilities' within that tradition, and phenomenology's attention to them involves its adopting a quite different set of philosophical goals. All this will be central to my third and final chapter.

3. *Epistemology's method differs crucially from Phenomenology's*

This then is Heidegger's 'diagnosis' of the traditional project in epistemology. It is also possible, however, to pull back from the relative detail of this treatment, and to consider his more general objections to the philosophical methods that underlie (as he thinks) this as well as other traditional projects. I may conveniently and appropriately enter upon this here, by way of further preparation for my concluding examination of Heidegger's positive phenomenological method. So let us consider what he thinks to be the fundamental failings that epistemology shares with other branches of traditional philosophizing, for these root inadequacies will turn out to be, not surprisingly, precisely the ways in which such philosophizing fails to be phenomenology.

Now in the third part of the previous chapter we saw that the phenomenological method is to be understood both in terms of a formal aspect—which consists in letting something that shows itself be seen from itself, rather than imposing any interpretation upon it—and in terms of the special 'objects' of this method, the phenomena—which turn out to be the modes of Being of entities rather than entities themselves. We saw too the way each of these aspects is related to the choice of everydayness as a starting-point, and as a standard of comparison for the positions of philosophers. Let us now consider how these aspects are related to the central topic of this current chapter, the traditional epistemological project and the philosophical method or perspective underlying it.

We may more conveniently begin with the second aspect: with Heidegger's interpretation of "phenomenon" as referring to the Being of entities, and his assertion that it is this that is the proper 'object' of phenomenology. Now we have seen that Heidegger claims the philosophical tradition has operated with a too-narrow conception of Being as presence-at-hand; I shall consider his explanations for this misdirection in a couple of paragraphs, and more thoroughly in the next chapter. But in the present context it is more appropriate to notice the way this thematic understanding enters into traditional philosophizing: it does so not as conclusion following direct investigation, nor even, usually, as explicit hypothesis or assumption. Rather, the understanding of Being as presence-at-hand operates in concealed fashion, underlying all explicit inquiry and never itself investigated or even noticed. We have seen, for example, that when Descartes insists upon extension as essential to any corporeal substance, he does so on the basis of an understanding of substantiality as constant presence-at-hand, an understanding he is not able to articulate. And this is why he is also unable to make clear the basis of the 'analogy' by which Being applies to his three types of substances.

The 'temporal' interpretation of this thematic understanding may help to make plausible the claim that it plays so widespread, fundamental, and unnoticed a role—for what could seem more obvious than that any entity can be adequately grasped in terms of determinate states at discrete moments? Heidegger takes this temporal bias, and the associated effort to achieve an explicit grasp of entities independently of any relational involvements, to be the concealed source that guides all the tradition's inquiries. And it is this that is responsible for the peculiarity we have seen in his treatment of epistemology: that he does not attack any step in the epistemologist's explicit reasonings, but would rather concede their adequacy (or inevitability) within the problem posed. It is the project itself—with its hidden reliance upon a particular implicit understanding of Being, and as the effort to complete, or to ground this understanding in itself—that is the object of Heidegger's attack.

A first difference between phenomenology and traditional modes of philosophizing will therefore be that the former gives explicit attention to the topic that is indeed decisive for the latter as well, though 'treated' only covertly by it. This neglect of Being by philosophy is in fact the subject of *Being and Time*'s first section: the question of Being 'has today been forgotten. . . . It is one which provided a stimulus for the researches of Plato and Aristotle, only to subside from then on *as a theme for actual investigation*.' (*BT* 21).

Later, in discussing Descartes' failure to explain the principle of unity underlying his three types of substances, Heidegger adds: 'Of course even the ontology of the medievals has gone no further than that of the ancients in inquiring into what "Being" itself may mean. . . . The meaning remains unclarified because it is held to be 'self-evident'.' (*BT* 126). In interpreting phenomena as modes of Being, and in claiming that these are the proper topics of phenomenology, Heidegger therefore means to distinguish this method from that underlying—and misleading—the philosophical tradition, which depends on an implicit understanding of these topics, without ever examining them. As we shall see, however, to 'examine' such Being, or to treat it explicitly, involves far more than merely speaking of it in one's theory—and indeed even more than (in the usual sense) 'thinking about' it. I shall return to this point in a moment.

Attention to the other, formal aspect of phenomenology brings out what in Heidegger's view is a second, closely related, failing on the part of this traditional philosophy. Formally, as we recall, phenomenology is to allow phenomena to 'show themselves in and from themselves'. Philosophers' failure to do so lies, to begin with, in their implicit dependence on a tradition, and on the interpretations it implicitly conveys. It is these traditional interpretations that are imposed on phenomena, absolving or preventing the traditional philosopher from confronting these phenomena themselves; reliance on such interpretations thus contributes to the failure to treat Being directly:

When tradition thus becomes master, it does so in such a way that what it 'transmits' is made so inaccessible, proximally and for the most part, that it rather becomes concealed. Tradition takes what has come down to us and delivers it over to self-evidence; it blocks our access to those primordial 'sources' from which the categories and concepts handed down to us have been in part quite genuinely drawn. (*BT* 43).

Heidegger supposes that the projection of Being as presence-at-hand had its origin in a genuine phenomenological openness to Being among the Greeks, but that this then hardened into a traditional view taken over unawares by succeeding generations of philosophers, so that their experience of entities and of Being was confined to an established channel whose limitations they were unable to notice.

Now such immersion within a tradition is an example of the abandonment to a 'they-self', which we met in the first chapter when reviewing the notion of falling. We saw that falling is an essential tendency we have, to avoid a direct confrontation with Being, and that alignment within conventions is just a route we may take towards this end. Thus traditional philosophy's presupposition of a present-at-hand ontology will ultimately be due to this falling tendency, which we shall need to understand more thoroughly. In particular, we shall have to see why we flee such confrontation with Being—why ontological insight is unsettling or disturbing to us. Phenomenology, by contrast, is to overcome this inclination to avoid facing Being. It is to achieve an 'authentic' openness to Being—to that of the present-at-hand, the ready-to-hand, and especially of Dasein itself—so that the foundational role of the understanding of these modes of Being is 'transparent' to it, and it can take back from the tradition and assume for itself the responsibility for this understanding.

In the next chapter I shall examine in more detail just how Heidegger thinks all this is to be done; I conclude here with a very general indication. Phenomenology, we have now seen, is to avoid the basic failings of the philosophical tradition, by allowing the modes of Being of entities to show themselves explicitly. Now I have emphasized that these modes of Being are already given, though in merely implicit fashion, in the understanding we have of them. And I have argued that the most basic level of such under-standing is that Being-in-the-world revealed in our everydayness. If the phenomenologist is to accomplish his task, then, it must be by making explicit, in some way or other, what is already implicitly available to him in his everyday condition. Phenomenology must resemble the theoretical attitude, in attempting to improve upon everydayness by achieving an explicitness not available in the latter. Because those modes of Being are given within our own under-standing, a grasp of our own Being will be of central importance in this effort: the phenomenologist must above all make explicit that understanding of himself which is somehow already given him. But he must do so in a way that avoids the traditional mistake of treating himself as something present-at-hand. Above all, he must not aim at that type of explicitness which would collapse his 'temporal stretch' into a sequence of limited nows. He must grasp this stretch, this way in which he is at once projecting and thrown and involved in his environment, in such a way as to retain all three dimensions; he must grasp it, in other words, from within, and not by stepping outside into an attitude that insists on detaching these three from one another. Heidegger will therefore require that the phenomenologist's achievement be realized at an 'existential' level—as we may now go on to see.

III

PHENOMENOLOGY

WE have now made our way through Heidegger's views on every-dayness (as our pre-philosophical condition) and on epistemology (as representative of the traditional mode of philosophy), and have seen how the understanding implicit in the former is used in crit-icism of the undertaking definitive of the latter. As things stand, it may seem that Heidegger allows to proper philosophy, or phenom-enology, only the negative task of returning us to everydayness from the misdirection of traditional philosophy, so that it has purely and merely a diagnostic or corrective point. The epistemologist attempts to improve upon everydayness by adopting an attitude that allows an explicit and decontextualized discovery of entities, and by justifying this attitude as complete and self-sufficient; has the phenomenologist exhausted his function when he has deflated this ambition, and noted our need for that (apparently less favour-able) everyday grasp of entities, with which he therefore counsels us to rest—for the most part—content? Or else, at most, it seems that philosophy might be called to reveal and to fix in an account that understanding of Being which is still only implicit in everydayness. For this everydayness has not yet articulated the concernful under-standing it involves; does the phenomenologist perhaps offer the added service of providing such an articulation, in the way that *Being and Time*'s first Division and my own first chapter have attempted to do? Even this latter expansion would allow only a quite limited role to philosophy. It would return us to our initial position from the pretensions of previous philosophy, and would only improve that position by offering a description of it, not avail-able to it before. Once again, the interest of these questions is heightened by their parallel applications to the intentions of ordi-nary language philosophers. Indeed, it seems likely that most of the latter allow to a proper philosophy only one or another of these goals; is phenomenology also to be only diagnostic and descriptive?

But my aim in this final chapter is to show that Heidegger does not in fact limit philosophy to these roles, but grants it the positive and all-important task of moving us beyond both everydayness and traditional philosophy to a third position possible for us, to which he gives the name "authenticity". In discussing this position I shall at last be arriving at the heart of the phenomenological method, touched on at the end of each of my previous chapters and now at last brought to centre stage. I shall also be attending much more thoroughly to the 'existential' elements in *Being and Time,* for it will turn out that the understanding the phenomenologist pursues requires not merely the theoretical mastery of some system, but a basic shift in the individual's mode of existence. And this will require me to survey many of the concepts and claims introduced in the book's second Division, though rather more selectively than in the first chapter's review of Division I. (My most important omission will be of the discussion of 'historicality'—i.e. of the way in which Dasein is in history. In very sketchy justification of this neglect, I may note that this historical element stands in a certain tension with the book's overall claim that there is an intricate essential structure to Dasein, immune to historical change. It seems plausible to suppose that Heidegger's late introduction of historicality made him less satisfied with this view, and so contributed to his decision not to complete the project.) We shall see that these existential themes—and the associated notion of temporality, which I shall also now elaborate more fully—are the most radically untraditional elements in Heidegger's system, and also those he uses at the very deepest level of explanation and criticism. As in the earlier chapters, it will be helpful to present Heidegger's position by contrasting it with a more traditional account of the same matters; for this purpose I shall here turn to Aristotle, whose presentation of philosophic wisdom as the highest good for man will prove useful in illuminating Heidegger's conception of phenomenology. In both cases we find a surprising connection between the pursuit of philosophical understanding and the achievement of the best of lives, although Heidegger's account of each of these is drastically different from Aristotle's.

My three parts will follow the sequence of those in each of the earlier chapters. First, I shall return to the opening topic of everydayness to uncover at last the roots or 'motives' to the falling that pervades it. This part develops this falling as a flight from a certain way in which our essential condition is dissatisfying to us—i.e. as an attempt to conceal or turn away from that unsatisfactoriness. This root of the falling that characterizes everydayness now shows at a deeper level how the latter can both be used as a standard for judging epistemological claims, yet also be criticized and resisted. Second, I shall use this 'existential' analysis to deepen the diagnosis of epistemology as well; this now appears as a more complex and ambivalent response to that dissatisfying character to our Being. On the one hand, this part uncovers as the 'positive possibilities' of this enterprise the respect in which it attempts to turn towards, and to deal directly with, that unsatisfactoriness which is more thoroughly fled in everydayness. It is here that we meet the genuine existential force of scepticism, and that aspect of epistemology which phenomenology will have the task of developing. But we now see too that the present-at-hand terms in which the epistemological tradition tries to handle this unsatisfactoriness make its response misguided, and that this misguidedness is more deeply attributable to the way this tradition is, secondarily, also still implicated in falling. Epistemology, as representative of traditional philosophy, is thus developed as a flawed intermediate position between everydayness and phenomenology. Third, I shall advance to this phenomenological method, developing it as Heidegger's preferred response to that unsatisfactoriness—though one not capable of eliminating it—and as guiding us along the only legitimate route out of falling everydayness. This is the route to authenticity, introduced long ago as antithesis to falling, and now finally to be described. In particular, we shall see how authenticity is most basically a certain way of living through time, and indeed the one in which our essential temporal structure is most transparently visible to us. Here at last we shall arrive at Heidegger's conception of the positive point to philosophy, and shall grasp the extent to which this is both continuous and discontinuous with the goals of the philosophical tradition.

1. Phenomenology confronts deficiencies avoided in Everydayness

a. *The unsatisfactoriness intrinsic to our Being: guilt and the nullities.* My first chapter had as its main task to introduce Heidegger's account of everydayness. But this account—provided in *Being and Time*'s first Division—was shown to be worked into a preliminary development of Being-in-the-world or care, as the essence or Being of Dasein as such; the structures of this Being are approached through, and are often described in terms of, their 'modes' in the position of everydayness. In attempting to distinguish the essential structures from the everyday modes, I paid particular attention to one of the four structural aspects introduced as basic to Being-in-the-world: Dasein's falling. I argued that this falling, though essential as a tendency or temptation for Dasein, is as a positive condition avoidable by it, if only exceptionally. Such 'actualized' falling is thus merely a characteristic of everyday Dasein—and also, in the rather different manner that the next part will develop, of a particular version of the theoretical attitude.

We saw that this falling amounts to a flight—from the disclosure of our Being as Being-in-the-world, into an absorption in entities within-the-world and in a certain way of Being-with others. In this earlier discussion I focused on that into which we flee, but my investigation now leads back, to the source or 'motive' for this flight. This lies in a way our own Being is inherently dissatisfying to us: Being-in-the-world, which grounds all encountering of entities within-the-world, is itself 'groundless'—indeed, it lacks a ground in two different respects, as we shall shortly see. While Heidegger's 'pragmatism' lies in the priority he gives to our concernful understanding, as the condition for all our activity, his 'existential' themes will centre on the claim that this concernful understanding is incapable of the two types of support we would wish for it.

Now we may wonder how so crucial an aspect of Being-in-the-world could have escaped our attention so far. Roughly, we have been occupied to this point with the internal structure of this concernful understanding, and with the dependence on this structure of both the everyday and theoretical ways of encountering entities. But now our scope is to be widened, as is Heidegger's own in his second Division, and we are to attend to what may be viewed as the external aspect of this structure—and of this structure as a whole. We shall see that acknowledgement of this aspect is a crucial prerequisite if we are to understand ourselves adequately, but that this aspect is unsettling to us, so that we tend to avoid facing it, and fall. This disturbing groundlessness of concern thus plays a quite pivotal motivational role, being that from which falling flees, and which authenticity is distinguished by facing. Examining it will open up the deepest level to the Heideggerian diagnosis of epistemology, and will restate the analysis in the previous chapter. It will also give access to Heidegger's basic conception of phenomenology, with its new assignment of goals and methods to philosophy.

Heidegger refers to this unsettling aspect as our **'guilt'** [Schuld], though he uses the term in a quite idiosyncratic sense. It refers to two interconnected ways in which our condition is inescapably lacking or deficient; this 'lack' is of a highly abstract and structural sort, very distant from the moral or religious inadequacies the term might initially suggest. Heidegger offers the following formal characterization of this guilt: 'Being-guilty belongs to Dasein's Being, and signifies the null *Being*-the-basis of a nullity.' (*BT* 353). To understand guilt we must grasp the two **'nullities'** [Nichtigkeiten] mentioned in this phrase. Generally, these amount to two different ways in which the 'contingency' to our world—the fact that it is in each case only one among many possible worlds—is dissatisfying to us. Why should these ends and projects concern us? Why should we interpret the entities around us with respect to just these involvements? Justification of particular projects is possible, in response to analogous questions, but this is only on the basis of a persisting and unquestioned concern for other portions of our world. Guilt is noticed when we question this concern or care as a whole, in a way that transcends any possibility of reply.

The nullities constituting our guilt are then two rather different respects in which this overall contingency and ungroundedness to our world can be troubling to us. And they lie respectively in the ways we are thrown and projecting, notions introduced in my early exposition of Being-in-the-world, as correlated with mood and understanding. Recall, first, that "thrownness" refers to the way we always find ourselves already in a world—already operating in terms of some system of assignments, yet one we have not ourselves constructed or chosen. This 'situatedness' is most evident from (and so is discussed in connection with) that aspect of Being-in called "state-of-mind", for when we realize that we are 'in' our world in part by way of that world mattering to us, i.e. being disclosed to us by our mood, it is especially apparent that our Being-in cannot be wholly within our power. However, to understand properly the sense in which we, because thrown, can never 'choose' or 'construct' or 'bring within our power' our Being-in-the-world, we must read these latter expressions in terms of the contrasting notion of projection. This, now recall, refers to the way we press ahead towards some possible way to be—towards some end or for-the-sake-of-which, as that by which we understand ourselves. It is as such projecting, or existing, that we must understand "choose" when we say that our thrownness consists in an inability to choose our own ground: this projective striving reaches out from a base it can never turn back to operate upon. 'As existent, [Dasein] never comes back behind its thrownness in such a way that it might first release this 'that-it-is-and-has-to-be' from *its Being*-its-Self and lead it into the 'there'.' (*BT* 330). As we must now see, it is precisely this thrownness, as the ungrounded ground of our projecting, that comprises the first nullity in guilt.

All our projection issues out of a way we already have been and become, which is impervious to all this striving it supports. Pursuing our ends, attempting to realize some broad for-the-sake-of-which, we are choosing or determining what we are and will be; this projection, indeed, provides us with our identity. But our pursuit of just these ends, our choice to be so, rests inevitably on a basis not laid by this prospective pursuit. Our struggle towards ends determines who we now are, but is due to a who we have been. And this stands always before any current determination of a self, showing that this self we define ourselves as, can never be simply identical to that self responsible for the defining. We 'make' ourselves by the activity of stretching ahead towards ends, but producer and product are continually distinct, and the responsibility for what we are slips always away from us, into our past.

Besides state-of-mind, there are various other phenomena in which this thrownness supporting our projection shows up in an especially clear and striking way. We are not responsible for the fact of our birth into the world, nor for that original condition from which our effort first begins. Moreover, this early effort is only gradually developed, through acquisition of skills and dispositions, into a full-fledged understanding of self and world, by which the infant becomes (in the full sense) Dasein—and this development depends in large part upon a training and education imposed upon us from without. We grow up into a system of assignments, and are first *constituted* by being aligned with the concerns and capabilities current in our society. Finally, even after our projection towards ends is fully under way, insofar as we are falling we pursue these ends in a merely haphazard fashion, being solicited at random towards one or another by equipment we happen upon, or in imitation of the others around us. In everydayness it is not *any* formed self that is responsible for our projection towards ends, not even one whose formation lies, for the previous reasons, so largely elsewhere.

Yet still, none of these points reaches to the root of thrownness, to what makes it an inescapable companion to our projection, continually renewed at each point as that pursuit of further ends evolves. For even in authenticity, when (as we shall see) the projection towards ends issues out of a self that has been formed and maintained in a prior activity of projecting, that activity was still other than this it supports. The basis for one's pursuit of just these ends stands always behind the person one becomes in this pursuit. This impossibility of an utter self-creation, this sense in which we can never be a 'cause of ourselves', is the first nullity in what Heidegger calls "guilt": 'In being a basis—that is, in existing as thrown—Dasein constantly lags behind its possibilities. It is never existent *before* its basis, but only *from it* and *as this basis*. Thus "Being-a-basis" means *never* to have power over one's ownmost Being from the ground up. This "*not*" belongs to the existential meaning of "thrownness".' (*BT* 330). We exist by projecting towards possibilities with which we identify ourselves, but this projection is grounded in an understanding at which we have already arrived. We are never able to choose our possibilities from the ground up, and our existence is in this sense out of our own control, possessing a momentum we do not ourselves generate. We find ourselves carried along, and never able to set or plant ourselves in such a way as to determine, once and for all and for ourselves, our own course.

This imposed momentum, which is indeed precisely the 'throw' we are always in, is disturbing to us insofar as we recognize or acknowledge it; mood, for example, discloses it as a burden: 'Although [Dasein] has *not* laid that basis *itself,* it reposes in the weight of it, which is made manifest to it as a burden by Dasein's mood.' (*BT* 330). What is burdensome to us is our inability to shake free of this settled basis that lies always behind us, and limits all our current projecting. Our moods reveal this inability most vividly, insofar as they interfere with, or impose a pervasive colouring upon, our activity of striving towards ends, while being themselves largely immune from any efforts to revise them. This thrownness, then, as our incapacity to generate our world or our selves for ourselves, is the first nullity in the guilt inherent in us as Dasein— the first sense in which our manner of existing is essentially lacking. It is the first way in which our Being, as Being-in-the-world, is dissatisfying to us.

The second nullity belonging to guilt, the nullity residing in our projection, is somewhat more straightforward:

... in having a potentially-for-Being [Dasein] always stands in one possibility or another: it constantly is *not* other possibilities, and it has waived these in its existentiell projection. Not only is the projection, as one that has been thrown, determined by the nullity of Being-a-basis; *as projection* it is itself essentially *null*. (*BT* 331).

And again: 'Freedom, however, *is* only in the choice of *one* possibility—that is, in tolerating one's not having chosen the others and one's not being able to choose them.' (*BT* 331). Thus, while the first nullity lies in our inability to choose the basis responsible for the choices we do make, the second consists in a limitation built into these choices themselves: that they inherently involve a ruling-out of alternative possibilities, and dictate that we now cannot be in those other ways. While the first nullity lies in the fact that *we* are not ourselves the reason (or 'efficient cause') for these possibilities, the second lies in the fact that there is *no* ultimate reason (or 'final cause') for preferring these possibilities to the others they inevitably preclude. Just as we can take responsibility only for individual projects within our world as a whole, and not for that world itself as the overall structure of our possibilities, so justification of possibilities can occur only in a localized way.

Speaking roughly (and with a term Heidegger himself would disavow), these possibilities we project towards make up the system of our 'values'; instances among them can be judged and shown preferable to alternatives, but only by reference to other values we hold constant; we cannot evaluate or justify the system as a whole, or show grounds for preferring it to those other complete worlds in which we could exist instead. Our world—that which is constituted by our aiming towards certain ends, and knowing certain ways to pursue them—is only one among many possible worlds. And just as it is not picked out as that one which we have chosen for ourselves, so it is not picked out as intrinsically finer or more worthy than any of those others. This nullity built into our projection is likewise disturbing to us, implying as it does that we must cut ourselves off from a vast range of possibilities, by virtue of our identification with some handful. We understand or define ourselves in terms of these possibilities we strive towards, and not only are they ones we ourselves have not made, they are not even intrinsically or distinctively *worth* striving for.

Heidegger argues, then, that these two nullities are built into our structure as Being-in-the-world: '*Care itself, in its very essence, is permeated with nullity through and through.* Thus "care"—Dasein's Being—means, as thrown projection, Being-the-basis of a nullity (and this Being-the-basis is itself null).' (*BT* 331). These nullities do not infect only our own Being, however, and do not make only our own condition dissatisfying to us. I have been remarking throughout how our understanding of our own Being involves a reciprocal understanding of the Being of entities within-the-world. As we grasp ourselves in terms of some end, we simultaneously grasp entities as the means to this end; because Being lies precisely in such understanding, there is a reciprocity between our own Being and the Being of equipment. It thus follows that the nullities essential to the former must show up in a parallel way in the latter as well, so that each groundlessness to Being-in-the-world is correlated with a groundlessness in the Being of entities.

The first nullity involves, we just saw, the dependence of our projection on a prior understanding, into which we have been thrown and which we cannot now construct or choose for ourselves. This grounding yet groundless understanding, however, has as its object not only our own mode of Being, but also that of other entities, so that we find ourselves likewise thrown into our ways of interpreting and encountering these entities, ways we can never establish for ourselves, but always merely find ourselves in the midst of. That a fork is to be used just so, a house to be organized into just these compartments and dwelt in in this way, are positions or stances towards these entities that we find ourselves already occupying. Our preparedness to deal with equipment along familiar routes or patterns constitutes an understanding of what these entities are, one that we operate on the basis of in all our projection or striving, and that is not constructed by that striving itself. Thus we have never secured for ourselves the Being in terms of which we encounter the equipment around us.

Second, to the extent that, on the basis of this imposed understanding, we do choose possibilities and project towards them, we have seen that we do so only at the expense of ignoring and precluding other possibilities. And this nullity too has its correlate in the Being of entities within-the-world, for this pre-emption of alternative possibilities *for us* involves a reciprocal ruling-out of other modes of Being that would be possible for equipment. In our choice of some for-the-sake-of-which, we constrain ourselves to encounter entities insofar as they bear upon that end, and must close ourselves off from the other roles possible for them—roles that again are no less intrinsically appropriate to the entities themselves. The familiar equipment about us could play quite different parts within other systems of assignments—and while just how and just why we make use of a fork can be justified within the context of *this* structure, which is our world, the choice of this whole system in preference to another assigning this entity to a quite different niche stands beyond all such justification.

In each of these ways, then, the unsatisfactoriness intrinsic to Being-in-the-world attaches as well to the Being of entities within-the-world. Each of us operates with an understanding of this Being that we ourselves are not responsible for constructing, and that is no truer to some way these entities inherently are, than many others one might equally well adopt. That our relationship to entities lacks the self-determination and the uniqueness we would naturally prefer, issues inevitably out of those limitations built into our basic structure, as thrown projection. In the second part of this chapter, we shall see that this application of the nullities to the Being of entities will serve as the 'existential source' for the epistemological project, while their application to our own Being would play a similar role in a parallel diagnosis of traditional ethics.

b. How anxiety faces this guilt. The nullities constituting our guilt are the ways, then, in which our essential condition as Being-in-the-world is dissatisfying to us. And falling, as we must next see, is a flight from recognition of this disturbing condition. For although we are always, in a way, familiar with our guilt (in that it is 'disclosed' to us, in a sense to be explained), it is only in a special state-of-mind or mood that we recognize it directly and explicitly. 'Proximally and for the most part' this guilt is disclosed even while we turn away from and avoid it. Now while this latter, fleeing response to the nullities is the proper topic of this part—because it is the everyday response—we can be helped to a better grasp of it and of the troubling character of the nullities themselves by looking briefly at that former, special mood in which guilt is faced more directly. (This mood, and that general mode of Being-in-the-world with which it is closely allied—authenticity—will be treated more fully in this chapter's third part.) This special mood is of course '**anxiety**' [Angst] (cf. *BT* 230 ff.; *WIM* 102 ff.). In it we feel '**uncanny**' [unheimlich], or 'not-at-home', in the sense that we lose our usual insertion (or 'at-homeness') within the system of assignments. More specifically, in anxiety we are stripped of our self-identification with those roles or ends towards which we ordinarily project, and consequently too of our ordinary relationship to equipment as the manipulable means to those ends. We lose our projective drive towards those goals that formerly compelled and defined us, and the equipment that was ready to our hands for use in achieving those goals, now lies inert and pointless around us. We see no reason to pursue those goals, or to employ that equipment in our customary way—and we 'see' this with a more sufficient and effective force than a purely theoretical avowal would involve.

This disengagement from our world, this way in which the world as a whole can cease to matter to us, imposes or constitutes an existential acknowledgement of the nullities essential to our Being. For it is only when we slip out of straightforwardly identifying with some particular end, that we fully recognize those two contingencies in our projection towards that end—contingencies that, unlike the end itself, genuinely belong to our own Being. In that Being, we are thrown projection, thrown into the projection of some world or other. That it should be just *this* world, that we should identify ourselves with just these ends and interpret our surroundings as means in just this way, is due neither to us nor to any intrinsic merit to this world. In its content our world is merely one among any number of possibilities, having no special claim upon us, nor we upon it. What does belong to us essentially and irrevocably is not any such content, but the manner of our thrownness and projection, including these very nullities that negate the claim of that content. In anxiety we are not-at-home in the world in which we happen to have been, and hence lose our tendency to grasp ourselves solely in terms of that world. We recognize the contingency to our world, and our condition of being thrown into projecting a merely contingent world, in both of these senses distinguished. And we recognize all this in the fullest or deepest way, by experiencing an interruption in the significance of that world. This constitutes an 'existential' acknowledgement of the nullities, in that it reflects them in the very manner of our existence—i.e. in our way of projecting. Only in such anxiety do we give more than merely theoretical regard to our essential groundlessness, and so to our own fundamental condition: 'In uncanniness Dasein stands together with itself primordially. Uncanniness brings this entity face to face with its undisguised nullity, which belongs to the possibility of its ownmost potentiality-for-Being.' (*BT* 333). Anxiety, then, is anxious not about any entity within-the-world, but about Being-in-the-world itself, which it understands appropriately, rather than in terms of those entities, or in terms of any particular ends:

That which anxiety is anxious about is Being-in-the-world itself. In anxiety what is environmentally ready-to-hand sinks away, and so, in general, do entities within-the-world. . . . Anxiety thus takes away from Dasein the possibility of understanding itself, as it falls, in terms of the 'world' and the way things have been publicly interpreted. (*BT* 232).

In the next parts, I shall develop this anxiety more fully, in its relation to epistemological scepticism, and to the phenomenological method.

c. How falling flees this guilt: preoccupation with the ontical. It is in its contrast with this special mood of anxiety that we are now at last in a position to grasp the source or motive of our falling tendency, and so too of the everydayness this falling infects. For we are impelled to fall precisely because our own condition is inherently dissatisfying to us, and because direct acknowledgement of this condition, in anxiety, is thus burdensome. Falling is precisely a flight from that recognition of our nullities, which oppresses us in the mood of anxiety. 'When in falling we flee *into* the 'at-home' of publicness, we flee *in the face of* the 'not-at-home'; that is, we flee in the face of the uncanniness which lies in Dasein. . . .' (*BT* 234). We flee, in other words, from that deep and direct recognition of the contingencies to our world, of the ways in which it and our relationship to it are less than we would prefer. This anxious recognition occurs as we drift apart from our world, and we avoid it precisely by reinforcing the links that bind us up with this world. Falling amounts, then, to our effort to recapture or to maintain our immersion within some particular system of assignments, an immersion that involves both whole-heartedly identifying ourselves with some particular end, and understanding other entities solely by reference to the way they contribute to (or detract from) that end. Such immersion thus fixes or stabilizes our own character, and that of those other entities, and conceals the contingency, the absence of essential content, that in truth attaches to their Being. By preoccupying ourselves with some particular way in which we and other entities can show ourselves, we are able to avoid acknowledging those nullities more deeply characteristic both of us and of them, and so 'tranquillize' ourselves—prevent these distressing aspects to our deepest structure from obtruding upon us.

But in what sense are we already 'familiar' with the nullities, in a way to motivate this falling avoidance of them? How can these nullities be 'disclosed' to us, even as we turn from them into everyday concerns? We can better grasp the structure of such falling by recalling Heidegger's distinction between two different levels to Dasein's understanding of itself: the existentiell and the existential. Each of these, as understanding, involves a grasp by Dasein of its own Being, and is thus to be distinguished from any (merely ontical) interpretation. But while an existentiell understanding grasps this Being in terms of particular possibilities or roles towards which it projects, an existential understanding grasps it in terms of projected ends as such.

The former level of self-understanding is the more immediate basis to any way we may interpret ourselves in our concernful activity. Such self-interpretation occurs in our concrete activities, but only because these are based in abilities that make up our self-understanding. So the carpenter, by actually hammering, interprets himself as a hammerer—and this episode of self-interpretation depends upon an underlying projection towards the role of carpenter, and competence over the means required for it. Yet this existentiell understanding of himself, while grounding all the carpenter's ontical interpreting of himself and his tools, does not by itself constitute a full ontological understanding either of his own Being or of that of his tools. This carpenter is not fundamentally just that—a carpenter; to the extent that he does understand himself solely by reference to that end, he is overlooking those structural elements to Being-in-the-world that he has in common with all other Dasein, and that make possible this existentiell projection towards just this end. Only because the carpenter is more basically thrown and projecting, and hence held in the nullities that respectively characterize these, can this existentiell understanding in terms of this end be possible at all.

But Heidegger claims that this deeper and grounding level of Being is likewise always grasped in a self-understanding: an existential understanding. We always do understand that our projection towards particular ends *is* a *projection*, and hence a 'choice' of these ends to the exclusion of others—and we understand that it occurs within a context into which we have already been thrown, and that is not also an object of this choice. And this more essential understanding also occurs not in any narrow episodes or acts, but in an ability or disposition we persistently possess. While the existentiell understanding is a competence for projecting towards some particular end, this deeper existential understanding is a competence for projection in general, a familiarity with the conditions and format for this activity. It is, we might say, a higher-order competence for developing and employing competences of that more specialized sort. And as such, it includes a familiarity with the nullities, since these are decisive conditions or limits constraining any such projection.

Thus Heidegger holds that any ontical self-interpretation, in which we act concretely within some definite role, always depends first on an encompassing existentiell understanding, and then in turn on a 'more primordial' existential understanding that grasps our essential condition of Being-in-the-world. Falling may now first be seen as a particular way in which these two levels of self-understanding can stand related to one another—or better, as a way they can *fail* to be related. In falling we do still possess that existential understanding of ourselves: we 'know how' to choose projects or ends. Indeed, our falling originates in this level of understanding, and in the disturbing acquaintance with the nullities, which it includes, and from which we try to distract ourselves. We find this distraction precisely in the existentiell understanding—which we turn towards and absorb ourselves in, to the exclusion of the existential. Thus falling involves a refusal to allow that higher-order capacity to become explicit to ourselves, and is accomplished by our immersion within the lower-level dispositions that capacity envelops.

The situation is thus parallel to—and can be clarified by—a case of two existentiell abilities, one similarly encompassed by the other: we may think of the carpenter's capacity to make a door, as subordinate to his ability to build a house. If the larger project is for some reason unsettling to him, perhaps because there are obstacles he is reluctant to face, he might 'lose' himself within the more immediate task. He might make the door while forgetting or avoiding its role in the overall project—by not doing what he does 'for the sake of' the encompassing, higher end. His ability to build the door is brought into play by itself, and not as a moment within the overarching ability. He does still know how to build the house as a whole, but fails to guide and judge his activities with respect to that end. It is in a similar sense that our existential understanding can fail to be explicit.

But there is a second way in which falling affects these two levels of self-understanding. The deeper, existential understanding has certain implications for the *status* of the particular ends towards which the existentiell understanding projects: these do not exhaust what we ourselves are. In falling we do not merely avoid the existential by absorbing ourselves in the existentiell, we also grasp the latter in a distinctive way, by ignoring and even denying the former's implications for it. In falling we refuse to allow our existential grasp of the nullities to become explicit, not merely by pre-occupying ourselves with existentiell possibilities, but also by conceiving the latter in a manner inconsistent with our nullities. For the nullities imply a contingency or 'looseness' in our identification with ends—a contingency that falling attempts to conceal or deny, either by ignoring the existence of any alternatives to these ends, or by refusing to concede such alternatives an equality of value or status. We suppose we straightforwardly *are* those roles towards which we project—and the more basic human situation of having been thrown into a groundless choice of such roles, is ignored and implicitly denied. Thus falling involves not merely avoiding an explicit and proper understanding of our Being-in-the-world, but even a purposeful misunderstanding, through an incorrect grasp of our existentiell possibilities.

Once again, this can be clarified by the analogy of two nested existentiell understandings: while immersing himself within the lower-level project of making the door, the carpenter may also over-value its end, by failing to place it in its overall context. He may allot more attention, energy, and time to this project than that context assigns it, and so may mistake its significance—not in what he thinks about it, but in the way he pursues it. His manner of engagement in this project may fail to accord with its role in the higher project, and indeed will naturally drift out of accord as that latter is forgotten.

Heidegger holds that this falling preoccupation with the existentiell implies a drastic mistake as to what we are. In the first place, it involves misunderstanding oneself *as* a mere entity within-the-world. If we understand ourselves simply by reference to that role or end towards which we project—if one takes oneself simply to be a carpenter, for example—we are identifying with a role or function contained in the system of assignments, as which we might then be (seemingly) adequately encountered by others. We all do very frequently encounter one another with respect to such roles or slots in this system; we thereby interpret one another as equipment usable for our ends. A sales clerk, for example, may be interpreted as a ready-to-hand means one employs in order to carry out a purchase. When in falling we grasp ourselves quite completely in terms of such roles, we of course do not directly treat ourselves as equipment in this way, since we project towards these roles and do not use ourselves (within them) as means to some further end. But we imply that others are justified in interpreting us solely by reference to these roles, and hence as means within their own systems of projection. And just as the interpretation of others as equipment fails to do justice to them as Dasein, so the existentiell self-understanding that implies the legitimacy of such relations to others, cannot be adequate.

Moreover, and for similar reasons, this self-understanding misguidedly grasps us *in terms of* mere equipment within-the-world. The role with which this understanding exhaustively identifies us, crucially involves the use of particular equipment: a carpenter, for example, is essentially an accomplished manipulator of the tools of his trade, and producer of still other ready-to-hand things. Or, similarly, an individual may understand himself as possessor or consumer of a class of equipment enjoying a certain recognized status. Once again, he is not quite understanding himself as a mere ready-to-hand entity; nevertheless, he grasps himself in terms of such entities, i.e. in terms of the equipment he knows how to manipulate in actualizing his role or end, or that makes up his conception of that end itself.

Such merely existentiell self-understanding is dominant in our everydayness: '. . . proximally and for the most part everyday Dasein understands itself in terms of that with *which* it is customarily concerned. 'One *is*' what one does.' (*BT* 283). The failure in such self-understanding lies, of course, not in the mere projection towards roles, but in treating these as exhausting what we are. When we do so we overlook the fact and conditions of projection itself, and in particular the nullities, which are more deeply constitutive of our Being. When we fall we cover over our own true relation to our world, and verge into viewing ourselves 'as or in terms of' entities merely within that world. It is important to keep in mind that such misunderstanding lies not (necessarily) in our explicit theories about ourselves, but in the way certain basic abilities are brought into play—or not. In the next part we shall see how this fall into the existentiell can lie at the root of epistemology, and in the last part shall learn how phenomenology aims to reawaken us to the existential.

d. How falling flees this guilt: bias towards the present. Now as we saw in the last chapter, Heidegger generally supposes the deepest level of analysis to be that in terms of temporality. And this is true in the case of falling as well—all the elements of the preceding account should themselves be explainable by displaying falling as a particular way of 'living through time'. This temporal level of account is thus officially important for the weight Heidegger gives it; it is also intuitively illuminating, by virtue of the fresh and invigorating direction from which it allows us to approach the phenomena it clarifies. So it will be helpful to show how our flight from the nullities involves us in a distinctive mode of temporality—and the more helpful because it will allow me to add further content to this important Heideggerian concept. This will in turn prepare for explanations to come: in the next part I shall describe the closely related mode of temporality in which the present-at-hand is encountered, and in the final part shall contrast them both with the temporality of authenticity.

We have seen that Heidegger speaks of temporality as involving the past, present, and future 'ecstases': three interlocking ways in which Dasein is always 'outside itself'. Here we must notice that there are various 'modes' in which we may stand in these ecstases, and that one of them is characteristic of our falling, and responsible for the features I have just been displaying. This falling mode of temporality most crucially involves an orientation or bias towards the present; as we fall, we are still stretched out into the past and future ecstases as well, but in a way that derives from a peculiar attachment to the present (cf. *BT* 397 ff.). In this section I shall show why such focus in the present should be a way of avoiding the nullities, and how this focus helps explain the various features of falling presented in the previous section.

The present ecstasis, we recall, is that in which we 'stand out among' the entities within our world, concerned or involved with them, desevering them in our sight and manipulations. But this present ecstasis may be occupied in different ways, which vary the character of this concern with equipment. Later, we shall see that in authenticity our concern issues out of an abiding hold on both of the other temporal ecstases, and that this produces a distinctively authentic present. In falling everydayness, by contrast, we sacrifice that hold, and seek to 'stand out' *only* in the present: to be wholly present among the objects of our concern, and not also stretched back towards what we have been, and ahead at possibilities we can be. And this too determines a distinctive mode of that present ecstasis.

What does it mean, to fail to hold on to the past and future ecstases, because focusing in on the present? We can make this more vivid to ourselves, by first reflecting on (what I shall call) the '*rhythm*' of our temporal stretch, and then feeling how falling's narrowing upon the present runs across it. This rhythm is produced by the intersecting intervals of the very many practical projects we have a competence or involvement in. I previously discussed the project of cooking a meal, and the temporal character of some particular absorption in it. But this project has a certain temporal structure simply as a project, which I did not then note; for convenience, I shall speak of this structure as the 'reach' of the project itself, by contrast with the 'stretch' of an individual absorbed in it. The project is made up of certain sub-projects, or steps, which are arranged in intersecting sequence for tactical reasons. The butter is put on to melt while the eggs are beaten; toast is begun so as to be ready with the rest of the meal. The 'joints' produced by this division into steps give a certain rhythm to this project, as it reaches towards the end at which it aims. Moreover, this project stands in typical relation to certain other projects, as all themselves steps within some greater reach. A day is one such greater reach within which those arranged projects produce a broader rhythm than that which each contains; the project of preparing and eating breakfast is itself just a step in this overall sequence, related to others with an intricate 'logic', and not merely juxtaposed alongside them. But these projects also interlock along very different lines. Some, for example, are very minor steps within a pattern that constitutes one's career; others, we must not forget, may be set within a pattern of relations not to equipment but to other Dasein. (For an example of the latter type of reach— an example in which the sequence is officially rigid and elaborate, and hence especially apparent—we may think of an older pattern of courtship, and the intricacy of steps arranged within it.)

Now the temporal rhythm of any such project is taken over by an individual whenever he involves himself in this project, pressing ahead towards its end with a ready competence over the steps to securing it. The network of projects in which an individual is in this way involved, will give to his life a complex and shifting rhythm. This rhythm is not produced only by the actual arrival of joints within adopted projects; the individual's competence involves a preparedness for the steps to come, and a familiarity with those already passed through, so that the competence itself contains that rhythm all at once. But of course none of these projects, and hence none of these rhythms, is itself necessary to Dasein: so far as all these are concerned, two lives may be absolutely unalike in their patterns. Yet there is at least one such rhythm, though a very attenuated one, that Heidegger thinks *is* necessary to us, and that he thus pays particular attention to. This is the reach towards our death.

I shall have to be especially brief with Heidegger's interpretation of '**death**' [Tod], but some mention of it is generally appropriate, and particularly serviceable here. All the intersecting projects I have so far considered have of course been end-directed, and it is their nested ends that provide most of the 'joints' to our temporal rhythm. But there is another type of end to all our projection and striving, and one that we share with every other Dasein, whatever the differences among our particular projects. All this projection and striving will end; one of our possibilities, and the one we cannot escape, is that of being incapable of any further projection. Now of course death is an 'end' in a quite different way than is the for-the-sake-of-which aimed at by a project: we do not, for the most part, attempt to actualize or achieve this possibility, but rather to avoid or delay it. Nevertheless, it is a possibility we understand, in the sense of possessing a competence or preparedness for it, rather as we are competent and prepared for some specific contingency that threatens one of our aims. Unlike such particular threats, however, the possibility of death is one imposed no matter what our adopted projects, and is a threat we cannot escape forever; it arises not from our environment, and not relative to certain chosen ends, but from and against our very nature as Dasein. It belongs to this nature or Being, not only that we exist by projecting, but that we shall not always possess this capacity, and hence not always be.

The possibility of death, then, belongs essentially to us, and is understood by each of us as a limit upon all our striving, a limit that importantly defines what we are, by placing in context all those other ends that we grasp ourselves through. This understanding of death thus contributes an *essential* structure to our temporality—a rhythm shared by lives different in all the particular projects that engage them. Moreover, this rhythm of our dying—the way we stretch ahead to the possibility of our death—is the very broadest rhythm to our temporality, and our very furthest stretch. For all our other ends and projects 'come before' this possibility; we reach past all of them in understanding our death. This does not mean, of course, that death will come only after we have achieved all those other ends, nor even that we conceive our death in this way. Death is a possibility that may arrive at any moment, to put an immediate end to our activity of projecting; in understanding this possibility, we understand also its inherent 'indefiniteness'. But even such an indefinite possibility can serve as a limit and context for all our projection: we understand that our other possibilities must be achieved, if at all, on this side of that limit.

These then are the 'rhythms' to our temporality, ranging from the very narrow and concrete (the project of cooking a meal) to the broadest and most indefinite (our dying). Using these as a sort of scale, I can now show more concretely what it means, for falling everydayness to focus in on the present, at the expense of past and future. Later, I shall also try to show just why falling should adopt this temporal bias, as a way of avoiding the nullities. For convenience, let us imagine this focus as progressively narrowing—and so falling as increasingly pronounced. It will then 'first' exclude from view that furthest stretch we make in temporality, that beyond all particular projects and their ends. In everydayness we fail to hold ourselves ahead towards that possibility which encloses and concludes all our others: the possibility of death. Our striving is not guided by reference to this possibility; we do not do what we do *because* we shall die. We press along in our projects neglecting this threat which might at any point break in to cut off their pursuit, and which eventually will so intrude, on these projects or others. And so we fail to maintain our stretch across all our future, but are preoc-cupied with a span nearer our present.

Next, this preoccupation may focus more closely: we may lose our concernful stretch towards our 'highest ends', and across those more general projects that have the longer reaches and incorporate the more subordinate ones. When we fall we fail to hold in view such grander projects which enclose and motivate the minor ones; we fail to do the latter 'for the sake of' their acknowledged ends. Examples of such broader projects might be one's career, and one's relationship to one's spouse—an orientation towards the present may prevent us from maintaining our projective striving upon such enterprises as these. This need not imply, of course, that we neglect or misperform the steps enclosed within as means; we merely do them in isolation from their own acknowledged ends. Our focus is too narrow to encompass these ends, and can only grip those briefer and more concrete sub-projects, with their sub-ends. We thus pursue these latter out of habit, or mechanically, and without being motivated by their fuller significance.

If next, however, our falling everydayness has not merely lost its hold on our broader temporal reaches, but is in active flight from any recognition of them (and we shall shortly see that and why this is so), even those minor projects that serve as steps within higher ones, may be avoided as bearing too much the reminder of the latter. Unable and unwilling to hold ourselves out towards our furthest ends, we shall then narrow our temporal stretch still more drastically, by absorbing ourselves in short-term projects that are quite detached from any broader implications—that are not even small steps towards our higher ends. We shall seek out discrete involvements in which we can preoccupy ourselves so thoroughly, and with such isolation, that there is for us only each present enterprise, complete in itself and suggesting no deeper purpose we might now be deficient in neglecting. And so in falling everydayness we find and maintain the very narrowest present focus when we absorb ourselves in self-confined projects; we thus avoid those past and future ecstases in which we would stretch ourselves out more fully. And because we are not holding ourselves out across any broader temporal reach, by pursuing these projects for any more general purpose, our transition between them shows a characteristic jerkiness, a lack of smoothness and continuity. These projects are not gathered or organized beneath any higher ends, and so fail to succeed one another in any purposive way. Their point lies precisely in their fitness for an isolating distraction, and this requires that they remain quite discrete little sub-worlds, succeeding one another as if by a change of channel. With an involvement in projects such as these, we have arrived at the narrowest temporal focus of the most fallen everydayness.

This then is the sense in which falling involves a bias towards the present, at the expense of one's past and future. And yet this bias does not imply that we stand only in the present ecstasis, and have completely or in every way withdrawn from those of past and future. Rather, in falling we stand out in the latter as well, but in a peculiar, 'deficient' mode which reflects that temporal bias. This is indicated, indeed, by the very fact that in falling we are *attempting* to narrow our temporal stretch; this itself implies a stretch towards a futural end. I shall briefly introduce these further points, and partially ground the previous ones in the text, by quickly surveying Heidegger's account of the temporality of falling curiosity, in section 68c of *Being and Time*. This involves, we might say, the complementary implications of the falling motivation for the way entities are discovered.

To begin with, quite generally, '. . . the third constitutive item in the structure of care—namely, *falling*—has its existential meaning in the *Present*.' (*BT* 397). In the case of curiosity in particular, as one manifestation of such falling, this bias towards the present expresses itself in a drive towards a **'making-present'** [Gegenwärtigen] of fresh or exotic entities. That is, we seek to achieve a currency or closeness of entities that have been distant and unfamiliar. Their 'distance' may lie in their unreadiness for use in any projects—then we appropriate them by placing them availably to hand. Or it may lie in their resistance to any explanatory account—and then we discover where to place them in our theoretical framework. In both cases, we make these entities present to ourselves with an immediacy not previously enjoyed; they no longer lie ahead of us as things yet to be coped with, or yet to be understood. This is the temporal aspect of the drive I have been calling "desevering". In the direct encounter within the present temporal ecstasis, curiosity finds it culmination and point.

But curiosity itself, as a striving towards such immediacy, quite obviously includes a futural ecstasis as well—and apparently still more essentially than it does the present, for once immediacy is achieved, curiosity ceases or shifts. We are not curious once we have achieved an immediate grasp, but only so long as we stretch towards it. Still, this way our curiosity stretches ahead towards the future is itself determined by the character of the present encounter it seeks, and by the overriding importance it gives to that encounter. Curiosity reaches ahead towards exotic entities solely in order to grasp them concretely and immediately; in curiosity we project towards possibilities solely in order to actualize them. And Heidegger takes this to imply that such falling curiosity reaches ahead towards possibilities in a way that fails to do justice to their character as possibilities—they have significance or worth only once they have been realized, and so not yet, while this projection towards them proceeds. 'Curiosity is futural in a way which is altogether inauthentic, and in such a manner, moreover, that it does not await a *possibility*, but, in its craving, just desires such a possibility as something that is actual.' (*BT* 397). We must wait until the third part to see more clearly what it means to project adequately towards our possibilities; this will of course be, to stand in the authentic mode of the future ecstasis. We shall also see there that the falling mode of this ecstasis is particularly inadequate with respect to our only essential end, our death. Here we need only recognize the preliminary point that the falling futural ecstasis is distorted precisely by a bias towards the present, which grants being only to actualities; it stretches ahead towards possibilities only in hurrying to transform them into current realities, so as to obviate its own futural stretch. In a parallel way, which I shall not pause to sketch, this bias towards the present holds our curiosity in a distinctive mode of the past ecstasis as well: one that avoids or distorts recognition of thrownness, by denying appropriate status to what one has been.

But it still remains to be shown why we should fall into such a bias towards the present. This temporal analysis of falling everydayness must be rounded out, by noting the account it allows of the motivation to this falling. We have already seen that we fall as a flight from the nullities, limitations essential to our condition, which we fully recognize only in the disturbing mood of anxiety. So how might a focus on the present allow us to avoid an anxious acknowledgement of these essential nullities? How might it allow us to neglect that existential level of understanding, to which these nullities belong? To begin with, recall that these nullities concern our projection and thrownness: we project towards particular possibilities only at the expense of others that are no less worth while, and we project on the basis of a way we have been and cannot now control. These nullities lie, then, in our relations to our future and our past, and will be grasped or avoided by the manner in which we stand in these two temporal ecstases. The further we stretch out in these ecstases, the more exposed we shall be to that troubling existential understanding. But by reducing these dimensions as far as we can, and by holding ourselves out in them solely for the sake of a fuller immersion in some present, we shall also reduce our exposure to the nullities.

This exposure is particularly severe with respect to our highest futural goals—those giving basic content to our conception of ourselves—because here we are closest to the end of our chains of justification. But by absorbing ourselves in some present context, and releasing our hold on these futural possibilities that assign us our identity, we are better able to avoid acknowledging the contingency to these possibilities, and to the identity they provide us with. One such higher possibility might be the role of carpenter, for example; to the extent that an individual holds himself out towards this role in an explicit projection, performing his current tasks for the sake of this higher end, his futural ecstasis has scope and transparency, and makes clear to him who he is. But standing out in this ecstasis will also expose this individual to a peculiar threat: he may be forced to recognize that there is no final justification for projecting towards this possibility rather than towards any other, so that this projection requires him to forgo other ends and other identities that are no less valid and no less deserving than the one he has adopted. Yet how can projection be sustained, once this contingency to its ends is recognized? The carpenter stands in continual danger of losing his projective momentum in the face of this recognition, and of slipping into an anxiety that paralyses all his activity by undermining the end it has been for the sake of. But by previously contracting his temporal stretch, by holding himself less in this futural ecstasis, or less transparently there, this carpenter can avoid being confronted with this basic contingency to his existence. And a parallel point could be elaborated with respect to the nullity lying in his thrownness. In both directions, a contraction in temporal stretch and preoccupation with the concretely present will allow us to avoid the anxious acknowledgement of our nullities.

This then is how the diagnosis of falling that I earlier sketched, will be restated at the level of our temporality. And this account of temporality has incidentally uncovered a phenomenon that plays a further role in motivating falling, a role we were not in a position to notice in that earlier diagnosis. This phenomenon is death, and it represents an additional limitation essential to our existence. Death is the furthest possibility for all our projecting: the possibility that all this projecting may end at any moment, and all our ends be foreclosed. When an individual holds himself out in the futural ecstasis to the furthest possible extent, it is to recognize this other contingency to all his projects and possibilities: the way they are all enclosed within that final end. And once again, this recognition can naturally induce an anxious loss of the power to project. How can we continue seriously to pursue our broader ends, when they may all be stripped from us at any point? Once again this anxiety may be avoided by contracting our temporal stretch, and preoccupying ourselves with the concretely present; in this way we reduce our exposure to that furthest and most disturbing possibility. Death, as well as the nullities in guilt, thus threatens us with anxiety, and motivates that bias towards the present which constitutes the position of falling everydayness.

e. Two routes falling flees along. In the first chapter I distinguished two directions taken by our falling everydayness: it flees into an absorption in entities within-the-world, and into an absorption in a certain way of Being-with others. As a last step in clarifying this new account of falling as a flight from recognition of the nullities, let us consider how both of these routes, in the versions adopted in everydayness (in the next part we shall consider those taken by the theoretical attitude), offer natural resorts for us while thus in flight.

Beginning with the second of these, we can fairly quickly see why such falling-in-with the 'they' and its understanding should help us to turn away from the 'groundlessness' of our Being: the very commonality of this public understanding, the way it is unanimously affirmed and conformed to, give it the appearance of fastening on ends and entities as they really are and must be, and conceal its status as merely one among many possible understandings.

When we are with one another in an everyday way, the bulk of our ends are projected towards in common, and entities are communally understood in their relation to achievement of those certified ends. There is a rough consensus as to the ingredients in a good life, and as to the role of equipment in its realization. This joint understanding is displayed in our public, concernful activities, and is shared in the discourse typical of our everyday relations to others; such displaying and sharing serve to strengthen the immersion of each within this understanding. We more easily care about our work when we see others busy at it about us, and when our talk with them takes its ends for granted. And so each of us is the less likely to recognize that he himself has never examined the means or ends involved in this understanding, and that these means and ends are adopted at the cost of excluding others, no less intrinsically worth while. In short, this everyday, falling Being-with strengthens our projection towards that existentiell understanding into which we have been thrown, and discourages the shift to an existential understanding of the limitations to our projects. Such Being-with helps to tranquillize us in the face of these disquieting nullities, and to hold us away from the anxiety in which we would adequately acknowledge them.

There is likewise a fairly obvious way in which an absorption in entities within-the-world, in the form of concernful dealings with equipment, can help avoid recognition of these nullities: by launching ourselves upon one of those referential pathways which project towards ends via the chains of involvements lying in equipment, and by allowing ourselves to be borne along with the momentum these routes themselves generate, we fend off the not-at-homeness which threatens to hold us aloof from involvements, and so to force upon us a recognition of our guilt. The ready-to-hand tools in our environment themselves solicit us into their involvements; they draw us onto those pathways upon which our sights are narrowed, by being focused at the existentiell ends for which that equipment is useful, and drawn off the existential contingency to those ends themselves. Thus such absorption in equipment is another natural route in our flight from the nullities.

A familiar phenomenon, much-noted in other contexts, is the special suitability of certain equipment for this second-order purpose of re-immersing ourselves in purposive involvements. That television is used as a remedy for boredom is a trite and obvious point, but one that finds a more elaborate and interesting development in these terms now at our disposal. Boredom, to begin with, is a close cousin to anxiety, for it too involves an abstraction from those projects that ordinarily engage us. It too amounts to a 'felt' recognition that there is no more reason to do one thing than another. Television is equipment well-suited to draw us out of such boredom, in at least a couple of ways. First, it can present to us in rapid sequence a series of other equipment and ends, and can arouse us to a brief but intense involvement in each in turn, holding none before us long enough for this concern to fade. In this respect television caters to our curiosity, as that tendency was explained in the opening chapter, and re-elaborated just now: it desevers or makes present for us one exotic entity after another, arousing a fresh but artificial concern which covers over the boredom that may have detached us from our more personal projects. But television—and other 'tools' too, such as novels—can accomplish this purpose in a rather different way as well. It can present the unfolding of a more extended 'drama', in the turns and developments of which we are encouraged to concern ourselves for a longer while. It can present, that is, some elaborate 'sub-world', a system of involvements, of ends and available means, which are familiar in type, though not in just this combination. We are enticed into a concern for these ends, and for the developing process in which they are pursued through the network of means—we share in this pursuit, and in the significance of each move in this framework. A sporting event is an example of such a 'drama' in which we may briefly share an artificial concern; it is distinguished by a relative simplicity, rigidity, and clarity to the system of its means and ends, as well as by a self-containment, or isolation from other systems of involvements. The clarity in a game's goals makes it easier for us to care, and their isolation from our higher concerns helps us avoid the existential doubts that most threaten us there. This too, then, is a route by which we may avoid an anxious recognition of the nullities basic to us, by stimulating an absorption in some narrowed sector of our world.

f. Everydayness is a modification of authenticity, and not vice-versa.
This part has shown that in falling everydayness the fundamental character of our Being is disclosed to us only as we turn away from that Being, while the latter is disclosed directly or explicitly in the

special mood of anxiety (together with, as we shall see, its attendant understanding and discourse). This central point helps to explain a quite significant turnabout midway through *Being and Time*. Previously our everydayness, with its constitutive falling, had been represented as our basic or essential condition, while authenticity was characterized as a derivative modification of this; in a line noticed back in the first chapter: '*Authentic Being-one's-Self* does not rest upon an exceptional condition of the subject, a condition that has been detached from the 'they'; *it is rather an existentiell modification of the 'they'—of the 'they' as an essential existentiale.*' (*BT* 168; cf. also *BT* 224). But with the introduction of anxiety (already near the end of Division I), this priority is reversed: 'That kind of Being-in-the-world which is tranquillized and familiar is a mode of Dasein's uncanniness, not the reverse. *From an existential-ontological point of view, the 'not-at-home' must be conceived as the more primordial phenomenon.*' (*BT* 234; cf. also *BT* 365). For it has now been discovered that we tranquillize ourselves in falling precisely in order to avoid that direct recognition of our essential nullities, which we experience when we are not-at-home or anxious. And as a flight from such recognition, falling must be dependent upon it, and must constitute a secondary way in which we may stand related to our nullities. The logically prior condition must be that of anxiety, which motivates—and sustains the impetus of—our fall.

The character of this reversal is closely connected with, and helps us at last to understand more fully, that issue which centrally concerned us back in the first chapter: the ambivalence in Heidegger's stance towards everydayness, as falling, yet still usable in the critique of traditional philosophy. In that chapter we saw that while everydayness serves him as a standard against which the positions taken by traditional philosophers are to be judged, it is the disclosure of Being in this everydayness that functions as such a standard, and not any position or belief we might then explicitly hold. That is, it is our everyday understanding of our own Being and that of equipment that is so used, and not any interpretation we might then accept or offer of these. And indeed, the falling that characterizes everydayness renders these interpretations suspect, and likely to be distorted in a particular direction.

By now, however, we have learned that even the understanding belonging to everydayness is affected by the falling flight from the nullities. We have seen how this effect is expressed, in the relationship between our existentiell and existential levels of understanding. While the existentiell understanding does always grasp our Being by projecting towards some for-the-sake-of-which, the everyday mode of this understanding identifies too tightly with this end, failing to acknowledge the contingency to all such projection. And this is due to the way such everyday existentiell understanding is insulated from the existential understanding on which it nevertheless still depends: in everydayness we avoid our existential understanding of the nullities basic to our projection, and refuse to allow it to affect, as it properly should, the manner of that projection towards ends. In falling everydayness, that is, we always have been aware of the looseness or contingency to our projection towards ends; we have recognized our own lack of responsibility for those ends, and the ultimate arbitrariness of them. This awareness confronts us with a basic feature of our essential condition, but one disturbing to us, which we seek to avoid; we achieve this avoidance by absorbing ourselves so thoroughly in our particular objects, that the looseness in our relationship to them is concealed.

Now for his initial purpose of attacking traditional (and so present-at-hand) interpretations of Dasein, Heidegger finds it sufficient to uncover our existentiell projection towards particular ends, a level of understanding already quite evident in falling everydayness. That it is there distorted by its detachment from the grounding existential level, is irrelevant for this preliminary task. In everydayness we grasp ourselves by projecting towards ends, and equipment by mastering its use, and these points are enough for the purpose of criticizing the traditional accounts, and their insistence upon a purely present-at-hand ontology. Nevertheless, there is another, fuller and more explicit way in which our Being and that of equipment can be disclosed—that way in which the existential level is not suppressed, but is allowed to reflect itself in the existentiell projection towards particular ends. For Heidegger's fuller purpose of uncovering our structure as a whole, it is only this understanding, and not that found in our falling everydayness, that can legitimately serve as a source or standard. And so as Heidegger's attention shifts away from the internal structure of our projecting and our world, and he begins to treat rather their external limits, he finds it necessary to adopt and describe a different understanding as criterion for judging or deriving accounts of Being: this is of course the understanding found in the position of authenticity. This authentic understanding then serves him as a standard for judging the inadequacies of everydayness itself.

Moreover, as we shall finally see, it serves him not only as a source for phenomenological findings about the most basic level of Being, but also as a goal or target for phenomenology's discourse. Phenomenology does not merely use this authentic understanding as a criterion for presenting interpretations of Being, it seeks actually to shift us out of our everyday understanding and into this other mode. For it is only when we stand for ourselves in this transparent relation to our own Being, that we can properly apprehend the structures phenomenology describes. Phenomenological thinking, then, must lead us beyond everydayness, despite the latter's great usefulness for this philosophical method. And so now we see the broad structure to Heidegger's ambiguous attitude towards everydayness: how he can on the one hand find in it a truth overlooked and concealed by the philosophical tradition, yet on the other not wish simply to return us there, but conceive of a different and favoured path from it, which is available to thinking. Of course this path has as yet been characterized only quite sketchily, and mainly in terms of a state-of-mind, anxiety—so that it must still seem inappropriate to refer to it as a thinking at all, or to link it with the phenomenological method. I shall be returning to these issues in the third part of this chapter, but first must focus a last time on epistemology, to complete my Heideggerian diagnosis of this, in a way this part's findings only now make possible.

2. Phenomenology does not attempt to eliminate these deficiencies, as does Epistemology

a. How falling can motivate the theoretical attitude. In the last part I might seem to have lost sight of this book's overall project. The existential themes I have just been elaborating are surely Heideggerian, but they must seem to have nothing to do with Descartes' project in epistemology, and so to be beside my main point. But as I shall try to show now, they in fact permit a deepening and a subtle reorienting of the account of the previous chapter: because the deepest level of *Being and Time* is the existential and temporal, so too must be the last stage of my Heideggerian diagnosis. Now back in that second chapter's presentation of this diagnosis, I noted that falling is supposed to operate at the earliest stage, but put off detailed treatment of its role. That notion, as well as its encompassing

context, have now been developed much more fully, so that we are positioned to take up this role it plays at the very roots of the Cartesian project—in the projection of Being as presence-at-hand, upon which epistemology depends. That is, we shall see how we naturally fall not only into everyday concern, but also into the theoretical attitude; the latter, in its defining aim towards an explicit and decontextualized view, is typically motivated by this same falling tendency we have seen at the root of everydayness.

Now to the extent that the Cartesian project, as a development of that attitude, is likewise implicated in the falling response to the nullities, it is 'existentially' misdirected and needs to be replaced by an alternative effort; this will be the core to Heidegger's ultimate critique of epistemology. But beside and over against this, there is the special way this project expresses that attitude, and here the presentation of the nullities will allow me to place epistemology within a more favourable light as well, by drawing attention to the extent to which it, like anxiety, refuses simply to ignore these nullities. Its response is inappropriate, but is not the utter flight or avoidance characteristic of everydayness and of other modes of theorizing. In this aspect that Cartesian project is continuous not with falling everydayness, but with the authentic thinking that will be the topic of my final part. Just as we discovered Heidegger's attitude towards everydayness to be ambivalent, by seeing that he also criticizes the understanding that was initially held up as standard, so now we discover a related ambivalence in his attitude towards the epistemological project, by noting beneath its misdirection certain 'positive possibilities'; these will lead on to our third stage, since phenomenology itself will have the task of developing them. In this first section, however, I must dwell on the negative, and on the background point how falling can motivate the theoretical attitude.

Let us begin by recalling the way Heidegger rallies us to diagnosis of the traditional project: 'Our task is not to prove that an 'external world' is present-at-hand or to show how it is present-at-hand, but to point out why Dasein, as Being-in-the-world, has the tendency to bury the 'external world' in nullity 'epistemologically' before going on to prove it.' (*BT* 250). And then, immediately, there follows his sketch of a key part of his diagnosis: 'The reason for this lies in Dasein's falling and in the way in which the primary understanding of Being has been diverted to Being as presence-at-hand—a diversion which is motivated by that falling itself.' (*BT* 250; cf. also *BT* 352). In the second chapter I focused on the defining aims of this projection of presence-at-hand, and tried to show how the epistemologist's problem develops out of these. Here I must go back a step, and try to show how this projection might itself arise out of our falling tendency.

Now Heidegger's general way of arguing here—attacking theory or epistemology by denouncing a 'motive' he claims it is due to—is likely to seem questionable in several respects. For in the first place, can there not be many motives, arising at many different levels, for engaging in theory? We may think of incentives as diverse as the need to earn a living, the desire for approval or admiration, and the will to emulate parents or friends. Moreover, as I have just hinted and shall later show, epistemological theorizing can also arise from motives not just unlike but opposed to that falling effort. So the Heideggerian diagnosis can claim neither that falling is the only motive towards theory, nor that it is always a motive. And there are also some difficult puzzles about the notion of motivation itself, which become particularly pressing in this Heideggerian context. What is it for the falling tendency to 'motivate' the theoretical attitude—how, concretely, are we to think of this relation between that odd and 'ontological' tendency, and that familiar, 'ontic' attitude? How can we tell, in particular cases, when the latter is 'due to' the former? Do not claims about motives fall under the scope of psychology rather than philosophy, and must they not be based in empirical study, which it seems Heidegger cannot have attempted? And perhaps most critically, why is this whole diagnostic approach not vulnerable to the charge of psychologism—of mistakenly supposing that a theoretical position can be undermined, by discrediting a motive for adopting it? For the following account to be acceptable, it must eventually respond to at least these several questions against it.

The previous part has developed falling as our tendency to flee the disclosure of Being, motivated by the unsatisfying character of the nullities fundamental to that Being; these nullities imply a certain 'groundlessness', both to our own Being and to that of entities within-the-world. Now how might adopting the theoretical attitude help us to avoid facing this groundlessness? In showing how everydayness might serve us in this way, I presented two natural routes by which our falling might lead to such everydayness: we may avoid facing Being either through a distracting absorption in entities, or through an immersion in the 'they' and its comfortingly predominant interpretations. And similarly now here, as we consider how falling might lead instead to a theoretical discovery of the present-at-hand, we may conveniently ask how either or each of these routes, as a means of avoiding the groundlessness of Being, could also encourage the adoption of the theoretical attitude, and its guiding thematization.

Beginning with the second route—falling as assimilating oneself to the 'they'—there is indeed a tie to this thematization, though one that is merely extrinsic, because historically local. For (Heidegger claims that) it is this way of projecting Being that has guided not only our philosophical tradition, but even the customary talk of our culture's they-self. Present-at-hand interpretations are comforting to us, because their widespread acceptance helps suggest they have an absolute status. But have I not already maintained that the understanding with which the public 'they' tranquillizes us is rather a concernful understanding of ends to be pursued and equipmental means for achieving them? Have I not claimed that it is rather by securing us in some definite relation to the ready-to-hand, that the 'they' helps conceal the contingency to all our projection? The everyday they-self, which we enter when we lose ourselves in the prevalent practices, will indeed avoid the nullities in these ways described in the previous part—in particular, by locking us more securely within those customary roles we play in producing or using equipment. It strengthens the hold of a single concernful understanding upon us. But this is compatible with our simultaneously adopting a quite different understanding as the basis for our explicit assertions—and this second understanding may also recommend itself to us as a part of public practices. Heidegger claims that the thematization of Being as presence-at-hand is typically accepted and reinforced in this way: as the basis of 'the way one thinks'.

Thus while encouraging our immersion in those practical roles current in the social context, and so reinforcing the security and stability of our self-interpretation in terms of these roles, the public they-self can also supply some present-at-hand description of us —for example as a species of organism—to be used in explicit accounts by us of our own nature. Similarly, the prevalence of those practices in which hammers are used for hammering can strengthen the grip of that ready-to-hand interpretation of this entity, compatibly with our being equally prepared to describe a hammer as most basically just wood and metal in certain spatio-temporal arrangements. So it is possible for us to receive two quite different understandings of Being, expressing themselves in different ways, in falling-in-with the 'they' and its public understanding: roughly, the one is a capacity to use (for example) a hammer, the other a capacity to describe the hammer in a theoretical context. Insofar as our flight from the nullities drives us towards such immersion in the 'they', we shall incidentally be led to that projection of Being as presence-at-hand which has, historically, come to characterize our public understanding. And of course scientific interpretations are indeed granted an especially widespread and confident public acceptance. So the tranquillizing impact of finding an understanding to be shared, to be repeated on all sides as settled and matter-of-course, will be effected as well by the theoretical as by the everyday understanding, and will qualify the former as an equally attractive resort for our falling. Here then is a glimpse of a first link—although an extrinsic and 'historically contingent' one—between this falling tendency and that thematization that grounds our theorizing.

But Heidegger believes there to be a more intrinsic connection between falling and thematizing; he wishes to make falling responsible not only for some individual's 'falling-in-with' this projection as that which happens to be publicly accepted, but even for the historical fact that it is *this* projection that has come to be so accepted (cf. *BPP* 66). The very aims that essentially guide our thematization, make it an intrinsically appropriate resort for us as we flee from the nullities of Being. And it is the second general route taken by our falling that comes into play in this way. For those aims—to discover entities explicitly and in themselves—are inherently attractive to the falling effort at an absorption in entities; they make possible a theoretical absorption which is different in type from that of everydayness, but which likewise permits an oversight of the nullities. A thematic grasp of presence-at-hand, like the everyday preoccupation with particular projects and their ends, helps us to overlook the equality of status to all the ways Being may be understood. It helps to reassure us that entities just are, straightforwardly, as we take them to be.

Thus the goal of the theoretical attitude is essentially such as to be attractive to our falling as well—there is what I shall call an '*affinity*' between the special attitude and the falling tendency. This relation is neither necessary, nor quite accidental: the attitude need not be adopted as a means to the end that falling pursues, but it is inherently suited to serve in this role. Nevertheless, it is also only in a certain aspect that theory's goal is attractive to falling, and so only in a certain manner of theorizing that this attitude will serve that tendency as means. For it is only this goal as accomplished, and not as still outstanding and worthy to be achieved, that our falling is attracted towards. And it is only that attitude as securely confident that it possesses an objective grasp, that will suffice as a means. It is these ways of entering this attitude in which that aspect attractive to falling is most prominently present; these are the cases in which it is most plausible to suppose that motive at work.

Let us go through these last points more carefully. In the previous chapter I suggested that thematization takes its character from a certain underlying intent: to encounter entities explicitly and in themselves. I then ascribed this intent back to our desevering tendency—to our effort to organize our surroundings, to put things 'in place'. A theoretical grasp of an entity would assure us of having quite fully desevered or controlled it, precisely because it purports to give more than just another perspective on that entity; it lays claim to an insight that will survive any shifts in context or project that might intervene before a later discovery of the entity. It is in this way, we saw, that thematization intends an improved discovery of entities, beyond that possible in our original everydayness. Now this improvement is also sought in our falling avoidance of the nullities, but it is sought in a different spirit or style. While desevering is operative more in the effort towards an objective grasp, than it is in a confident possession of this grasp, only the latter can suit our falling. While desevering is a will to control and organize entities, falling is a will to believe that they have been controlled and organized already. The activity of pursuing a privileged truth is not in itself acceptable to falling, because acknowledgement that such truth is still outstanding can as much heighten as conceal the contingency to one's current understanding. So by contrast, it is when theory claims to have placed things objectively, as they are in themselves and not relative to any context of concern, that it most indicates a falling motive. It is when the theorist is most securely satisfied that he is discovering his objects in the one way they really are, and that he has fixed and stabilized these objects within a most

privileged system, that he turns away from the existential understanding that discloses their Being as incapable of any such secure
grounding.

This point has an equally important complement, in a way often
noticed before: a theorist quite confident of his objective grasp is
neglecting not only the nullities in his objects, but also those in
himself. He attributes an unwarranted priority not only to the way
entities are encountered by him, but also to the attitude in which he
encounters them. For just as one's concernful understanding discloses at once the Being both of equipment and of oneself, so too
the thematic projection implies a correlative understanding by the
theorist of himself. In thematizing Being for objects, he simultaneously understands himself as subject—as thinker of the fundamental concepts that accomplish this projection, and as discoverer
of the objects in the realm this opens up; in projecting capably along
the path leading towards these ends, he understands himself by
reference to that role. But if such a theorist supposes that as subject
he discovers his objects in the one privileged way, he takes this role
to have priority over others—to be *the* way of encountering entities,
and not one whose choice is ultimately without ground. He takes it
to be singled out from other possibilities, to be an intrinsically
highest end. And so he can be 'justified' in his choice of it, and
tranquil in his neglect of the other, 'less valuable' possibilities. This
role, of a subject discovering things in themselves, is thus particularly suited for the work we saw everyday possibilities can also
perform: it makes it easier for the theorist simply and exhaustively
to identify himself with this end, and so to overlook the contingency
to this and any other possibility. In both of these complementary
ways, then, thematization is a natural resort for us as we flee the
disturbing disclosure of Being—and it is so by virtue of its defining
aims, and not merely for its public acceptance.

And yet, as I noted before, the theorist need not have resorted to
this attitude from out of that motive; quite other routes can also
issue in theory. These 'affinities' between theory and falling do not
entail that the former is (always or ever) actually pursued for the
sake of the latter; the affinities need not be 'operative' in this way.
And if we think of a motive as an event, preceding and producing
the effect we attribute to it, it will be hard or impossible to show that
in some (much less many) cases 'the' motive for theory is that falling
tendency; indeed, it is hard to see how we should even set out to

investigate this claim. Fortunately, however, this Heideggerian diagnosis does not depend on the view that falling is such a preceding cause. For what will be important is whether the theorist is *also* falling—whether he pursues his theorizing in a falling 'style'—and not whether falling motivates his theory in that causal sense. More specifically, the diagnosis will attack the theorist insofar as he affirms his positions in a way that overlooks his nullities; it will not be necessary that he so affirm them *in order* to overlook those nullities.

Nevertheless, I shall continue to speak of such modes of theorizing as 'due to' or 'motivated by' falling, because while this relation can perhaps not be established so firmly as to bear a heavy load of argument, it can at least be made plausible enough to support such locutions. For to begin with, we must remember that for Heidegger a purpose or motive can be far less explicit than our deliberate intentions—this follows from his account of the implicitness of our projection: we act out of a concernful drive towards an overall end, though often without any explicit thought of this end. So a falling avoidance of the nullities can be one of our motives for theory, even if we have never reflected upon those existential limits. And to confirm that this motive is present, we should look not to some original event of decision, but to an overall pattern of avoidance, which the style of some theorizing aligns it with. Moreover, we must remember that falling lies at the deepest, 'existential' level, as part of the structure we share just as Dasein; it is a temptation we all have in common, despite the divergence in the ends we contingently adopt. And this suggests that the temptation might be especially prevalent, and especially significant wherever it does occur.

Using this procedure, we can detect the falling motive at work in a distinctive style or aspect theoretical inquiry sometimes reveals. We have seen that the sciences have developed through thematizations that increasingly free the basic descriptions of entities from the influence of any relativizing involvements. So colours are specified by numerical wavelengths, and not by hues that can be differently experienced in differing contexts. This development tends towards an ideal that is best represented by mathematics, in which disagreements can be conclusively resolved by decision procedures producing the same results for workers in radically different cultural and personal situations. Now how and when might a falling motive be traceable here? When one enters a field whose thematization has been highly developed in this way, when one works within this thematization under the assumption that it allows one to grasp the way objects really and only are, and when one prides oneself on being 'just right' and 'in the truth' in the positions one takes in this field, that motive is suggested. We may imagine, for example, a logician, who delights in his ability to demonstrate his claims and to refute decisively any alternatives or objections to them, who supposes that he finds here an absolute truth, and that in possessing this truth he has achieved a privileged position, preferable to all those not matching this high objectivity. And when such a style of engagement in theory occurs against the background of those everyday modes of falling I described in the last part, we find a full pattern of avoidance which justifies our assigning such a motive to theory.

These points can be developed in one direction by returning to the positions (within theory) of realism and idealism, and noting their respective affinities to this falling tendency. To the extent that this tendency does motivate the theorist, he will tend to overlook any factor that would expose the contingency implied by our nullities. So he will tend to ignore the role played by a founding projection of Being, in allowing his discovery of objects. If he carries this to its extreme, this theorist will neglect not only the deeper, concernful understanding, but even that thematization on which his theories more immediately depend—he will then arrive at *realism,* the most natural position for the theoretical attitude, when it is adopted from this falling motive. Such realism takes entities straightforwardly to be as its attitude discovers them, and thus hides the contingency more truly their own. And in taking its attitude to be in contact with the one way all entities inherently are, it presumes a priority for this stance, which contradicts the fundamental equality to all our possibilities, and the fact that the choice of even this attitude is unjustifiable. So Heidegger supposes a crucial attraction of realism to be, that its mistakes are precisely these ones we purposefully wish to make.

But falling can also accomplish these aims through a less extreme position: one acknowledging that a thematic projection must ground any discovery of the present-at-hand, but failing to see how this projection is grounded in turn in the concernful understanding. Although this *idealism* notes that its objects are as they are only by virtue of its own thematization, this does not guarantee that it confronts those nullities that falling flees; these nullities lie not in the thematic projection, but in our deeper concernful understanding. Idealism does, to be sure, recognize one or more contingencies of a different sort. If a Kantian version that allows only one such thematic projection to be possible for us, it already denies the realist claim to be discovering entities as they intrinsically are—but it still permits the theoretical attitude to claim the next best thing to a perspectiveless sight: the one necessary perspective. If a version that allows this projection to shift as our conceptual frameworks evolve, it further denies that there is one best perspective for discovering objects—but it continues to imply that we are most basically theorists, the occupants of some one such stance. Thus even in those versions of idealism that admit the greatest looseness in our relationship to entities, the effect is still to fix or stabilize our own identity, as knowers. But of course viewed in the context of our Being-in-the-world, such theorizing is only one possibility for us, which we must sustain ourselves in through a groundless projection. By citing this concrete role as definitive of us, the idealist closes himself off from this disturbing status. And he does so because he has failed to look down to the level of our concern.

Regarding both realism and idealism we must bear in mind a general point, to be developed more fully in the final part. Not only do our nullities lie deeper than the thematization that idealism recognizes, but they are only adequately confronted at a corresponding level: not by a merely theoretical recognition of any projection or any contingency, but only by a grasp that is deeper than theoretical, because existential (i.e. at the level of our concernful understanding and state-of-mind). Theory can, of course, help us towards this deeper recognition—as indeed we shall see when we examine the relation between phenomenology and authenticity. But if it conveys only an interpretation of ourselves, and only an ability to speak differently about our structure and properties, it remains at too superficial a level, and neglects the crucial effect that philosophy should properly attempt. This warning applies, we shall see, to Heidegger's interpretations as well, but it has far greater force in application to realism and idealism; here theory itself implies that the theoretical grasp is sufficient—that it is a grasp by what we ourselves are, and thus the needed modification of us at our basic level. The content to their interpretations wrongly implies the adequacy of a certain manner of grasping them, because this is the manner appropriate for that type of entity we would be, were that content correct. Thus realism and idealism encourage us, in this basic way, to neglect the search for a really adequate self-understanding. And so both realism, which interprets all entities from within the projection of Being as presence-at-hand (which it fails to notice), and idealism, which views them decisively by reference to that projection (which it notices no more than), can serve to turn our view from our basic guilt.

By way of a final clarification of this falling motive towards theory, we may now again view it in those temporal terms that Heidegger believes to give the deepest level of analysis. In this light, the theoretical attitude aims at an even more drastic narrowing of our temporal stretch, than that typical of falling everydayness; it is distinguished by an effort towards a purified present, and it is as such that it is most tempting as a target for our falling tendency. We took a first look at this temporality of theory back in the second chapter, where I argued that theory's confinement to the present prevents it from accounting for our meaning or understanding. And in the previous part I described the analogous bias towards the present that is found in everydayness: we are preoccupied with short-term projects, and pursue them in isolation from any broader context or further purpose. I showed how *this* present focus is motivated by our flight from those troubling nullities, which are encountered in the ecstases into past and future; by restricting our stretch in these temporal dimensions, and throwing ourselves into the most immediate concerns, we avoid the disturbing limitations intrinsic to our projection and thrownness. Now, we shall see more fully how the theoretical discovery of the present-at-hand likewise involves a focus upon a restricted present, and that here too this focus may be motivated by a falling flight from our basic nullities.

The theoretical attitude, as we recall, aims to encounter its objects with an explicitness and an independence from context that are not originally present in our everyday discovery of the ready-to-hand. The latter lacks these characteristics precisely because it encounters equipment within the scope of projects, and hence on its way to ends at which its sights are primarily directed. This remains true even where that narrowed focus makes the reach of these projects quite short: our attention is still not upon these tools in their own right, but is slightly diffused through the project as a whole. Achieving the explicitness and the decontextualization at which the theoretical attitude aims, therefore requires restriction to a still narrower present than that found in any involvement in projects. This attitude seeks to grasp its objects immediately, in an intense and momentary survey—it seeks to stand out towards them in a present ecstasis that is most thoroughly detached from past and future, most free from any bearing these might normally have on the character of a present encounter. For these reasons, the pursuit of objectivity is the pursuit of *presence* (cf. *BPP* 315).

We may distinguish two aspects to this goal of presence, corresponding to the aspects to the goal of objectivity. With respect to some object of his experience, the theorist wishes to encounter it as it is in itself, independently of any context in which it may contingently occur. He thus aims to bring this object both solely and completely before him: just it, and all of it, is to be present to his attention. This aim is for a 'presence of the object'. But simultaneously, with respect to the attitude in which he surveys an object, the theorist wishes his grasp to be entirely explicit. His attention is to be transparently focused on it, and not clouded or diverted by other concerns; he is to be purely an observer. And this aim is for a 'presence in the attitude'. As we might also express these two goals, the theorist wishes to 'give its full due' both to each entity—by encountering it in the one privileged way most adequate to its nature—and to each moment of his experience—by dwelling fully in it, and neither hurrying by nor taking it in the wake of what came before. These two goals suggest one another, and together determine an ideal way of being in time, towards which the theoretical attitude aims; we may again recall Descartes' account of 'clear and distinct perception', as a paradigm statement of this ideal.

But this radical narrowing of our temporal stretch will also be attractive to the same falling motive that explained the less drastic focus of everydayness. In affecting this isolation from past and future, the theoretical attitude turns its back on the nullities belonging to its thrownness and projection; it supposes that it has overcome the contingencies to the discovery of entities, for these lie in the way this discovery is shaped by dependence on a past one cannot control, and by an orientation towards ends one cannot fully justify. By restricting its ecstases into past and future, and seeming to encounter its objects outside the context provided by these ecstases, the theoretical attitude is able to suppose that it has overcome its dependence on an ungrounded perspective. And this is reflected in its claim to both types of presence just now distinguished. The full presence of an object to our view is to allow it to show itself to us in the one best way; our full presence in attending to it is to allow us to experience this moment most adequately. In both cases, we forget the ultimate equality of incompatible possibilities: there is no best way for objects to appear, or for us to use our moments. So the theoretical bias towards the present can also be motivated by a flight from the nullities—and it is more likely to be (partly) so motivated, the more satisfied the theorist is that he has arrived at the reality of his objects, and so stands in a most privileged position. But what then of the traditional project in epistemology, which arises precisely out of a dissatisfaction over these points?

b. Epistemology can face the nullities that falling flees. We have seen that the Cartesian project is a quite special application of the theoretical attitude: it is this attitude's attempt to turn back upon itself, to confirm its own claim to objectivity. And so epistemology arises with the task of establishing that this attitude it embodies has a transparent access to objects. We must next re-examine this way that project is a special undertaking by the theoretical attitude, on the basis of what we have now learned about falling. Is this motive I have just been attributing to a certain familiar style of theorizing, to be extended straightforwardly to epistemology as well? Or does the manner in which this represents a development of that attitude, cause it to stand in a different relation to our falling tendency?

We must begin by distinguishing among the several basic positions that may be taken within epistemology: one theorist may suppose himself in possession of a positive solution to the Cartesian problem, and so also of objective truths; another may be engaged in inquiring after such a solution (whether or not prepared for the discovery that none is possible); still another may concede or embrace scepticism, and so deny that objectivity can be had. Now there are also innumerable ways, different along many dimensions, of engaging or involving oneself in these positions—quite different ways of accommodating them within the framework of one's projection towards ends. Thus one epistemologist may stake his self-esteem on his success with that problem, another may pursue it peripherally; one may judge success by his reputation through the profession, another by standards more his own. Perhaps most often there is no intrinsic relation between a possible position, and a possible mode of engagement, and the latter are distributed across the former indifferently. But in the last section we saw how such intrinsic relations are possible for theorizing in general, and indeed for the positions of realism and idealism within theory. And now here we can see such connection between those three epistemological positions, and the basic existential stances towards the nullities.

Now by virtue of the overall theoretical attitude they are engagements within, the basic epistemological positions all share an affinity with the falling avoidance of the nullities. We saw why it is tempting to lose oneself in a theoretical absorption in objects, and to narrow one's attention to a present moment of reflection. To this end, what is most crucial is not the content of the theories one accepts, but the opportunity an absorption in any theory affords, of isolating oneself in a pure present, cut off from past and future and the contingencies they bear. Thus the falling theorist can embrace any of the positions distinguished, for relief from the unsettling nullities. Nevertheless, there are also affinities between these positions (i.e. the content they are constituted by), and the basic existential stances—affinities that either reinforce or counteract this more general affinity between falling and theory.

A first of these positions can be placed rather quickly in this way: the positive conclusion that we can and do have objective knowledge has an obvious affinity of its own to that falling absorption, quite like what we have already noted in realism. For this positive response has reaffirmed the theoretical attitude, in its claim to an explicit and decontextualized view, and has returned to a position of ease within the present-at-hand. But on the other hand, and more complexly and interestingly, we can find in the *other* basic positions within epistemology a more positive value in this existential dimension—one that Heidegger seems never to concede them, but that arises naturally out of his position as I have sketched it. For in its very drive after grounding, in its refusal simply to rest within and to take for granted that present-at-hand understanding, i.e. in precisely the way it is a second-order development of that understanding, we find in the epistemological project a sparking dissatisfaction that may be rooted in recognition of the null basis belonging to our Being. This dissatisfaction has been extinguished and left behind by the convinced positive response, but is alive in different ways in the other positions. Although the present-at-hand exhausts the horizons even of these latter epistemologists, so that they cannot see explicitly down to those more basic nullities, they do at least question the adequacy of their access to the present-at-hand, and so refuse to find in it that tranquillizing security it so naturally provides.

Let us consider these remaining positions in turn, beginning with the open-ended search for solution to the problem—what the phrase "epistemological project" more narrowly implies. We can make the 'existential value' of such inquiry more plausible or vivid to ourselves, by thinking back to the significance this project may first have had for us, before its freshness was lost and it assumed the status of a formalized puzzle. When we call up in this way the sense of dissatisfaction that Descartes' First Meditation seems so aptly to address, we might well describe it as the sense of having grown up into an understanding we have never ourselves chosen, of finding ourselves now in mid-flight, and of wishing to begin again properly at the beginning, to uncover and ground what has all along been operating beneath the surface of the choices and discoveries we have made. Such a description of our motivating dissatisfaction draws it near the first nullity Heidegger attributes to our guilt: the nullity involved in our thrownness, our condition of being unable to get back behind this thrownness to project our way of Being thoroughly, from the ground up. Can we not view Descartes' undertaking as a response (in the first place) to the dissatisfaction with just this condition—and a response, moreover, which does not immediately turn away from this condition by fleeing into the illusory groundedness of the public interpretation, but rather attempts to confront it head on, and to improve it?

Descartes' project, viewed in this aspect, is an attempt to address this first nullity; it begins with the acknowledgement that we have been borne along all our lives with a momentum not our own, so that we have never made ourselves responsible for what we are. More particularly, we have not taken responsibility for the way entities are understood and interpreted by us—for it is this nullity in objects or entities, and not in ourselves, that epistemology is most concerned with. (Later, I shall suggest that ethics may be linked to concern with the nullities in ourselves.) Our views of the entities around us are based in a system of theories and concepts we have never constructed or chosen for ourselves. Indeed, Descartes has recognized also that it is a merely public interpretation we have been thrown into—a conception of our world taken over unawares from the others we have grown up among—though he views this inheritance as a set or system of ontical beliefs, and not as a grounding ontological understanding, as Heidegger claims it to be. But of course Descartes is not merely attempting to arrive at accounts (of entities) that are his own, and not rooted outside or behind him. He also wishes to encounter these entities in the one best way—privileged not just as being his own, but for anyone. In our Heideggerian schema, this intent is directed against the second nullity, lying in our projection; Descartes is dissatisfied not just with the fact that he has been thrown into a particular interpretation, but also with his inability to justify this interpretation over against the alternatives to it. This comes out clearly as he proceeds: his famous doubt involves the worry that many possible accounts are equally justifiable, and that he has no evidence that would allow him to give priority to just one. Here too, then, Descartes' project begins in a deliberate refusal to accept the public understanding with falling's tranquillity.

Descartes' response to this dissatisfaction also bears some of the force of a reaction against our falling everydayness—and so also an abstract resemblance to the Heideggerian response we shall be meeting in the next part. Following Descartes, we are to begin by attempting to cancel this momentum that has so far carried us along; we are to bring ourselves to a temporary pause, by freeing ourselves from the thrust of those conceptions that have so far determined our course. And by bringing ourselves to rest in ourselves in this way, we shall have reached that privileged position from which we can make a new start for ourselves, setting our own bearings, and supplying our own momentum. By pausing in this way, and breaking the impetus that was imposed from without, we shall be able to assume a responsibility for ourselves we never before possessed. We shall have overcome, it seems, our thrown-ness, and have positioned ourselves to uncover the right or proper way of standing related to entities. Such may be part of the force and attraction the Cartesian project initially holds for us. And rather than representing a falling flight from the nullities, as has formerly appeared, it seems in this aspect to involve an attempt to face and overcome them.

Now with this break in momentum, the position of epistemological inquiry has withdrawn its confidence from current theories. But it still holds open the hope that some such theories might eventually be affirmed after all; it is still willing and eager to settle down into some such secured system. In its content, this position thus stands in an ambivalent relation to the theoretical attitude it occurs within: on the one hand valuing and pursuing the goal of this attitude—an objective grasp—but on the other accepting it only as a goal, and not as a condition already achieved. Because it is this goal only as accomplished that aligns theory with falling, the position of epistemological inquiry thus has only an indirect or distant affinity to such falling. And as we turn now to the final basic position within epistemology—the sceptical reply to its question—we can see that even this indirect link has been cut. The position of scepticism is more thoroughly at odds with the theoretical attitude it is couched within, because it renounces that attitude's goal even as a possibility. And so it has still less affinity to the falling temptation, being not even *en route* towards the secure objectivity the latter would prize. In this aspect, the sceptical position is instead related to a quite different existential stance: anxiety. Just as anxiety is an abstention from practical projects, due to recognition that no mode of concern for equipment has priority over any other, so scepticism abstains from (knowing) assertions, out of conviction that no such accounts can arrive at some way objects are in themselves.

It seems possible, then, to allot to the epistemological project a more favourable role within Heidegger's system than he himself is ever willing to concede it. We may view it as linked to recognition of the unsatisfactoriness involved in our essence as thrown and projecting. And while this recognition may be abandoned by the positive conclusion to that project, the positions of inquiry and scepticism preserve it; they tend not towards a fleeing lostness in the 'they' and its stable accounts, but precisely out of and against such lostness. In this way we find for epistemology an '*existential*' source (in the ordinary sense of the term; but also in Heidegger's technical sense: a source at the level of our existence as care). This lies in the nullities essential to our structure, and more specifically in the ways these nullities render our relations to the entities about us deficient and disturbing.

And with this, we also find in epistemology those 'positive possibilities' that phenomenology, despite the radical character of its criticisms of this and other branches of traditional philosophy, will accept the task of developing. That there should be such possibilities is a supposition underlying Heidegger's treatment of the most diverse philosophers; consider, for example, his insistence that his 'destruction of the history of ontology' has a positive, constructive aspect:

> ... this destruction is ... far from having the *negative* sense of shaking off the ontological tradition. We must, on the contrary, stake out the positive possibilities of that tradition, and this always means keeping it within its *limits*; these in turn are given factically in the way the question is formulated at the time, and in the way the possible field for investigation is thus bounded off. (*BT* 44).

It seems only appropriate to extend this sympathetic strategy to epistemology as well, despite Heidegger's own more unrelenting aversion to the field.

c. Yet epistemology is an inadequate response to these nullities. This friendly amendment can only be allowed, however, if we immediately acknowledge the ways in which Descartes' efforts in particular, and those of the epistemological tradition generally, are *misguided* responses to that unsatisfactoriness, even though they may approach it directly. That is, in the terms of the above quotation, we must bear in mind the 'limits' to the epistemologist's problematic: those ways in which his own formulation of his difficulty has shut him off from a really adequate response to it. These ways hinge about a single crucial point, by now well familiar to us: there is a gap between the level at which an epistemological position occurs, and that at which the prompting nullities lie. And the affinities that bridge this gap still cannot allow these positions to meet those nullities adequately. This point has several interrelated aspects.

A first has already been discussed in detail, though in a different context. We have noted that Heidegger's principal objection to epistemology accuses it of misinterpreting Dasein by treating it as present-at-hand. Here we encounter a more particular version of this failing: the epistemological project mistakes that root unsatisfactoriness, which is in fact a groundlessness in our concernful understanding, as rather a groundlessness in our system of beliefs about entities, or in our thematic understanding. Descartes, for example, begins with intuitive discontent over the ungrounded public understanding into which he has grown up—but then, out of his immersion in the theoretical attitude, he goes on to interpret that understanding as just such a system of beliefs, i.e. as a set of present-at-hand objects, presented to that present-at-hand subject which he himself is. He is impelled to do so, we have seen, because his guiding attitude will allow him to discover only what can be concrete and current. So he supposes that this understanding is an unsatisfactory *possession,* which he needs to replace with a better. But instead, this public understanding has the temporal breadth of any full way of Being-in-the-world: it is not crystallized in some set of beliefs we possess, nor (as with Kant) in a handful of concepts presupposed in our theories, but is diffused through all our implicit but intentional behaviour and experience—it guides this behaviour as a disposition towards particular ends, and as a readiness for recognized moods. The epistemologist, then, though confronting an existential dissatisfaction with his thrownness into contingent projections, immediately misinterprets it as a lack in something present-at-hand, and so immediately assumes a task Heidegger believes misguided.

Entangled with this misconception of the character of this lack is a second misconception of the level of a proper response to it. Because the epistemologist mislocates the nullities in the beliefs of a knowing subject, he supposes that the only transformation required of him is at the level of his theorizing—at the level of the positions he 'possesses'. And so the goal he pursues is his acquisition, as a Cartesian subject, of the most privileged or well-grounded of theories. But we have already noticed, and shall see further, that while (the phenomenologist's) theory can help us *towards* an adequate response to the nullities, this response is not given with any such theory, but lies in a transformed mode of concern. Indeed, the theoretical attitude itself—not to mention any particular positions that may be adopted within it—does not amount to a basic enough transformation of our existence to constitute a genuine alternative to our falling everydayness. Whether we theorize or not, and the content of the theories we adopt, may have affinities to the authentic or falling modes of existence, as we have seen. But it is only these modes of existence that genuinely meet or avoid the nullities, and those affinities do not at all enable theory to do so on its own.

There is still a third important way in which the epistemological project is an inappropriate response to its initiating dissatisfaction—though this point now applies more specifically to the opening project of inquiry (and still more bluntly to the positive solution), while not to the sceptical conclusion. This lies in the very fact that the project tries to eliminate the dissatisfaction by providing the grounding that is felt to be lacking. Heidegger claims this is not possible: 'Thus "Being-a-basis" means *never* to have power over one's ownmost Being from the ground up.' (*BT* 330). When we see how the nullities arise with our temporal structure, we see their inevitability; conversely, it is because the theorist has misinterpreted their character, or the level at which they occur, that he can believe he might manage to correct them—it seems feasible to collect a best system of positions. But we shall see that phenomenology instead aims to induce a non-fleeing recognition of our nullities, that yet does not try to overcome them. It should help us to face these limits in our thrownness and projection, and to engage in our worldly projects in a way that reflects our acknowledgement of those limits. In attempting to eliminate our nullities, the epistemological project neglects our true task of learning to live in a ready recognition of them. (And indeed, as we saw, in aiming to arrive at a position in which these nullities will no longer trouble or distress us, this project aims at an eventual tranquillity and security, which is precisely what falling everydayness has sought, though in a more delusive way.) Thus here too epistemology's praiseworthy effort to confront these disturbing features of our position, is followed through inappropriately.

Now these three criticisms of epistemology, and indeed the general angle of approach this whole part has taken, may induce a certain discomfort, which would find expression in the charge of psychologism, mentioned above. For should not epistemological positions be judged in their own right, by reference to the goal they inherently pursue, and not according to any motives claimed to underlie the theorist's adoption of them? Why is this Heideggerian diagnosis not as much beside the point as it would be, to attack a philosopher's positions by pointing out that he has an unappealing character? Why, more specifically, is this diagnosis not as crude as the charge that epistemological doubt is neurotic? This odd angle of attack is indeed not peculiar to Heidegger, but characteristic of existentialists quite generally, and responsible for some of one's immediate resistance to them. They shift the grain of philosophical discussion, so that points and arguments all tend in a different direction—and it can easily seem this is no more than a change of subject, and to a non-philosophical subject.

But to begin with, the previous chapter has already presented arguments of a more traditional thrust, attempting to show that the project of self-validation that theory sets running, cannot achieve its own object. These arguments have thus pressed towards what seems a sceptical conclusion, as a position within—or conclusion to—that project itself; it was difficult to distinguish Heidegger from the sceptic epistemologist. If adequate, then, those arguments would somewhat blunt this charge of psychologism, so far as it applies to the Heideggerian attack on the positions of inquiry and positive solution. But it would remain in full force against Heidegger's attempts to undermine the sceptic; it is here that we especially require a defence for his 'psychological' line of attack. And considering this here will allow me to develop the ways Heidegger is and is not a sceptic—and also to pull together some threads left loose through this part.

The gist might be put in this way: on the Heideggerian view, scepticism is true, but it is in the first place a derivative truth, and in the second a truth that needs to be embraced in a peculiar, self-undermining way, if it is to be combined with an insight into the more crucial truth it is grounded upon. Scepticism is true, because it is indeed the case that our theories can never give us access to some way things might be in themselves; always, it is an unjustifiable thematization of Being that guides our theories of entities. But this truth is not the most basic truth about our condition—it itself depends on the truth that we are temporally stretched along, so as to be rooted in an unchosen past, and reaching out towards a limited future. The last chapter showed how it is this temporal dispersal that ultimately precludes a transparent grasp of the purely present-at-hand. This temporal stretch, however, is itself only recognized when we acknowledge those troubling links to past and future, and do not absorb ourselves in an isolated present; this will be so in the condition of authenticity, which I shall describe more fully in the next part. Yet that contrasting absorption is precisely the goal of the theoretical attitude, where this is entered in a straightforward or whole-hearted way: the theorist typically aims at a radical *presence* of himself to his object or his theory, a presence that distracts from the nullities in his temporal spread. And so that deeper truth of our temporal condition is compatible with only a nonstandard mode of theorizing—one that resists this attitude's inherent tendency to forget the temporal embeddedness of its insights.

These points apply to theoretical positions of all types, for example to those of the physicist. They indicate the style of the 'authentic science' whose possibility Heidegger suggests at *BT* 415. Only the scientist who embraces his positions in this contextualizing way, will preserve recognition of that deeper truth about his condition—a truth that reveals the limits to all the claims he is making about objects. Only such a scientist can intend his claims in the spirit appropriate to the type of validity they can have. These points apply even to the claims that Heidegger himself makes in *Being and Time*; in the next part I shall show how this intricate system must be viewed, so as not to be subject to the attack on theory as falling. And these points apply also to the theoretical position of scepticism: if, while accepting this position, we are not to lose sight of the deeper truth it is founded upon, we must affirm it in a distinctive style or spirit: not as pure contemplators, removed from our life-concerns into an absolute and most privileged state, but rather as arriving at this position within the context of unjustifiable projects we have been thrown upon. Such a style of acceptance maintains insight into the temporal dispersal that grounds the truth of scepticism; in so doing, it embraces this sceptical stance in an awareness of the 'existential' status of this stance, as a view we adopt in the course of our engagement in projects.

Conversely, to say that a theory is motivated by falling is to say that it does not face that deeper truth, and hence does not place its positions in this temporal context, or grasp them in awareness of the way they indeed are true. I must wait until the next part to develop with more reasonable fullness the nature of this temporal or contextual grasp, which is necessary if we are to view our truths with the type of transparency possible for us. But as we anticipate this, I shall quickly sum up the implications of these points for the charge of psychologism. In condemning a theoretical position as due to this motive, Heidegger is indeed applying a standard somewhat extrinsic to that position itself. For he is attacking it for its failure to grasp a different truth, lying (as he thinks) deeper than the one at which the theorist deliberately aims. But we should note first that this standard is at least an 'epistemological' one; it is not ultimately an aesthetic or moral criterion, whose relevance would be more obviously doubtful, but demands insight into or confronting with the 'reality' of our relation to entities. And second, the truth this standard concerns is one not wholly distinct from the position itself—for it shows how or in what sense the position can be true: not 'absolutely', in a couple of senses. Ontical claims about entities are grounded in (and 'relative to') an unjustifiable projection of their Being. More deeply, *any* claim (including even the preceding ontological one, or scepticism) is not a best way of standing related to entities, in which we transcend our temporal dispersal, and the nullities in our thrownness and projection—it is not a truth for contemplation in an absolute and timeless present. If the theorist ignores the existential context for his claims, he intends them in a sense they cannot sustain.

In general, then, the Cartesian project must be given an ambivalent role within the Heideggerian system. On the one hand it is allied with the attempt to face directly, and to refuse to flee, that unsatisfactoriness intrinsic to our condition; in this respect it amounts to an effort to move beyond our base condition of falling everydayness. But on the other hand, insofar as it is locked within the scope of the theoretical attitude, and mistakes that unsatisfactoriness as merely the correctable lack of a self-grounding by that attitude, it itself also falls, and fails properly to recognize or appropriately to respond to the nullities infecting our relations to entities; in this respect the epistemological project still belongs within the falling everydayness it attempts to surmount. In the next and final part we shall consider that response to these nullities which Heidegger thinks the proper one—and at the same time, and at long last, shall see the full extent and basic character of that mode of thinking with which he wishes to replace the traditional project, having, as I have now at last fully done, first presented his diagnosis of it.

d. A parallel diagnosis applies to traditional ethics. Before proceeding to these final topics, however, I shall turn aside briefly to sketch an analogous existential diagnosis for another main branch of traditional philosophy. (Unfortunately, this discussion will have to be even more schematic than usual, but I hope at least to make easily imaginable how the preceding could be more elaborately extended to this other field.) If the nullities as they apply to the entities about us can plausibly be claimed as the root to the epistemological project, it seems even easier to view these nullities as they apply to ourselves, as giving moral philosophy its impetus. For in the most abstract terms, what is the latter but the attempt to choose deliberately for ourselves the way we are to be, and by discovering, moreover, that one way preferable to all others? While epistemology confronts these nullities as they limit relations to 'objects', and prevent us from encountering them as we would do, ethics treats the nullities as they bear rather upon our pursuit of defining ends. We are inevitably troubled by the recognition that these ends are ones we have been thrown into pursuing, and by the suspicion that they are not ultimately preferable to others they require us to forgo. And moral philosophy at least addresses these deficiencies directly, and takes on the task of providing and defending some procedure that will single out certain courses of action as preferable to others. So here too the philosophical project may be viewed as a direct response to an acknowledged sense of dissatisfaction, and may be set over against that falling response which flees into ends that have been sanctioned by the 'they', and that therefore tranquillize us with the illusion that they are firmly based. The moral philosopher is not content with such falling security, and questions whether those public possibilities into which he has been socialized are genuinely preferable to the others he can imagine.

And yet, here too Heidegger must find the philosophical undertaking to be misguided, and in the same three general ways. For first, moral philosophy misunderstands projection towards ends as avowal of—and action by reference to—a moral system, or a certain theory of the good life. That is, here too the philosopher misses the deep locus of his motivating dissatisfaction, and misinterprets it as a lack in something present-at-hand. So he imagines it to be a deficiency in his practical principles, or in his concrete behaviour in the 'world'. Second, he thus also believes that the proper response to this dissatisfaction can consist in possessing some set of ethical beliefs, and in conforming his definite actions with these beliefs. He fails to suspect or to face the more sweeping transformation of his Being-in-the-world that authenticity requires—a transformation in the way he stretches out through time, and not merely in the sediment of positions and actions this projective activity leaves behind. And third, such philosophy attempts to eliminate the sense of dissatisfaction that sets it under way, by showing conclusively that certain possibilities are indeed to be pursued at the expense of others. It thus misses the way the needed existential transformation instead involves 'living with' the unattainability of just this ideal.

We find here the reasons for Heidegger's repeated announcements that his notions of falling and authenticity are not moral or valuative (cf. for example *BT* 211, 265). 'Moralizing' is indeed a manifestation of falling: an attempt to tranquillize oneself and others in the choice of one factical possibility to the exclusion of others. It revealingly expresses itself, for example, in a 'resentful' attack on the possibilities lived by others, where these possibilities possess an attraction that threatens one's satisfaction with one's own, and aggravates awareness of the nullities; by convincing oneself that these threatening alternatives are excluded, or shown inferior, by their immorality, one is able to content oneself again with one's own, and to avoid once more the disturbing contingency to projection. And moral philosophy, like epistemology, in aiming towards the ultimate removal of the relevant nullity, seeks in the long run to play this same role, by reassuring that the choice of some one possibility is grounded, after all. As we shall see, authenticity is not distinguished as a projection towards any such privileged or certified end, and its achievement in no way alleviates one's guilt. Once again, it will generally consist in an ability to maintain one's projection in the face of explicit recognition that it cannot be grounded. And such recognition goes beyond the theoretical position of 'ethical relativism'—which would be, yet also would not be, accepted by Heidegger himself, in the ways we have already seen for epistemological scepticism. Here then are the roughest outlines of a Heideggerian critique of any moral philosophy that still involves elements of the falling moralizing; in many further ways, this critique would run largely in parallel to the one I have sketched for epistemology.

3. Phenomenology: the positive task of the new philosophical method

a. The Being of tools and objects is revealed by breakdowns in our relations to them. I now at last turn to consider that other departure from falling everydayness which Heidegger believes the proper (and indeed the only successful) one and to which, under different aspects, he gives the names "phenomenology" and "authenticity". I shall focus, that is, on Heidegger's conception of the proper method for philosophy or for thinking, although the recommended route is of a rather different character from these latter activities, as they are usually conceived. In the third parts to the preceding chapters I have taken first looks at this phenomenological method: first in its role of making explicit an understanding of Being already implicit in everydayness, and second in its contrast with the philosophical method represented in epistemology, viewed as implicitly presupposing a traditional understanding of Being. Now, having more adequately grasped the falling that underlies both everydayness and epistemology, we are at last in a position to deal comprehensively with phenomenology, since this is most crucially a way of turning towards that which falling flees. In this crucial dimension we shall see that phenomenology is intimately connected with that opposite to falling which Heidegger calls "authenticity". I shall begin my discussion of these topics by considering a series of specific ways in which it is possible to 'make explicit' an understanding of Being that proximally and for the most part is only implicit, and is, indeed, even fled. This helps us to approach the type of explicitness, or of transparency to truth, with which Heidegger wishes to replace that sought in traditional philosophy.

We have seen that phenomenology is for Heidegger 'an allowing of Being to show itself from itself'. But by itself this formula most likely suggests little to us; how, concretely, is this to be accomplished? Insofar as this rewriting of Husserl's "To the things themselves!" does not suggest empirical research—that is, a study of entities within-the-world, which it certainly does not—its point probably remains obscure to us. But attention to Heidegger's own procedures can help to give this notion content. Let us now look at ways in which the three modes of Being may be brought to show themselves: those of the ready-to-hand, the present-at-hand, and Dasein. In each case Heidegger focuses on some breakdown in the normal understanding of this type of Being, a breakdown that makes this understanding explicit, and reveals it as having all along made possible the encountering of entities within-the-world, in whose favour it was then neglected. (Cf. *BPP* 309, which stresses the role of 'the privative' in making clear the positive.)

Let us look first, then, at those breakdowns that bring to light the Being of ready-to-hand equipment—the mode of Being that is structured as a world or system of assignments. Heidegger describes his general interest here in this way:

Has Dasein itself, in the range of its concernful absorption in equipment ready-to-hand, a possibility of Being in which the worldhood of those entities within-the-world with which it is concerned is, in a certain way, lit up for it, *along with* those entities themselves? [If so,] then the way lies open for studying the phenomenon which is thus lit up, and for attempting to 'hold it at bay', as it were, and to interrogate it as to those structures which show themselves therein. (*BT* 102).

Heidegger goes on to point to cases in which equipment is broken, missing, or in the way as occasions in which the normally hidden phenomenon of world, and its internal structure, can come explicitly into view. For example, when the turning indicator on one's car is broken one is reminded of its various assignments, an implicit familiarity with which has all along grounded one's use of it as a turning indicator: I am now struck by the linkage between this lever and the lights at the corners of the car, and by the role these play in informing others of my intended direction; I am vividly impressed with the way these have all along allowed me to manoeuvre safely at crossroads, and to proceed easily and without thought across town to my destination. When this quite minor piece of equipment breaks down, so to an extent does my ability to operate smoothly and effortlessly within the larger context that includes interrelated equipment and also the ends they are for the sake of. And with the partial breakdown in such an ability, its scope, and the internal structure to the understanding it involves, may be glimpsed as something that has been operating all along. We then suddenly 'see' that our more explicit striving has always occurred on the basis of an implicit mastery of routes or means, a mastery by which we are related to entities in ways ordinarily ignored. As Heidegger puts it:

But *when an assignment has been disturbed*—when something is unusable for some purpose—then the assignment becomes explicit. . . . [W]e catch sight of the 'towards-this' itself, and along with it everything connected with the work—the whole 'workshop'—as that wherein concern always dwells. The context of equipment is lit up . . . as a totality constantly sighted beforehand in circumspection. With this totality, however, the world announces itself. (*BT* 105).

In lighting up these assignments, the breakdown lights up the Being of equipment, i.e. a phenomenon. Phenomenology will therefore have as a technique appropriate to it, attention to breakdowns of this sort.

Now although the projection of Being as presence-at-hand occurs in a quite different way, it is possible to locate and to give an analogous role to breakdowns in this way of understanding Being, too. Such breakdowns occur, for example, in periods in which a science's basic concepts are undergoing revision. At such times it is particularly clear that all positive research accomplished by such a science takes place on the ground of a particular way in which the Being of that science's entities has been sketched out beforehand. Where mere research is dominant, on the other hand, this ground is apt to be overlooked. Thus when Heidegger wishes to show that all sciences rest on an understanding of Being, he points to the way in which the basic concepts constituting such an understanding are today so widely in flux:

The real 'movement' of the sciences takes place when their basic concepts undergo a more or less radical revision which is transparent to itself. The level which a science has reached is determined by how far it is *capable* of a crisis in its basic concepts.... Among the various disciplines everywhere today there are freshly awakened tendencies to put research on new foundations. (*BT* 29).

As we have also seen, however, this projection of Being as presence-at-hand has only a secondary status, according to Heidegger; for this reason, and also because he takes it to have been commonly recognized, at least since Kant, he shows relatively little interest in characterizing its details, and correspondingly little interest in attending to its breakdowns.

b. Anxiety is the breakdown in which our own Being is revealed. By contrast, the Being of Dasein itself is of course the central topic of *Being and Time*, so that any such breakdown that is suited to bring out this Being will be of extreme importance. It is anxiety that plays this role. While equipmental breakdowns were road-blocks to our understanding of (i.e. to our ability to manage or operate smoothly along) a certain segment of the referential totality constituting our world, anxiety may be viewed as a breakdown in our state-of-mind, as the way in which the world as a whole matters to us. While equipmental breakdowns light up the internal structure to the world, and the Being of equipment, anxiety lights up an external aspect to this world, its 'groundlessness', and along with it our own Being. In this chapter's first part I gave an opening account of anxiety, but only in its formal character of turning towards those nullities in our condition from which falling flees. Now, because of its role of illuminating our Being, by which it will prove of particular importance for phenomenology and authenticity, I must try to present it more comprehensively and concretely.

Anxiety, then, is a state-of-mind or mood, but a very special one. Other moods disclose segments of our world as mattering to us in particular ways; for example, fearing discloses a certain type of detrimental reference it is possible for some entity to have, and allows us then to encounter such entities as threatening. In anxiety, on the other hand, the mattering that typifies other moods occurs in what Heidegger elsewhere likes to call "a deficient mode". That is, all the involvements that make up the structure of the world cease to concern us: 'Here the totality of involvements of the ready-to-hand and the present-at-hand discovered within-the-world, is, as such, of no consequence; it collapses into itself; the world has the character of completely lacking significance.' (*BT* 231). This does not imply, however, that the world ceases to be disclosed to us—indeed quite the contrary, for as all entities within-the-world lose their involvements it is the world as such that 'obtrudes' itself. The world, which has previously been grasped only in an implicit mastery of its intricate routes and ends, is now lit up all at once for us, as our immersion within it is lost. While each other mood absorbs us in a particular style of concern for some part of our world, and thereby precludes the detachment that would allow us to notice the whole, anxiety has no such focus on particular entities, and so permits or forces a relation to that whole. Referring to this way in which anxiety, unlike fear, arises with respect to 'nothing' within-the-world, Heidegger says:

The obstinacy of the 'nothing and nowhere within-the-world' means as a phenomenon that *the world as such is that in the face of which one has anxiety*. The utter insignificance which makes itself known in the 'nothing and nowhere', does not signify that the world is absent, but tells us that entities within-the-world are of so little importance in themselves that on the basis of this *insignificance* of what is within-the-world, the world in its worldhood is all that still obtrudes itself. (*BT* 231).

But it is possible to make this notion of anxiety a bit more vivid. What we are to imagine is that all those diverse referential pathways that lead out from us towards our various ends cease to absorb or concern us, and that we cannot set ourselves into any of them in that smooth and effortless way we normally do without notice. I could go out the door for a walk, but why bother? I could pick up the phone to call so-and-so, but what's the point? In losing our everyday assignment to such equipmental dealings and the projects they are couched within, we take explicit notice of them all in a way we ordinarily do not. We see all these routes radiating out from us, while previously we had already been launched upon one or another.

There is indeed a related, *everyday* way in which we often take notice of such projects, and we can improve our grasp of anxiety by contrasting the two. We very often evaluate our projects from the point of view of still broader projects, weighing their value as steps within the latter. How would a walk now contribute or detract from my more general intentions for the day? And we may of course conclude that there is no reason to bother with such an activity just now, a decision we might express in the same words attributed above to anxiety. In considering a project 'from a distance' in this manner we view it explicitly in a way we cannot when immediately launched and engaged upon it. And such recognition may also be forced on us by such equipmental breakdowns as I earlier described. But all such detachment from projects, and such explicit noticing of them, is crucially different from the position of anxiety. For in each such case we stand back from one project only by standing within another; the perspective from which we view the former is detached from it only by being engaged instead in the latter and thus not serving as a perspective upon it as well. By contrast with anxiety, then, such everyday recognition, including that induced by the equipmental breakdowns mentioned before, is confined to sectors of our world—to parts of its internal structure viewed from elsewhere within it—and does not make explicit the nature of our relation to that entire network of routes and involvements.

We must not suppose, however, that the more thorough detachment in anxiety involves merely a quantitative difference from these everyday cases; this thoroughness is responsible for a crucial difference in kind. When we decide against some particular project in our everyday way, we in effect are determining that it lacks a sufficient ground or justification in those broader pursuits from within which we view it. Our higher ends within the latter do not sufficiently support an involvement in this route; such involvement is, in this sense, 'ungrounded'. And this ungroundedness is, most crucially, noted not in a belief about this project, but in our lack of any impetus into it—by the absence of any felt pull through the project and towards some attracting end. Other projects, however, may of course be discovered to merit involvement, by being seen to contribute to these higher ends. So *this* disengagement will not naturally persist.

When, by contrast, we are abstracted from *all* our projects by the mood of anxiety, we necessarily encounter a far more radical kind of ungroundedness. We have now lost all our impetus; our ends have lost all their former attractive force. Individual projects are no longer discovered to lack justification only relatively to others in which our concern is already established. Rather, we have now lost all basis for such relative assessment, and thus lack any starting point from which we might proceed to discover some projects as grounded. By halting our momentum along our accustomed routes, anxiety has deprived us of our everyday procedure for achieving some new involvement. Lacking attraction towards any ends, we can find nothing in any particular projects we might entertain, that could support or induce an adoption of them. We seem trapped in a position from which every enterprise must continue to seem ungrounded. But further, this anxious disengagement reveals to us something of more general significance, something that has been true of our everyday situation all along. It reveals that the whole of our everyday involvements, viewed as a total world with which we have been concerned, has always lacked that type of grounding which is possible only internally to it. To the extent that this whole system has ever had any basis, it has been only in the fact of our involvement within it. There is no justification for this system as a whole, of the sort we ordinarily seek and can find within it.

And so in anxiety this system of involvements comes into view as ungrounded, as having no support beyond that usual impetus through it, which we now have lost but can remember. This ungroundedness to our world which is sighted in anxiety is of course the first nullity introduced as belonging to our guilt: the nullity lying in our thrownness, which is itself precisely that impetus along referential pathways which has now, momentarily, subsided. Anxiety discloses this ungroundedness not in the abstraction of a theoretical claim, but by holding us apart from our world and forcing us to see, by contrast, the only basis we have ever had for our attachment to it. It holds us out of the 'throw' that alone sustained that attachment; we now confront the nature of this throw by directly experiencing its absence. It has been only our thrownness into this world that has made it ours, and not the judgements or weighings of our personal choice. Indeed, we are so far from having chosen this world for ourselves, that being now off its rails we are unable even to set ourselves back upon them. What personal basis has been left us for doing so? We must rather depend upon being thrown once again towards ends we can take no responsibility for, since only on the basis of this throw, and these ends, can any choice or self-expression begin.

This anxious disengagement from our projects thus reveals in an especially deep and vivid way a contingency that has characterized the latter all along; it reveals the extent to which these projects are not really our own, and can indeed never fully become so. Our engagement in them is a mere accident of our thrownness. In losing our everyday assignment to such projects we thus lose too our ability to identify ourselves securely in terms of them, and so to avoid an acknowledgement of our disturbingly loose relationship to them. It is not, however, that we have some further content beyond these projects into which we have been thrown; when these are stripped from us by anxiety, we do not discover in ourselves some more basic remainder, but only those nullities themselves, which prevent straightforward identification of ourselves with any particular projects. Anxiety drives home that we are not any of our factical roles, but that we are not anything beyond our projection towards some one or another of these roles, either. Precluding identification with any such factical, merely contingent projects, it brings into view the activity of projection itself, which is truly essential.

In anxiety, then, it is not some portion of the referential totality that is lit up (as happens when equipment breaks down), but the world as a whole, and the everyday manner of our Being-in it. That is, it is our own Being as thrown projection that we catch sight of, and in particular what we might call an external aspect to that Being—a way in which all our particular projects are lacking in grounds and can slip away at any moment. And so in this third, and by far most important type of breakdown through which phenomenology can uncover Being, there is revealed precisely that dissatisfying aspect to our own Being which is that from which falling flees, and that which traditional epistemology undertakes to eliminate.

c. Phenomenology does not aim at a merely theoretical grasp of our existential structure. But in noting that phenomenology, in order that it may bring to light the various modes of Being (of equipment, of objects, and of ourselves), will focus on breakdown conditions of these types, I seem merely to have described a technique available to this method, without approaching its true centre. ('Technical devices' are contrasted with the method itself on *BT* 50.) Attention to these breakdowns in our everyday understanding is surely by itself not sufficient to single out phenomenology as the new mode of thinking that Heidegger claims it to be. Such breakdowns can be studied from various perspectives, with varying purposes. What is peculiar to the phenomenologist's manner of treating them? We must attempt now to draw nearer the heart of this phenomenological method, and to recognize its fundamental divergence from the mode of thinking involved in epistemology and in the other branches of traditional philosophy. When we have done so it will be clearer still why such breakdowns should be especially significant for this method.

We have seen that these breakdown conditions are useful to phenomenology because they help the latter to make explicit an understanding of Being that is usually only implicit. But what precisely does such 'making explicit' amount to? Is this primarily a matter of the understanding now being put down in words, being captured in some definite formulation? Does phenomenology ultimately strive after a *theory* that is the more acceptable the more exactly it corresponds to the previously implicit understanding of Being? Must this not be phenomenology's aim, given that *Being and Time* itself—which surely must be the archetype for this method as Heidegger understands it—seems so obviously to aim at presenting just such an account?

We may begin by taking note of statements in *Being and Time* suggesting that phenomenology does make Being explicit by fixing it in a theory. Early on Heidegger discusses the everyday, merely implicit understanding of Being in this way:

As we have intimated, we always conduct our activities in an understanding of Being. . . . We do not *know* what "Being" means. But even if we ask, "What *is* 'Being'?", we keep within an understanding of the "is", though we are unable to fix conceptually what that "is" signifies. We do not even know the horizon in terms of which that meaning is to be grasped and fixed. (*BT* 25).

Phenomenology, apparently, has as its task to 'fix conceptually' the meaning of Being, and will improve on our everyday position in just this way. The distinction between the terms "existentiell" and "existential", while usually understood (in the sense I elaborated back in the first part of this chapter) as that between grasping oneself via roles, and grasping oneself via the activity of projecting in general, is sometimes rather presented as a distinction between understandings that lack or possess a conceptual formulation. An existentiell understanding of oneself, says Heidegger, 'does not require that the ontological structure of existence should be theoretically transparent. The question about that structure aims at the analysis of what constitutes existence.... Its analytic has the character of an understanding which is not existentiell, but rather *existential.*' (*BT* 33). It here seems that an existential understanding is precisely a theoretical, conceptual one, and that it is in this that it possesses the explicitness or transparency that an existentiell understanding would lack. So the phenomenologist, in aiming at such an existential analysis of Dasein, must apparently improve on our original everydayness by contributing a theoretical account. And indeed, *Being and Time*'s own procedure seems clearly to confirm this; its methodical delineation of the four aspects of Being-in, for example, seems just such an analysis of the structure of our Being.

If application of the phenomenological method to Dasein does principally aim at such a theory, it would follow that this method must be quite independent from that mode of pre-theoretical (and so, apparently, 'existentiell') understanding to which Heidegger gives the name "authenticity"—and which amounts, as I have often anticipated, to that mode of existence in which we turn towards the nullities fundamental to our Being, rather than fleeing them in the manner of everydayness. For we shall soon see that such authenticity by no means presupposes intellectual appropriation of a theoretical system—so that phenomenological understanding would be in no way a precondition for it. And conversely we can already see that the grasp of system that this understanding apparently involves, by no means presupposes the authentic condition: the latter will include, not surprisingly, the state-of-mind of anxiety, yet surely it would be possible for a patient student to master the system of *Being and Time*, even including its discussions of anxiety itself, and so achieve the 'existential' understanding, without ever succumbing to such a mood. Generally, on this conception of the phenomenologist's task, his interest in the above-mentioned break-downs, including anxiety, will lie in their usefulness to him as events that are especially instructive about the structures he pursues, and that can be observed as well in others as in himself—or perhaps even more fruitfully in others, as then his own intellectual capacities are less likely to be distorted by these breakdowns themselves.

It seems then that Heidegger's analytic, if successful, must conclude by fixing the Being of Dasein in a system of propositions that delineates the structure of this Being—and that this system will be such that it can be passed on to and mastered by others whether or not the latter have achieved that authentic stance. And so my earlier hints of a link between phenomenology and authenticity have apparently been refuted. Put generally and loosely: Heidegger's phenomenology will be an 'existential' phenomenology only in the sense that it deals, as with the objects of a detached inquiry, with structures and problems of the sort treated elsewhere in the existential movement. But it will not aim at a basic transformation in the manner of our existence, as others in that movement might do; the adoption of the phenomenological method to handle these topics has apparently reintroduced a more traditional conception of our philosophical goals, as indeed seems so clearly reflected in the system and jargon of *Being and Time*.

But Heidegger in fact warns more than once against this natural approach to his work—against the temptation to grasp it in a detached and theoretical way: 'The answer [to the question of Being] is not properly conceived if what it asserts propositionally is just passed along, especially if it gets circulated as a free-floating result, so that we merely get informed about a 'standpoint' which may perhaps differ from the way this has hitherto been treated.' (*BT* 40). And again:

Whenever a phenomenological concept is drawn from primordial sources, there is a possibility that it may degenerate if communicated in the form of an assertion. It gets understood in an empty way and is thus passed on, losing its indigenous character, and becoming a free-floating thesis. Even in the concrete work of phenomenology itself there lurks the possibility that what has been primordially 'within our grasp' may become hardened so that we can no longer grasp it. (*BT* 60–1).

And indeed, if Heidegger were pursuing such a traditional, theoretical grasp of our structures, the question would immediately arise, why he would not then be treating these structures as present-at-hand, in precisely the way he so strongly condemns. This puzzle may well have occurred to us earlier, in response to that prior critique, for if the theoretical attitude inevitably interprets its 'objects' as present-at-hand, it seems that *Being and Time* cannot help but distort Dasein's Being, merely in offering a theory about it. If phenomenology is to 'grasp' that Being, it cannot be by fixing it within this theoretical view; eventually, we must see how this method can 'transcend' these limits on theory. First, though, I shall make more explicit how that prior critique would extend to (and rule out) the account of phenomenology that I have just been weighing. In general, this account tries to apply to that method precisely the present-at-hand interpretation of language, whose inadequacy was argued in the previous chapter. It misinterprets the sense in which phenomenology is to offer a *logos* of phenomena, or the sense in which it is 'discourse'. It interprets phenomenological discourse as a mere set of present-at-hand propositions, and inter-prets phenomenological understanding as some concrete relation to this set. So we can see its inadequacy by repeating, from a some-what different angle, some of the points made in the previous chapter.

We may distinguish two particular forms the misinterpretation of such understanding may take. First, and more crudely, it may suppose phenomenology to seek mere '*formal mastery*' of a system of propositions. The 'truth' of phenomenological analysis would consist in a correspondence between such a set of propositions and the existential structures they treat. And to grasp this truth, to achieve phenomenological insight, would then be to assimilate this system and to become capable of producing for oneself the proposi-tions in which that truth had been captured and crystallized. It is fairly obvious how this interpretation tries to explain truth and understanding in present-at-hand terms: the phenomenological account is associated with these concrete tokens in which it is expressed, since these tokens are taken to bear the concrete rela-tion of correspondence to the facts themselves; grasping this ac-count is then identified as mental possession of these tokens, a possession confirmed by one's ability to produce them on demand. But it seems pointless to argue the inadequacy of this interpretation on the ground it views discourse as present-at-hand, since it is so obviously deficient in a much more straightforward way. In explaining understanding as formal mastery of these tokens, it allows it to be achieved in too great an isolation from the items to which these tokens refer; it approves a capacity to manipulate these tokens with respect to one another, without a prior experience of their relation to their referents, or a further ability so to apply them. But a merely theoretical understanding need not be so thoroughly detached from its objects. This is therefore too crude and unchallenging a form of the above interpretation of phenomenology as aiming at a theoretical grasp.

For second, and more plausibly, this interpretation may rather suppose that phenomenological understanding requires, in addition to such merely formal mastery, an immediate acquaintance with the existential structures its propositions concern, and a capacity correctly to apply the latter to the former. It would involve, as I shall put it, an '*objective grasp*' of these structures themselves. Thus it would include, for example, an ability to recognize in oneself and others an occurrence of anxiety, and to analyse its essential features. Its competence would not be limited to a facility at man-oeuvring within the conceptual structure of *Being and Time*, but would encompass the connection between these concepts and the existential structures to which they refer. And so this 'merely theoretical' understanding would bring us into contact with the subject-matter itself, would 'touch ground' there in a way that the previous version failed to do. And yet, as in the previous case, this interpretation of phenomenology's goal rests on an illegitimate account of truth and understanding, an account of them in merely present-at-hand terms. The previous and more superficial interpretation viewed linguistic tokens as concretely embodying the truth about our structure; thus a capacity to produce the tokens could be identified as an understanding of that structure itself. The more developed account likewise identifies phenomenological discourse with these tokens, but adds that we must not only grasp the tokens themselves, but witness their correspondence to that structure—view this structure along the lines delineated by the phenomenological system. But an understanding that consisted in such witnessing of a correspondence, would necessarily distort the character of that structure; in seeing why this is so, we shall see why it is appropriate to speak of such understanding as involving an 'objective grasp' of the structures it treats. Briefly, to witness the correspondence between words and their referents in this theoretical way, requires that those referents be encountered as present-at-hand 'objects'—i.e. in that typifying isolation and explicitness. And this in turn requires that they be encountered 'from without', since in themselves these structures, as aspects of our Being-in-the-world, possess precisely that contextuality and implicitness which such theory attempts to overcome.

We can see this more concretely by taking as example one of our existential structures—our projection—and considering how an 'objective grasp' of this would go. To project is to stretch oneself out towards some way one can be, through a pathway of means over which one is competent; it crucially involves a peculiar 'temporal stretch'. When projection is captured in a theory, however, and described in a sentence such as the preceding, it is met from an attitude that itself renounces this stretch, in seeking to achieve an explicit and contextless view of projection itself. For this attitude attempts to grasp the phenomenon with the same immediacy with which it surveys the description 'corresponding' to it. The theorist believes he will have grasped our projection when he achieves an 'overview' of it; a 'synoptic' view that encompasses all its structure, and pulls it entirely within the scope of a momentary survey—just as a view from a high building scans all at once the organization of a city, discovered only in bits and pieces from the streets below. The sentences describing a phenomenon are intended to enable us to take just such an overview of it. But such focused scrutiny is only achieved in an attitude that compresses its own temporal stretch, forgoing that reach towards ends which would give to the encounter an off-hand and secondary status.

And this results in distortions of projection itself, as it is grasped in the theoretical attitude: while theory may note and emphasize that projection possesses this peculiar stretch, and while it may even delineate segments within this stretch with corresponding parts of its own analysis, it also compresses the phenomenon by supposing it capturable within a distinctly-bounded formula. It supposes our projection something that is adequately surveyed in the focused glance that sees the formula's application to others or to oneself—a survey that contracts its stretch and pulls together its structural elements to bring them within the scope of a glance as brief as that of the formula itself. It is in this sense that projection is made into an 'object' by a theoretical interpretation. This general intent of the theoretical attitude, this implicit supposition that projection can be comprehended in so focused a way, may even be contradicted by a theory's own account of projection—which may insist that projection is not merely present-at-hand, that it has a quite different ontological and temporal status than entities of that type—but the stance in which theory itself requires us to stand towards projection is still always forcing it into that mould.

Even this more sympathetic way in which an understanding of existential structures can be 'merely theoretical' thus fails to do justice to these structures themselves. For while—unlike a merely formal mastery—this 'objective grasp' of these structures does bring us into a direct relationship to them, its theoretical nature forces these structures into the role of present-at-hand objects, implicitly distorting their genuine character. Such an objective or theoretical understanding cannot, then, be the aim of Heidegger's phenomenological method; *Being and Time* cannot be trying to convey this type of grasp of our Being as Dasein, for such a grasp would distort that Being it treats. The system and analysis of that work must rather be intended as a means to a quite different mode of acceptance; Heidegger must intend his claims to be appropriated in a different style, with a different manner of insight, than is sought by the philosophical tradition.

d. Phenomenology requires facing the nullities, in the position of authenticity. It still remains, however, to characterize this phenomenological method positively. What will such understanding be, if not mastery of the structure or system proposed in *Being and Time*, and if not even the ability to recognize these structures within oneself and others? Clearly, I must draw my interpretation from the positive account Heidegger gives of the *logos* involved in phenomenology. And recalling this account, we see that what is crucially missing in the above, theoretical reading must be the requirement that the existential analysis 'light up' or reveal the essential aspects of our Being for the reader of his work. Indeed, even the *truth* of this discourse is supposed to consist not in its correspondence to structures 'there' in us, but in its capacity to uncover those structures for us; thus, in the Greek terms we have met before: 'The 'Being-true' of the *logos* as *aletheuein* means that in *legein* as *apophainesthai* the entities *of which* one is talking must be taken out of their hiddenness; one must let them be seen as something unhidden (*alethes*); that is, they must be *discovered*.' (*BT* 56–7).

Now the theoretical or objective grasp did, in a sense, uncover phenomena, or bring them out of their hiddenness, for it brought them into an explicit and focused view. But we have seen that Heidegger cannot mean this by phenomenological understanding. To see what he rather intends by such 'uncovering' or 'revealing', let us recall what that contrasting 'hiddenness' involves. Being, which is phenomenology's theme, lies hidden precisely because we have typically turned away from the disturbing disclosure of that Being, into our base condition of falling everydayness: 'To Dasein's state of Being belongs *falling*. . . . That which has been uncovered and disclosed stands in a mode in which it has been disguised and closed off by idle talk, curiosity, and ambiguity. . . . *Because Dasein is essentially falling, its state of Being is such that it is in 'untruth'.*' (*BT* 264). The truth of phenomenology, then, will consist in its capacity to 'light up' for its student those aspects of his Being that falling has inclined him to avoid. The reader must be helped to turn himself towards, to confront directly, those features of his Being that he has previously fled; in particular and most crucially, he must confront the nullities fundamental to that Being, which are the original motives for flight from it. Phenomenology, then, must uncover phenomena in the sense of leading us to adopt the opposite response towards them from that taken in falling everydayness. Heidegger's name for this antithesis is of course "authenticity". Despite our earlier line of reasoning, then, there is indeed an intimate connection between phenomenology and authenticity. Phenomenology finds its point in directing its student towards authenticity, and it is the latter, and not any theoretical system, that constitutes the existential understanding at which the former ultimately aims.

But of course this does not yet make satisfactorily clear why phenomenology should require authenticity. I have traced the connection between them at too formal or schematic a level, and need to show more concretely how authenticity would correct the deficiencies involved in a merely theoretical grasp of phenomena. Before doing so, however, I must pause to sketch some of the content to this Heideggerian '**authenticity**' [Eigentlichkeit]. Most generally, this is a turning-towards those nullities from which falling flees. Heidegger's more common name for this non-falling mode of existence is "**resoluteness**" [Entschlossenheit—the German is revealing both in its affinity to "Erschlossenheit" ("disclosedness") and in its secondary connotation of 'openness', which will suggest a non-attachment to existentiell roles of projects]. As a contrasting mode of Being-in-the-world, resoluteness is constituted by different modifications of understanding, state-of-mind, and discourse than those found in falling everydayness. Rather than understanding ourselves 'as or in terms of' entities within-the-world, i.e. in terms of concrete roles we contingently play within the world, in resoluteness we understand ourselves as 'guilty', hence in terms of those nullities that indeed are essential to us. Rather than absorbing ourselves in such moods as fear, which lock us within contingent ways in which entities will matter to us, in resoluteness we hold ourselves open for anxiety, which discloses the nullities underlying all such mattering, and hence the more basic character of our Being. And rather than going along with that idle talk which tranquillizes by concealing the groundlessness of the public interpretation it conveys, in resoluteness we are reticent, having been 'called back into the stillness of [ourselves]' (*BT* 343). Heidegger brings these aspects together in this way: 'This distinctive and authentic disclosedness ... *this reticent self-projection upon one's ownmost Being-guilty, in which one is ready for anxiety—we call "resoluteness".*' (*BT* 343). We thus arrive at a first outline of authenticity: it is that mode of Being-in-the-world in which we most directly and unflinchingly face our own Being, and in particular those nullities intrinsic to it.

It is not only our own Being that is directly disclosed in authenticity, however; even the Being of entities within-the-world shows itself most appropriately in this mode of disclosure. For '. . . this *authentic* disclosedness modifies with equal primordiality both the way in which the 'world' is discovered (and this is founded upon that disclosedness) and the way in which the Dasein-with of Others is disclosed.' (*BT* 344). In order to explain this, I must first correct a likely misconception concerning this authentic condition. My discussion so far, with its emphasis that authenticity is precisely a refusal to lose ourselves by falling into an absorption in entities, may suggest that in resoluteness we detach ourselves from any involvement with entities. But Heidegger emphasizes that this is not so:

Resoluteness, as *authentic Being-one's-Self*, does not detach Dasein from its world, nor does it isolate it so that it becomes a free-floating 'I'. And how should it, when resoluteness as authentic disclosedness, is *authentically* nothing else than *Being-in-the-world*? Resoluteness brings the Self right into its current concernful Being-alongside what is ready-to-hand, and pushes it into solicitous Being with Others. (*BT* 344).

Authenticity, that is, does not involve an abstraction from the system of assignments, or disengagement from the world of concern, but rather a different manner of involvement in that world. In authenticity we do not cease assigning ourselves to (i.e. projecting towards) various ends, as roles we seek to play within the world, but we assign ourselves to these in full recognition that they do not constitute what we most basically are; thus we assign ourselves to these with a ready openness to giving them up and to substituting quite other roles. Similarly, in authenticity we are not transfixed and incapacitated in the condition of anxiety; factical moods continue to determine the manner in which our world matters to us, but as 'ready' for anxiety we do not exhaust ourselves in such moods, but acknowledge the contingency to all such modes of concern.

This different relation in which authenticity will stand to the for-the-sake-of-which, as that element in the system of assignments towards which all the rest is oriented, modifies as well the disclosure of the Being of equipment—since this Being is disclosed precisely in our capacity for employing such entities for our ends. The authentic openness to shifts in these ends—the refusal to cling to them as secure indicators of what we really are—will have as its complement an openness to shifts in the assignments constituting the Being of equipment, and a disinclination to take any current assignment as the secure essence an entity must and can only have. Moreover, there is an obvious way in which authenticity will analogously modify the way presence-at-hand is disclosed, despite the special affinity we have noted between falling and this way of projecting Being. For although it is especially tempting to do so, we need not take our discoveries of present-at-hand properties as findings of the real or basic nature of entities; here too we may hold ourselves open to shifts in the thematizations grounding these discoveries, and may hold in view the temporal context to all our claims.

e. Only in authenticity is our temporal stretch transparent to us. Let us now return to consider more carefully why this authentic or resolute position should be necessary for an adequate grasp of our existential structures. So far, I have relied on the abstract point that authenticity faces or acknowledges our essential nullities, while falling everydayness avoids and conceals them. In its projection, for example, the former acknowledges the looseness in its relation to all its ends, rather than immersing and losing itself in its concern for them. Now we have seen that these nullities are indeed most important features to our essential structure, so that a recognition of them will be required for phenomenological understanding of that structure. But it is not yet clear that phenomenology must face these nullities in precisely this authentic way; nor is it clear that such authenticity involves recognition of the many other features of our existence that phenomenology seeks to understand.

In order to cement this relation between the phenomenological method and the authentic condition, let us see how the latter can supply the deficiency we have already observed in an 'objective' or 'merely theoretical' grasp of phenomena. The inadequacy to any such detached relation to these phenomena lies, as we saw, in the incompatibility between the temporal stretch of the phenomena themselves, and the temporal focus at which the theoretical attitude aims. The latter attempts to grasp its objects in a momentary survey, an intent we may observe in its effort to 'capture' these objects in discrete linguistic tokens. But when these 'objects' are aspects of our Being-in-the-world, this attempt involves a distorting compression of the temporal stretch that is essential to them. Phenomenological understanding must obviously avoid such distortion—but how is this to be done?

The response that immediately suggests itself is that this essential temporal stretch to such features of our existence as projection and thrownness will only be adequately witnessed 'from within' such projection and thrownness themselves. In projecting, for example, we are stretched out ahead towards our ends; if the theoretical attitude fails to do justice to this reach, where else but in the activity of projecting itself should we seek to correct this inadequacy? Thus it might seem that phenomenology must aim to return us from the theoretical attempt at self-understanding, to that everyday condition in which we are simply immersed within the projective reach towards ends. But if phenomenology were to do only that, and were to effect no changes in that everyday condition, in what sense would it have succeeded in 'lighting up' or revealing the existential structures, which are only implicitly understood in that condition? In denying that the explicit grasp aimed at by the theoretical attitude is compatible with the character of these structures themselves, it seems we must have renounced any hope of improving upon our everydayness, or of raising to any greater perspicuity the background understanding the latter involves. Moreover, the everyday mode of projection is falling, which means that it is not merely by accident that it is implicit or opaque to itself in this way, but from the design of avoiding the contingency intrinsic to that projection. And this design encourages a compression in the temporal stretch of our everyday projects, of the kind much more drastically achieved in the discovery of the present-at-hand. All of this suggests that while a merely theoretical grasp of projection must implicitly distort its temporal character, we cannot be satisfied with our everyday relationship to that phenomenon, either. Is there some third possibility?

We want, as we might put it, a 'subjective grasp' of our existential structures, which yet involves a greater explicitness and a greater acceptance of their temporal character, than does our ordinary immersion within these phenomena. Such a 'subjective grasp' of projection, for example, might achieve explicitness by engaging in projects with a clear view of the end at which they aim, rather than losing its sight of the reach to these projects, by immersing itself in the details of means and equipment. And such a 'subjective grasp' would do justice to the full scope of projection, by stretching itself out in this way towards its furthermost ends, and pursuing more immediate projects and ends with a clear recognition of their merely subordinate role. Although Heidegger would surely disavow the expression "subjective grasp", because he takes 'the subject' to be a present-at-hand distortion of Dasein's true nature, it is this mode of projection that belongs to the position of authenticity, and that gives us that hold on this phenomenon which his phenomenological method seeks. In projecting in this authentic way, we achieve a '*transparency*' in this existential structure, which allows us to be clear about its character 'from within' the activity of projecting itself. And more generally, the condition of authenticity is comprised by those modes of *all* our 'existentialia' in which those structures achieve an explicitness and an adequacy to their own basic character which they more commonly lack. While I cannot try to show this with respect to each of these many structures, I shall quickly sketch the authentic modes of our three temporal dimensions, since Heidegger takes these to give the fundamental level of existential analysis.

The authentic mode of our futural ecstasis is '**anticipation**' [Vorlaufen] (cf. *BT* 306, 386); it is that mode of projecting I just now roughly indicated. In it we reach out towards our final possibility, our death. We hold this possibility in view in the course of all our striving towards ends: we pursue our particular projects in the steady recognition that this possibility that bounds all our other ends, is of such a character that it may arrive at any moment. We thus recognize that this possibility has a permanent presence, and does not only arrive in being at that moment in which it is actualized. This possibility that is always with us, is 'the possibility of the impossibility of existing', or the possibility that all our projecting may be cut short at any moment; it thus threatens, and forces us to confront, our very 'ability-to-be'. And so facing this distinctive possibility induces a parallel recognition of the sense in which all of our other ends are as possibilities: their significance for us must lie in our ongoing striving towards them, and not in some persisting state in which they might be achieved and attain actuality. For the indefinite possibility of death precludes our identifying ourselves with such actualized states, which may never arrive. We are thus pulled back from our falling position of '**awaiting**' [gewärtigen] our possibilities (cf. *BT* 386; *BPP* 289)—a position in which we understand ourselves by reference to not-yet-actualized states, supposing we shall find our significance only once they are attained. By anticipating death in this fashion, then, our relationship to all our other ends is transformed as well; our projection towards them now acknowledges their character as possibilities, and the way in which our projection towards them gives definition to who we are. Our projective stretch into the future achieves a transparency and adequacy as to its own character, which were missing in the everyday mode of this ecstasis.

The authentic mode of the past ecstasis is '**repetition**' [Wiederholung] (cf. *BT* 388; *BPP* 287); it is that way in which thrownness can acquire a similar transparency and adequacy. Just as authentic projection involves an acknowledgement of the true character of the futural possibilities in terms of which we identify ourselves, so authentic thrownness gives adequate regard to what we have been, and to the role this too plays in determining who we are. Our thrownness is troubling to us because of the nullity it involves: we have been set into our projects, from out of a past that grounds our projection and cannot be determined by it. We cannot choose who we will be, 'from the ground up'. In falling everyday-ness we respond to this intrinsic limitation by avoiding it. We ignore the role played by what we have been in determining what we now are, and renounce any effort at continuity with our past, preferring to detach ourselves from it by absorbing ourselves in immediate concerns. This falling mode of our past ecstasis is '**having forgotten**' [Vergessenheit] (cf. *BT* 389; *BPP* 290); in it our thrownness is hidden or avoided. In authenticity, by contrast, we face this tem-poral dimension as well. We achieve a transparency in this ecstasis towards our past, by maintaining our relationship to what we have been and done, despite the disturbing fixity to these, and our inability now to improve them by any projective striving. We ac-knowledge that this past has a presence now, because it guides the course of our ongoing effort; we recognize that this effort therefore involves a 'repeating' of what we already have been. Just as antici-pation 'stands out' at the horizon of our futural ecstasis, and allows to our possibilities their proper presence within our current activity, so repetition reaches back to our past, and grants to it too a place in what we now are. Our involvement in some present concern has the character of anticipation when we explicitly reach through it to our most distant ends; similarly, it has the character of repetition when we explicitly come to it from being who we have been.

The authentic mode of the present ecstasis is 'the **moment of vision**' [das Augenblick] (cf. *BT* 376, 387; *BPP* 287); it is that way of concerning ourselves with our present projects, in which our rela-tionship to them achieves a transparency it ordinarily lacks. This authentic present is possible only on the basis of anticipation and repetition, for it amounts precisely to an involvement in our en-vironment that does not lose itself there, but holds onto the ecstases into past and future as equally definitive of who we are. To be clearer about this, we may begin with the contrasting falling mode of this ecstasis, which Heidegger calls "making-present". We have indeed already met *this* inauthentic ecstasis, in the first part's review of the temporality of falling. It was appropriate to do so, because this ecstasis is so decisively important for falling in general, being the original movement by which we lose ourselves in the ready-to-hand or the present-at-hand (cf. *BT* 376). In it we absorb our-selves so thoroughly in our current projects and in the equipment employed within them, that we lose our stretch through the other temporal dimensions, and fail to pursue these projects with an abiding attention to what we have been and shall be. We thereby understand ourselves solely in terms of these projects, and in terms of the entities encountered within them. We 'make these entities present' in the sense that we allow only them to be present to our attention; this constitutes an 'ecstasis' into the present in the sense that our attention 'stands out among' these present topics of concern. By contrast with the inauthentic modes of the other two ecstases, such making-present does not involve a narrowing or retracting of its ecstasis—it is not in this way that it falls short of explicitness or transparency. Rather, it is precisely because we stand so thoroughly out at the horizon of this dimension that this stretch is itself overlooked. There is no independent self, provided by the ecstases into past and future, to serve as a 'starting point' for this stretch, and thus to make clear the existence of a stretch or gap at all. The result is therefore the same as in those previous cases: this temporal dimension lacks transparency in its falling mode, and we lack an explicit understanding of it. And this is also, of course, true of the falling relation to theoretical claims, as this was discussed in the preceding part.

By contrast, the 'moment of vision' occurs in conjunction with anticipation and repetition, so that we 'come out' to our projects and equipment from a prior understanding of what we have been and shall be. These other ecstases provide a stable identity on the basis of which those projects are entered; they give rise to a '**situation**' [Situation] within which entities are assigned their particular significance, rather than being allowed to seduce us into some concern they customarily imply. In this way we acquire a certain independence from these entities and our dealings with them, and can be clear about our relationships to them, from 'within' that relationship itself, in a way we ordinarily are not. Similarly, this is also the authentic way of standing in the theoretical attitude towards objects: not losing ourselves in a purely present absorption, but seeing our claims and beliefs in their temporal context of our thrown projection, and hence in a transparency to their ultimately contingent status, which we typically lack.

Each of these temporal dimensions, then, possesses a stretch that cannot be adequately grasped in the momentary survey from the objective stance. To comprehend them in a way that does not inherently distort this essential spread, we must therefore 'stand out' in these dimensions ourselves—not, however, in the falling modes, which involve distortions and concealments of a different type, but in those authentic modes that provide transparency and explicitness to these structures themselves. Taken together, these authentic ecstases constitute a certain consistency or coherence for one's life—not in its chronological course as viewed from without, but in the way in which each present activity is explicitly pursued within a full context of what one has been and will be. One holds in one's hands the reins of all the various projects one is upon. By contrast, the narrowed focus of falling everydayness detaches each episode from what lies behind and ahead, and breaks a life into a succession of passing involvements, none with a bearing on others. Such falling temporality, however, cannot fully achieve this collapse of our temporal stretch; the latter persists, so that falling has more the character of concealment than of transformation. This uneliminable essential stretch is only revealed to us in that authentic self-consistency which Heidegger calls "resoluteness".

Thus phenomenology, in order to convey an understanding of our existential structure that does not in one way or another conceal or distort that structure, must attempt to move its audience into authenticity. It can only convey comprehension of its existential subject-matter, by producing an existential effect on its student. 'Mastering' the elaborate system of *Being and Time* cannot be an end in itself, but only a step towards a radically different way of appropriating its insights—Wittgenstein's image of his propositions as a ladder to be cast aside has an obvious relevance here. Heidegger's phenomenology, then, is more thoroughly or intrinsically 'existential' (in the ordinary sense) than it previously seemed. Despite the far more traditional flavour this method gives to his work, he still aims at that 'edification' which his predecessors in the existential movement have more obviously and colourfully sought.

And so—as my previous accounts have indeed already implied— phenomenological understanding will be 'existential' (in the Heideggerian sense) not insofar as it is theoretical or conceptual, but rather insofar as we overcome that immersion within narrowed projects and roles which falling has encouraged, and so locate our merely 'existentiell' projection towards such roles within a grasp of our fuller structure. Such existentiell understanding will not be replaced, and indeed the success of an existential analysis will be gauged by whether it has been brought to bear on the reader's relationship to his own existentiell projects, and not insulated from them as a merely theoretical position: 'Yet where are we to find out what makes up the 'authentic' existence of Dasein? Unless we have an existentiell understanding, all analysis of existentiality will remain groundless.' (*BT* 360). Of course, phenomenology is not the only route to authenticity—Heidegger says that there is already within us a 'call of conscience' which itself draws us out of our fallenness and towards authenticity. He mentions that authentic Dasein can become the conscience of others (*BT* 344); the preceding discussion has implied that phenomenology is one way in which this occurs. And for phenomenology to accomplish this task, it will make a much fuller use of those breakdowns than was suggested above. These cannot be merely useful events from which it collects its data; phenomenology must rather induce these breakdowns in us, or prepare us to attend to them properly when they chance to occur. For such situations force us to encounter deeply enough, i.e. existentially, those phenomena of which *Being and Time* speaks. Only by virtue of anxiety, in particular, are we deprived of our tranquillizing self-identification with existentiell roles—including even the role: master of the phenomenological system—and directly confronted with those nullities more essential to us than any such roles.

f. General review, through a contrast between Heidegger and Aristotle on philosophy's aim. By way of recapitulating some of the main points in this positive account of phenomenology, and recalling its roots in the earlier presentation of concern, I shall conclude by contrasting these sectors of Heidegger's system with the corresponding positions in Aristotle. This comparison is particularly illuminating, both in the similarities and in the differences. Indeed, the whole range of Heidegger's system stands in most interesting relationship to Aristotle's, taking over and transforming concepts and claims with surprising regularity. I shall lead up to their contrasting accounts of philosophy by quickly surveying some of these other connections, which help to explain the divergence between those accounts.

At the very beginning of my discussion, the 'pragmatic' presentation of everydayness contained some strongly Aristotelian aspects. Heidegger claims that we basically encounter entities as ready-to-hand equipment—that is, as decisively characterized by some use or 'in-order-to'. The present-at-hand interpretations that science has taught us to think fundamental, are in fact logically secondary. Thus, what this entity—this hammer, for example— basically is, must be grasped by reference to an end it is for, and not in terms of that material composition of which the chemist might speak. In insisting upon such a teleological account of these entities, Heidegger reverts to an Aristotelian conception of them, from the currently prevalent view. In fact, Heidegger applies this account more widely than Aristotle himself: he applies it as well to those 'natural' entities in which Aristotle finds a quite different teleology. Heidegger also interprets a tree, for example, by reference to the use we make of it (cf. *BT* 100), while Aristotle considers it to have an end 'of its own', independently of any purposes with which humans might approach it. Insofar as there *is* such a 'natural' or intrinsic teleology for Heidegger as well, it is found only in Dasein itself—and it is in their respective accounts of the end-directedness of human beings that the most suggestive contrasts appear.

As we continued with Heidegger's presentation of everydayness, we saw that the teleological account of equipment depended upon a more basic teleology within Dasein itself. It is because we understand a tool as possessing an in-order-to, that the tool's Being involves a reference to this end—and that prior understanding consists precisely in our own projection towards ends, and mastery of the means of achieving them. Here too there is a general continuity with Aristotle: the formal and final cause of an artifact are predetermined in the intentions of the craftsman, and these intentions occur within the scope of his own pursuit of some end. Unlike the artifact, the directedness of this human being towards his end involves an intrinsic capacity to move towards it, although in some this capacity is more 'excellent' or effective than in others. So far these accounts are broadly parallel, but crucial differences arise concerning the status of these human ends. For Artistotle, there is a single highest end which all human beings are alike in pursuing: happiness. This end is essential to us, as a tool's use is essential to it, but unlike the latter, our end is not imposed from without, but determined by our own 'nature'. Achievement of this determinate end is the best life available to us, and the excellent individual is precisely the one with the clearest conception of this goal, and the greatest ability to reach it. The aim of at least part of philosophy is to help us to acquire this excellence, and thereby this best of lives. But for Heidegger, our situation is fundamentally different. There is no such highest end assigned us by our nature, which philosophy is to help us to achieve. All the ends we do and can pursue, including those 'highest' within our system of assignments, suffer from those two types of contingency belonging to our essential 'guilt': these ends are not ultimately preferable to others they make us forgo, and we cannot claim an original responsibility for producing or adopting them. In these ways, the particular ends we strive towards are arbitrary, and ungrounded in either our essential nature, or in the choices of some original self. On the other hand, there *is* a 'final' end of a quite different kind in Heidegger, and moreover one that is essential to and distinctive of us. But this is death, the finality of which is of so different a type from Aristotle's, that Heidegger's insistence on calling it such must seem a peculiar joke. And yet it is at least a joke with a lesson, for this 'replacement' of happiness with death is a focal point for many of Heidegger's basic divergences from Aristotle.

Aristotle, then, claims that the final and essential end for human beings is happiness, and that all the other ends we seek are pursued as means to it. And Aristotle takes this to imply that this happiness at which we aim must be an '*actuality*', in that it must be that state or condition in which we 'hold ourselves in' our essential end, and so actualize ourselves as human beings. In fact, the determination of happiness as such an actuality is used by Aristotle as a crucial criterion for specifying the particular content of this happiness: it must be a condition that is complete or sufficient in itself, that aims at nothing beyond itself, but contains its whole point or purpose within. All our previous striving has tended towards this condition, and will find its reason or justification only once this condition is achieved. While this end still lies beyond or outside us, while this actualized state lies still in our future, our being is merely that of '*potentiality*'. The condition of happiness must completely overcome this merely potential directedness into the future; in happiness we must find a present that is sufficient in itself. Using this criterion of actuality, of the purely present, Aristotle concludes that happiness must above all consist in the activity of contemplation, for it is this, more than anything else of which we are capable, that possesses the required self-containment or self-sufficiency. Because such actuality is the end that essentially defines human beings, it is only by achieving this condition that we become, for Aristotle, what we essentially are.

But because Heidegger assigns to Dasein a final end of a radically different type, his discussion takes a drastically different route through this same territory. Death is our final end not in the sense that all our others are means to it, but in that it bounds these others: they, and our pursuit of them, must all occur on this side of death. Our final end, however, can come at any moment; it is permanently or continuously possible for us, and this affects in turn our relationship to all our other ends or possibilities. As actualized states, the latter may or may not be achieved, and once achieved they are always susceptible to being lost at any moment. To suppose that such actualizations of our ends constitute the justification for our current directedness towards them, would be to overestimate the expectability and the stability of those realized states. When we recognize the sense in which death is our final end, we are then brought into a different relation to all our other ends as well: we see that their significance for us lies in their status as possibilities, in our continuing effort towards them, as we press out of this present and towards the future they represent. It is not in a self-contained present that we become fully human, but in an open directedness into a future that may never be realized. It is not contemplation, then, but an existential 'resoluteness' that is recommended by a study of the structure of our ends. And yet surprisingly, such resolute directedness into our future turns out to be connected with philosophical understanding in a way that compares once more with Aristotle.

For Aristotle, contemplation is the primary component in human happiness because it is that activity which is complete in itself, and which aims at nothing further or futural; it is in this sense that it is purely present, and purely actual. Not all intellectual activity is of this character. When we are engaged in an ongoing investigation, or pursuing some line of argument or chain of reasoning towards its conclusion, we are *en route* to an end that lies beyond this activity itself. Moreover, that self-containment required for actuality can be precluded by the character of certain possible objects of our thought: in attending to an entity that is only potentially, because it is in motion towards that end at which it actualizes itself, our apprehension lacks completeness because it does not yet encompass what that entity fully is. Similarly, in attending to an entity whose cause or explanation lies outside itself, our scrutiny is referred beyond itself to a grasp of that fuller account. And so our thought achieves pure actuality, and can qualify as genuine contemplation, only by occurring as an accomplished grasp of an entity that is itself purely actual, or unmoving, and that does not have its reason or cause outside. Aristotle concludes that contemplation must contemplate God, as pure actuality, and unmoved mover. And yet this contemplation is also, in a sense, a grasp of itself, for it is itself an approximation to that activity which characterizes this God it contemplates; in apprehending God, it apprehends that condition it has itself very nearly achieved, so that contemplation in a sense includes an understanding of what we ourselves most essentially are. The highest good or happiness therefore consists, for Aristotle, in that highest form of philosophical understanding, which includes self-understanding.

In Heidegger, we find a comparable coincidence between the best of lives and philosophical achievement. That resoluteness which he advocates on the basis of his account of our existential structure, is at the same time a necessary component of phenomenological understanding. For it is only in this authentic condition that we are sufficiently 'transparent' to ourselves for that structure of our existence to be fully perspicuous to us. In particular, only when we explicitly hold ourselves out in the temporal ecstases towards past and future, does our fundamental and distinctive temporality come into direct and undistorted view, and along with it those nullities we ordinarily seek to avoid. Phenomenology can do justice to the nature of existence only if it carries us beyond a merely objective grasp of these structural features, and allows us to grasp them explicitly 'from within', in the transparency of their authentic mode. And this grasp reveals to us Being—not only our own, but that of the entities which are on the basis of our disclosure of them.

While for Aristotle happiness requires contemplation, for Heidegger phenomenology requires authenticity. There are deep continuities between these positions, and between the manners in which they are arrived at. But we have seen that there are also deep differences which hinge on contrasting accounts of the nature of time, and of the manner in which we are and can be within it. Aristotle's assignment of priority to actuality, and to the condition in which we most fully achieve it, is an instance of that preoccupation with the present, and presence-at-hand, which Heidegger takes to have characterized the philosophical tradition since its beginnings. We have seen in some detail how it lies at the root of the Cartesian project in epistemology. Here it is this insistence on the priority of the present-at-hand that leads Aristotle to his connected accounts of the best human life and of the highest philosophical understanding. And it is Heidegger's denial of such priority, and his argument that we are and must be in time in a quite different way, that are basically responsible for his alternative suggestion of authenticity and phenomenology.

Authenticity, then, amounts to a particular mode of disclosure, primarily of our own Being and of the nullities fundamental to it, but also of readiness-to-hand, and even of presence-at-hand. It is, moreover, a privileged mode of disclosure, in that it reveals each of these by turning towards it and acknowledging the dissatisfying character inherent in it, rather than by fleeing and attempting to cover over that character. Phenomenology is to be understood as that mode of thinking which lights up these phenomena or modes of Being by inducing us to adopt this privileged authentic stance towards them. *Being and Time* will have succeeded as phenomenology, that is in letting these phenomena show themselves, only to the extent that it allows the reader's own Being to be 'transparent' to him in this manner. Only in authenticity is this Being lit up for us in the way that phenomenological understanding requires. In thus guiding us to authenticity, phenomenology makes the only proper exit from everydayness, an exit that does not eliminate the unsatisfactoriness that everydayness flees, in the way traditional philosophy has always attempted to do, but that lives in the world in full acknowledgement of this dissatisfying character. This then is the positive task that Heidegger assigns to philosophy.

INDEX

The following references are not intended to be exhaustive, except for those listed after proper names. Italicized numbers cite my principal introductions of Heideggerian terms; others pick out the most important later developments of them.